"In this compelling new book, Naomi Drew outlines practical, disarmingly simple ways to assure that our children will live in a better, more peaceful world. What could be more important than heeding her call? The time to act is now."

—Barry Lenson, author of *Good Stress, Bad Stress*

"Together, we truly can build a better world, and Naomi Drew shows us how in this inspiring and practical book. Every family seeking hope and healing will find it here."

—Meg Cox, author of *The Heart of a Family: Searching America for New Traditions That Fulfill Us*

"This may be the most important book you will ever read. It not only shows how we can raise a generation of peaceful children, it shows how we can each take part in creating a more peaceful world. Join Naomi Drew in the most important race of our times—the Race to Peace."

—Michele Borba, Ed.D., author of *Building Moral Intelligence: The Seven Essential Virtues That Teach Kids to Do the Right Thing* and *Parents Do Make a Difference*

Hope and Healing

Peaceful Parenting in an Uncertain World

Naomi Drew, M.A.

CITADEL PRESS
Kensington Publishing Corp.
www.kensingtonbooks.com

CITADEL PRESS BOOKS are published by

Kensington Publishing Corp.
850 Third Avenue
New York, NY 10022

All Kensington titles, imprints, and distributed lines are available at special quantity discounts for bulk purchases for sales promotions, premiums, fund-raising, educational, or institutional use. Special book excerpts or customized printings can also be created to fit specific needs. For details, write or phone the office of the Kensington special sales manager: Kensington Publishing Corp., 850 Third Avenue, New York, NY 10022, attn: Special Sales Department, phone 1-800-221-2647.

CITADEL PRESS is Reg. U.S. Pat. & TM Off.
The Citadel Logo is a trademark of Kensington Publishing Corp.

Designed by Leonard Telesca

First printing: September 2002

10 9 8 7 6 5 4 3 2 1

Printed in the United States of America

Library of Congress Control Number: 2002104318

ISBN 0-8065-2408-1

To all of the people who were lost on September 11th.
May their spirits guide us in the quest for peace.

To all the children of the world, for they are our hopes,
our dreams, our future.

Contents

Foreword

The problems facing the world today are enormous. The obstacles that block the road to world peace appear so high, seemingly insurmountable.

Yet through our words and deeds, we must never allow ourselves to think, "There is nothing we can do to make the world safer and better. The problems are too immense and we are too small and powerless." If we start to believe that, if that is the message we send to our children, we have already lost the struggle and our children will live in a world no better than our own.

Fortunately, another path lies open to us. If we keep hope alive and continue to take action for peace and understanding, even in small ways, we will prevail. It is a battle we can win.

I would like to stress that I am not being unrealistic when I say that, through hope, we finally will achieve world peace. Quite the opposite. Hope, coupled with action, is a most practical thing. I see that principle at work everywhere.

John Wallach, a journalist who covered the Middle East for twenty-five years, got an idea on how peace might finally be achieved in that conflicted part of the world. He saw that every Israeli child is taught to hate and mistrust every Palestinian. And. every Palestinian child is taught to hate and mistrust every Israeli, thus setting up a no-win situation. John reasoned that if he could induce the governments of Israel and nearby Arab nations to send their brightest and best fourteen and fifteen year old youths to a camp John had created, a camp where these youth would live together, play together for three weeks, engage in intense interactive sessions where they would discover their common humanity, then there might be a chance of achieving a lasting peace. He calls these youth, men and women, "Seeds of Peace," and has established a camp and organization with that name.

I visited the camp and came to know some of these young people. It impressed me that when they got to personally know their "enemy," they discovered that not only did the "enemy" have a face, but had feelings and dreams and ambitions and a desire for peace, no different from their own. They began to learn how not to hate. And they have become convinced that peace is possible.

Most exciting to me was hearing a young girl say, "Can you imagine what it can be like if one day some of us are the heads of our governments?" I can imagine what it will be like.

There is precedent for those who have learned how not to hate. These people changed their worlds. Anwar Sadat did. He was the president of Egypt twenty years ago and was a key leader in arranging the Camp David agreement during Jimmy Carter's presidency. This agreement proved to the world that nations who have warred for centuries can live in peace.

Sadat had been brought up to hate the Israelis. As a young leader he led protests and publicly promised to never shake the hand of an Israeli as long as they owned an inch of Arab land. When he was in solitary confinement in a Cairo prison for being a part of a plot to assassinate King Farouk, he used the quiet and alone time thinking, meditating and studying the scriptures of his faith tradition. He was transformed within, and when he eventually became the president of Egypt, he knew what he had to do. He went to Israel, met with their leaders and began the peace process which lasts to this day.

An individual can make a difference.

Another example is Nelson Mandela, until recently president of South Africa. Fifteen years ago, most people would have bet their lives on the certainty that South Africa would have destroyed itself. Yet while in prison this man whom the government feared most and had imprisoned, worked through and past his bitterness so that when he was released from prison and eventually elected president of his country, he had gained the respect of the various competing coalitions and literally saved South Africa. A Roman Catholic priest noted that the reason Mandela succeeded was that he had suffered, and he forgave. Thus the power.

For several years I had the privilege of knowing Robert Muller, until his retirement head of all non-political functions at the United Nations. Starting with the UN in 1947, a year after its beginning, Robert Muller had been in nearly every country in the world. He had observed the worst of the worst first-hand. And yet he is the most optimistic man I ever met. He believed things would get better.

I once asked him why he was so optimistic, why he had so much hope. He said, "It's the only way that works." And I believe he is right. Nothing is gained through negativism and pessimism. And he also said that the more hopeful and optimistic we are, the greater the chance that each generation will do a little better than the last generation.

When we see the difference individuals can make by changing their minds and hearts, we are amazed and inspired. Time and time again, we see this force at work.

There is hope for the world, a kind of hope that is not only reassuring, but also profoundly effective. We must teach our children, and we must remind ourselves, that while world events may appear to be out of our control, we still have hope. Hope, kindled and honored deep within our hearts, can translate into action and make a better world.

It is my hope that this worthy book, with its deeply felt message of hope, will serve as a bright beacon of peace along the way. May it help lead us through our current dark days toward a better and more peaceful tomorrow.

Dr. Arthur Caliandro
New York City
April 2002

Acknowledgments

To all the following people I extend a warm hand of thanks. You have each played an important part in the writing of this book. May you all have peace in your lives:

To my husband Mel for his total support, care, love, and incredible contribution.

Betty Levin, for her overflowing enthusiasm, support, and for the invaluable information she provided.

Virginia Abu Bakr, for bringing her wisdom, spirit, and insight into this book.

Lyn Evola, for her generosity, support, and inspiration.

Gareth Esersky, for believing in the books I write and understanding their essence.

Richard Ember, for his insight, wisdom, and support.

Dr. Arthur Caliandro, for his beautiful foreword.

Barry Lenson, for his support and kindness.

All the parents in this book, for the openness and insight they so willingly shared.

All the children in this book, for their honesty, and for the hope they continuously give me.

All the invaluable insights from experts I interviewed for the special resource section: William Ury, Patrice Gaines, Michael Lerner, Teresa Benzwie, Arnie Ropiek, Marcia Prager, Imam Chebli, Jim Vogt, Ron Lewis, Heidi Kaduson, Rhea Almeida, Michele Borba, Coleman McCarthy, and Bob Moore.

The teachers, guidance counselors, psychologists, and other professionals I interviewed, for their wisdom, time, and insight.

Meg Cox for her support and networking, and for her belief in this book.

Ann Walsh and Pat Windom, whose wisdom guided me to greater depths, and has given me wings.

Kirin Mishra and Amy Kronice, sources of the Saraswati spirit in my life.

Susan Albert for her research, support, and information.

My boys, Michael and Tim Drew, who have always inspired my desire to bring peace to this world.

Joan Sichel, for her valuable contributions and her wonderful guided meditation.

Gail Siggelakis and Eileen Zweig, for their support, friendship, and insights on many chapters of this book.

Linda Bradshaw, art teacher at Hopewell Elementary School, and to the children there who created the beautiful cover of this book Will Young, Courtney Youse, Emily Brown, and Hallie Schaeffer.

We request to all the countries in the world:

Peace in the world
Peace in our countries
Peace in our homes
Peace in our hearts.

> —Farliz Calle, age eighteen,
> a leader of the The Children's Peace Movement
> and Nobel Peace Prize nominee

We call on the human family to address the root
causes of violence and build a culture of peace and
hope. We know that another world is possible, a
world of justice and peace. Together we can make it
a reality.

> —Nobel Centennial Appeal, signed by twenty-three Nobel
> Laureates on December 10, 2001

Introduction

What oxygen is to the lungs, such is hope to the meaning of life.

—Emil Brunner, Swiss theologian

Patience, my heart:
Night's length will pass,
And we shall see tomorrow rise
with shining faces.

—Faiz Ahmed Faiz, Pakistani poet

In his acceptance speech for the 2001 Nobel Peace Prize, United Nations Secretary General Kofi Anan said, "We have entered the third millennium through a gate of fire. If today, after the horror of 11 September, we see better, and we see further—we will realize that humanity is indivisible. New threats make no distinction between races, nation, or regions. A new insecurity has entered every mind, regardless of wealth or status. A deeper awareness of the bonds that bind us all—in pain as in prosperity—has gripped young and old."

Now, a year after the horror of September 11th, we are jarred once again as we recall what happened on that day. None of us will ever forget the details of where we were and what we were doing when we got the news.

I was home recuperating from the flu when the phone rang at 9:15 A.M. It was my husband, and in a shaken voice he said, "Something horrible has happened—a plane just crashed into the World Trade Center. It's on fire. Hurry, turn on the TV . . . "

The first image I saw was the north tower of the World Trade Center in flames, and in moments, a plane crashing into the south tower. Then the words, "The Pentagon is on fire, and a plane has just crashed in Pennsylvania."

"My God!" I said, and burst into tears. Then I hung up the phone and frantically tried to reach my son Michael, who lives in New York. Ironically, September 11th was his birthday.

The lines were completely blocked and there was no getting through, so in desperation, I ran to the computer and e-mailed him. "Mike, are you okay? Please write back as soon as you get this." And then I prayed.

In about a half hour, I received this e-mail, which I will save forever, "Don't worry, Mom. I am safe." I sobbed as I read my son's words.

My younger son Tim lives close-by, so my calls to him weren't as urgent. I told him to come right over, then my husband arrived, and next my brother. Numb and shaken, we decided the only thing we could do was go to the nearest Red Cross center and donate blood.

When we got there, we were amazed to see a line of people already snaking round and round the small building. There were hundreds and hundreds of people—of every age, race, and color—students, factory workers, teachers, secretaries, executives, lawyers, mothers, fathers, and grandparents. A sampling of America itself had gathered in that teeming parking lot to do the only thing they could—donate their blood. A man in a turban walked through the crowds handing out water. "I'm here on a visit to the United States," he said. "I had to come and help."

That day was like a prism that reflected at once the best and worst of humanity.

Now, one year later we are still struck by a profound awareness of the fragility of life. And we are faced with the ever-more-pressing question—what can each of us do to foster peace? But before we can look at creating peace in the world, we must look at creating peace in our own lives. Why is this so necessary? *Because peace starts with each individual.* It starts with the ways we relate to ourselves and others, and from there it radiates out to every life we touch.

This book will provide you with ways to begin creating peace in yourself, your family, your community, and in the world itself. The key to peace on every level is *you.* As you read each chapter, you will find concrete, practical ways to weave the skills of peace-making into your daily life and the lives of your children.

This is an action-oriented book. The possibility of peace lies not only in our beliefs and desires, but most importantly in our actions. The hope you seek will come each time you put peace-making into practice through your words, behaviors, and in the ways you relate to others.

Remember this: Peace is not just the absence of war; it is an active, dynamic process in which we take specific steps to coexist cooperatively with one another. Creating peace takes determination and intentionality. Time is of the essence, so the race to peace must begin now—and it needs to start with *you.*

We need to take extreme care not to slip back into our old ways of separation, apathy, and powerlessness. Instead, we must allow the events of this year to be the catalyst for transforming our lives, our families, and the world at large. Too many of us have held on to a wish of getting back to normal. But what is normal? In some ways, normal was being asleep, not seeing the world in its complexity and wholeness, not seeing the confluence of light and dark that exists in all of us and in all of life. We believed we were separate—from one another and from events of the world. Yet as we now know, we were never really separate at all; we just lived with that illusion.

We believed that we lived apart from the rest of the world, in a kind of protective bubble that was cut off from the realities that other people faced, such as famine, war, and terrorism. Yet when you think about it, we weren't as insulated as we thought. Columbine, Oklahoma City, Paducah, numerous other school shootings, the attack on the USS *Cole,* and the bombing of the World Trade Center in 1993—these events and others like them started to crack the veneer of our illusions. In actuality, we are living in one of the most violent times in history. The twentieth century saw a hundred million victims of war and another hundred and seventy million victims of political violence. And over the past decade, the surge of youth violence in the United States has shaken us to the core. Former Surgeon General Dr. David Satcher called youth violence "our nation's problem, and not merely a problem of the cities, or of the isolated rural regions, or any single segment of our society." In his 2001 report for the Centers for Disease Control (CDC), Satcher called youth violence "ongoing and startlingly pervasive," affecting *all* of our children.

Although a decline in youth violence has been reported, the CDC tells us that the figures these reports are based on don't tell the whole story. Here's a statement from the Surgeon General's report to the CDC in 2001:

> Youths' confidential reports about their violent behavior—reveal no change since 1993 in the proportion of young people who have committed physically injurious and potentially lethal acts. Moreover, arrests for aggravated assault have declined only slightly and *in 1999 remained nearly 70 percent higher than pre-epidemic levels.* In 1999, there were 104,000 arrests of people under age 18 for a serious violent crime—robbery, forcible rape, aggravated assault, or homicide. Of these, 1,400 were for homicides committed by adolescents and, on occasion, even younger children. . . . The number of adolescents involved in violent behavior remains disconcertingly high, underscoring the urgency of this report. This is no time for complacency.

The CDC stresses that this problem spans all geographic areas and socioeconomic groups. And according to 2002 figures from the Children's Defense Fund, 3,000 children a year die from gun violence—that's nine children a day across the United States.

We are raising our children in a culture of violence. Yet *we have the power to change things.* In this moment these words may sound inconceivable, but as you read further, you will find ways you can play a critical role in changing the conditions that lead to violence—starting right in your own home.

Ending the cycle of violence *is* within our control. Again, the words of Dr. David Satcher: "Youth violence is not an intractable problem. We now have the knowledge and tools needed to reduce or even prevent much of the most serious youth violence." Doing this starts in each of our homes, then moves out into our neighborhoods, our nation, and ultimately the world. The same skills needed to resolve interpersonal conflicts and reduce violence are those applicable in the halls of diplomacy. Peace in our world depends on the willingness of each of us to play our part.

REASONS TO HOPE

Harvard University has been running an extraordinary program for the past twenty years called the Project on Preventing War. Its director, William Ury, has traveled the world, helping opposing groups of every manner to resolve conflicts. He has done this successfully in schools, corporations, communities, and nations; he's worked with families, trade unions, African bushmen, and world leaders. And what's become increasingly clear is this: Effective tools for preventing and resolving violent conflict on all levels already exist. We have at our disposal methods that have been used successfully throughout history time and time again—conflict resolution, mediation, listening, compromise, and early intervention.

So why aren't we using these skills more now? The answer, according to Ury, is that one major thing stands in the way: our fatalistic belief system. We believe, erroneously, that war is inevitable and peace impossible. The occurrence of war becomes a self-fulfilling prophecy. Ury poses this question: "What if all those innocent children, women, and men dying from a stray bullet on our streets, from a terrorist bomb or an air raid—what if they were dying needlessly from a disease as preventable as smallpox?" The disease of violence *is* preventable, and it's a disease we can all start fighting now.

How do we know this can work? William Ury says: "For the first 99 percent of human history, the norm was not organized violence, but coexistence; only in the last 1 percent did violence become the way of resolving differences." Yes, our ancestors engaged in wars and acts of violence, but their violence was less concentrated and far less frequent, and methods of prevention were employed far more often. The acceleration and institutionalization of violence that characterizes modern times is not representative of our history. It is actually a distortion of it. And the last hundred years have been the bloodiest since human beings have come to inhabit the earth.

In terms of violence, what differentiates us most from our forebears is that they were more prone to utilize methods to prevent it—cooperation, sharing, and negotiation. Too often during the past century, we have seen violence used as if it were the only option, and the most expedient way to achieve our national goals. So instead of putting our resources, energy, and creativity into utilizing nonviolent options, we arm ourselves to the teeth and create increasingly more lethal weapons. And now it looks like we are gearing up for an unending state of war. About this, Congressman Dennis Kuchinich says, "Let us pray for our children. Our children deserve a world without end. Not a war without end."

We have, in essence, accepted a culture of war and violence. Our fatalistic way of thinking has infected our homes, schools, communities, and the world at large. But we must realize that *it doesn't have to stay this way.*

You are the key to change. The preponderance of violence we live with now will diminish only when enough of us take action to end it, starting right in our own homes and communities. The personal and global are inextricably linked. Dr. Myriam Miedzian, director of The Parenting Project and author of *Boys Will Be Boys: Breaking the Link Between Masculinity and Violence,* speaks and writes about ways that violence is gender-related. In a speech at Princeton University in 2001, she said that although violence in girls is on the increase, 90 percent of the homicides committed in the United States are by men, and much of the violence in the world is initiated by males. Why is this the case? Because all over, sons are raised differently from daughters. Even though girls have shown a startling propensity for aggression, theirs tends to be verbal and social, while males are far more physically violent. The reason? Our boys are not taught to empathize. Cut off from their own emotions, they become numb to the feelings and needs of others. When this happens, physical violence becomes easier to commit.

Obviously this isn't the case with every boy we raise, but according to William Pollack, author of *Real Boys,* empathy in many males starts to extinguish as early as second grade And these boys grow up to be our leaders. Yes, more women are entering the halls of government, but the majority of those who govern are still men, and often women who govern take on the qualities of their male counterparts. Dr. Miedzian says, "We desperately need to develop leaders who have empathy and can think through the consequences of their actions. We need conflict resolution skills to close the gap between our technological and social skills. This will impact us locally and on an international level. What we need in the schoolyard and in the political arena are the same."

The changes Dr. Miedzian speaks of must start right in our own homes. They must start with the way we raise our sons—*and* our daughters. They must start with the example we set. And foremost, they must start with our *actions*.

There is an African proverb that says: "When spider webs unite, they can halt even a lion." The propensity toward violence will be halted when enough of us move beyond our fear, indifference, and fatalistic thinking to form webs of action. What kind of action? That is what you will discover in the pages of this book. Change starts with the personal, and ultimately spans out to the community, nation, and world. We are all interconnected, and our actions are more far-reaching than we realize. Throw a pebble in a pond and watch the ripples radiate out and out and out. Our actions are like those ripples.

THE POWER OF THE INDIVIDUAL

As you read this book, you will find many inspiring stories of people—"regular" people—who have made a positive impact on the world because they were unwilling to accept the status quo, and they chose to take action. These are people of all ages and colors—children, adults, and senior citizens. They are examples of hope in the face of resignation, action in the face of apathy.

The rising violence in our world has thrust us into a race to peace, one we can only win with everyone's involvement. What gives me hope is that many of you will join this race. I believe so much in your capacity for goodness and action, and I've seen firsthand what's possible when people are motivated. A transformation that took place in my own life was my most profound lesson, and what inspired me to begin was my children.

Twenty-one years ago, when my boys were five and eight, I started looking at the world they were growing up in, and what I saw frightened me. I saw a world becoming increasingly more violent, and moreover, a world that possessed the weapons of mass destruction. The ramifications of this first overwhelmed me, but ultimately propelled me on a search for the answer to the question: *How can we make the world safer for all of our children, and what is my part?*

As a "regular person," I had no idea that someone like me could possibly make an impact beyond my immediate scope of work, family, friends, and community. Stepping out of my normal boundaries felt really scary. But even more frightening was the prospect of what could happen if I didn't. The path our world was on threatened the future of our children—as it does now—and as a mother, I could not accept this. If a car was coming full speed in the direction of my boys and I did nothing to stop it, I wouldn't be able to live with myself. Here, we were faced with an even larger danger—nuclear weapons.

What could I possibly do? I started meditating on the question, and as I did, I was led to books, articles, people—a plethora of information that brought me closer and closer to knowing the answer. The most important book I came across during that time was *Human Options* by Norman Cousins. It was my first exposure to the idea that "regular" people like you and me could literally change the world. Cousins stressed how urgent it was for each of us to take action, and to not leave creating peace up to other people or our governments.

I took a leap and wrote Cousins, asking him if there was anything someone like me could do. In his response, he had no easy answers, but he said something that reached into me like a bolt of lightning and propelled me on the path I have not veered from for over 20 years: "As long as there are people like you who care, there's hope for the future."

These words were my call to action. They were the power source that energized me to take one step after another and start making a difference. I had to do something—but what?

I started researching peace organizations and immediately found one in my community. Then came conferences, workshops, meetings, and connecting with other people on the same path, most of whom were parents. I started teaching conflict resolution to my first-grade students, and the lessons I developed eventually became my first book, *Learning the Skills of Peacemaking*. One thing led to another, and without my even intending it, that book became one of the first in America to introduce the skills of peacemaking into public education. It has now been translated into six languages and is being used all over the world. If someone had told me that this was going to happen, I wouldn't have believed them.

Before long, I wrote another book for educators, *The Peaceful Classroom in Action*, and people in my workshops started asking me when I was going to write a similar book for parents. Their urgings led me to write *Peaceful, Parents, Peaceful Kids*, my last book. After September 11th, it became clear that another book was in order, one that would give parents new skills for coping with this drastically changed world. So now I offer you this book, in hopes that it will inspire you to join me in creating peace for children everywhere.

One thing I know for sure is this: *If I can make a difference, anyone can.* So now I pass on to you the same words that first inspired me:

"As long as there are people like *you* who care, there *is* hope for the future."

THE NATURE OF HOPE

Hope is something we create; it comes from within ourselves, not from external circumstances. Suzy Yehl Marta, founder of Rainbows, a grief support network, says, "Hope is at the center of all loss. This feeling is what carries us from darkness into light. Hope suggests that suffering does have a purpose. Hope says we *do* have the strength to survive what has happened. Hope is much more definitive than a wish. To hope is to have a determined, clear vision for the future and how it can be" (*From the Ashes*, p. 218).

A determined, clear vision for the future—that's what will unfold as you read this book. A vision of peace for all of our children and the ways to make it possible. We each possess the power to do this, and as you read, you will find out how.

The first thing you'll need is a notebook. Entitle it: "Journey to Peace, Hope, and Healing" and keep it handy while you read. You'll need this notebook to do the exercises recommended in each chapter. Each one will provide you with specific ways to begin creating peace in yourself, your family, your community, and beyond. So don't skip these exercises; they are well worth the time.

Four essentials will accelerate your journey toward peace, hope, and healing:

• *Suspend disbelief.* Put aside old concepts of what is possible and what is not. So many people feel resigned, believing that peace isn't possible. But as long as the sun rises in the sky each morning, there are hopes for peace. When the voice of doubt fills your mind, let it pass rather than allowing it to fuel your anxiety.

Focus instead on the vision that brought you to this book. Nelson Mandela changed the world from a prison cell, but too many of us believe we can't make a difference. To that I say, oh yes you can! One person *can* make a difference. Every big movement has started with grassroots actions of individuals like you and me. If not us, who?

• *Let your vision be a source of inspiration and energy.* Visualization and verbal affirmations will strengthen the power of your vision. If your goal is to be at peace as an individual and have peace within your family, then create a mental picture of what that would look like. Picture every detail. Write down what you envision, and create a corresponding affirmation like: "I am at peace within myself and I have a peaceful family." If you want to think really big, add, "The world is at peace." We might not know the way to make this happen yet, but our collective visions may just lead us to discover how. Also remember this: Everything of value that has ever been created by human beings has started with somebody's vision. So suspend disbelief, focus on your vision, and let this book be a touchstone to hope.

• *Trust in the power of goodness.* There are more good people than bad in this world. Remind yourself of this and tell it to your children. Look around and you'll see a preponderance of goodness confirmed every day: kind people who reach out to lend a hand, compassionate people who care about the common good. Let the awareness of this strengthen you and give you hope. Include in your vision the knowledge that good people who care really *can* make profound changes in this world, and they already have. Trust this vision, just like you might trust a prayer.

Trust also that "impossible" things have been created and "impossible" obstacles overcome in this world by good people. On days when your vision of peace is challenged, think about other seemingly "impossible" good things that have come to fruition.

Mahatma Gandhi accomplished the impossible. Believing India could gain independence through nonviolent means, he stood firm in the face of countless voices that said it couldn't be done. Gandhi believed that love was the most powerful force in the world and he believed in the power of goodness. By remaining true to what he held closest to his heart, Gandhi made manifest an "impossible" vision, and in doing so he literally changed the world. Share his story with your children. It is critical that they learn from the earliest ages to trust in their own power, and to honor the the visions they perceive. Teach them to believe that, with enough hard work and determination, what they envision *is* within reach.

Nelson Mandela had the "impossible" vision of a South Africa free of apartheid. Inspired by Gandhi, he held to his dream of achieving freedom largely through nonviolence. Like a beacon of light he rose above voices of hatred and helped dismantle this deeply engrained system of oppression. Mandela said, "Playing small doesn't serve the world. As we are liberated from our own fears, our presence automatically liberates others." This is the essence of believing in what's possible. It is the type of courage that allows goodness to speak with strength and pride in the face of negative forces.

Remember these stories when doubt rears its head, and allow them to inspire you beyond your trepidations. As you read this book, you will meet many wonderful people who acted on their visions to make this world a better place. Chapters 8 and 9, in particular, are filled with their stories. Inspiration is contagious. As you become inspired, pass it on. We need to spark each other's hope and desire to take action. The race to peace will be won when enough of us join in, and by sharing your inspiration and commitment, you will be an inspiring force for others.

• *Be willing to take action.* We live in a society where people want everything fast and easy. Yet creating the things we value most is a slow process.

A wonderful children's story called "The Garden," by Arnold Lobel, beautifully illustrates this point. In the story, Toad plants some seeds and expects them to grow immediately. He goes out to his garden the following day and grimaces in frustration at the empty soil and shouts, "Seeds, grow now!" But his impatience yields nothing. He repeats this several times with the same result. Finally Frog advises Toad to water his seeds each day, tend them patiently, and then see what happens. After following Frog's advice, Toad learns that seeds grow only if we lovingly tend them over time.

Many of us are a lot like Toad. We have lost the discipline to persevere. In theory, we want a peaceful world for our children to grow up in, but what are *we* doing to make it happen? The things of this world we want most—hope, healing, and peace—will come only with our patience and determination. "Instant" doesn't work with the important things.

Being willing to take action to create peace means taking the small, arduous steps day after day. And as you read this book, you will find out what they are. You will meet many parents like you who are living the skills of peacemaking and teaching them to their children. Every person you encounter is real—none are based on composites, even though many of the names have been changed.

At the end of this book there is a special resource section that is, indeed, very special. In it you will hear the advice from top experts about your most pressing questions. How do we raise moral, compassionate children in a cruel and violent world? How do we explain the contradictions to our children—we say we want peace but we're at war? Can regular people really make a difference? You will find the answers to these questions and others, each one based on in-depth interviews.

As you read, please remember that creating peace is a process that requires time and faith, but the results will be long-term and life changing. I so strongly believe in your innate power. Now plunge into this book with an open mind, an open heart, and a vision of unlimited possibilities, and remember—*you* are the key to peace. God bless you.

PART I

HEALING

Chapter 1

Expressing Our Emotions: Moving Beyond Fear and Anger

If you truly care for humanity, include yourself in their numbers, by giving your own inner feelings the voice and the dignity they so deeply deserve.

—Clarissa Pinkola Estes

There is something in every one of you that waits and listens for the sound of the genuine in yourself. It is the only true guide you'll ever have. And if you cannot hear it, you will all of your life spend your days on the ends of strings that somebody else pulls.

—Howard Thurman

DEALING WITH PAINFUL EMOTIONS

It was early October and we were all shell-shocked. The Twin Towers lay in smokey ruins and the death toll grew larger each day. Many people from my home state of New Jersey had been killed, including loved ones of friends and colleagues. My reaction was one of extreme hypervigilance: I continuously immersed myself in reports of these events. If something else was going to happen, I was going to know about it right away. But doing this was making me more fearful. The world felt totally out of control and every minute was a reminder of how much things had gone awry. Finally, one luminous autumn day, something inside me said, "Enough!" I knew if I turned on CNN one more time, I'd end up even more numb and shell-shocked. So I walked out the back door, stood in my yard, and stared blankly at the sky. Suddenly all these buried emotions started coming up. I had this overwhelming sense of grief, fear, and despair. I let each painful feeling rise to the surface, and as I did, what was at the bottom was revealed: *the fear that life might not go on.*

That was it—the core of my sense of dread, the feeling I'd been trying to buffer myself against in all my news gathering and hypervigilance. I breathed deeply and let the dread rise to the top. And as I did, my body and mind started to unclench. The fear itself was alive and present, and with it a sense of raw awakeness. I looked squarely into the eye of what I was most afraid of, breathed deep, and allowed it to be.

In the acceptance of what scared me most, I was able to start to let go. That's when I began noticing things I had not since September 11th. In my numbness I'd been missing what was right before me. I stared up at the graceful trees that surround my house and noticed sunlight shining through the tops, making the leaves translucent. A breeze wafted through the foliage, and light glinted off each bush and blade of grass. I stood there breathing it all in, fully present to this moment of extreme paradox. The fear was still present, but so was this ineffable sense of light and beauty.

When I went inside, I picked up a picture of my sons and held it to my chest. Love and gratitude coursed through me, and then the words, "Things are all right *in this moment.*" I knew that the floor I stood on was solid, the walls of my house still standing, and my loved ones safe and well. Then I finally grasped it: *This is the only moment we ever really have.* I have no control over what will happen next or what's already passed, but I *do* have control over this moment. And by keeping perspective, I can make this moment, and this moment, and this moment okay.

*   *   *

We have all had so many painful feelings over the past year, and now as some of them resurface, know that there are things you can do to move through them. Husband and wife team, Dr. Les Fehmi and Susan Shor Fehmi, M.S.W., run the Princeton Biofeedback Center, where hundreds of people go each year to learn ways of dealing with stress, fear, and other difficult emotions. Dr. Fehmi says, "Our culture has taught us to run away from pain, and now we're unprepared." Most of us have learned to suppress uncomfortable emotions, but doing so ultimately backfires. Suppressing emotions can wreak havoc on our immune system and undermine our ability to fully enjoy life.

"In our society we don't want to go where it hurts. Yet we need to learn to love our pain as much as we love our pleasures," the Fehmis advise. Pain is part of being human. By acknowledging it, embracing it, and allowing ourselves to express it, we strengthen our bodies and spirits, and become more resilient. Repressing what's inside wears us down. Allowing emotions to rise to the surface is like breathing fresh air for the first time. We free up all the energy it took to hold our feelings in.

Helen Keller once said, "Everything has its wonders, even darkness and silence." Yet we run away from darkness, avoid silence, and fear acknowledging the places where it hurts to look. Ironically, in the acceptance of our fear and pain is the opportunity for freedom.

It's hard to accept negative feelings in a society where we've been conditioned to push things down and "get on with life." And we *have* gotten on with life in the past year, but have we done it at the expense of our authenticity? Have we tried to push away what scares us most and bury ourselves in our busy lives? Have we taken a "don't go there" attitude about the feelings that trouble us most? If your answer to any of these questions is yes, then know that each time you push away a painful feeling, you're cutting off a part of yourself. This is our opportunity to let feelings that may have been buried beneath the surface come up for air. Here are four powerful steps to help you do this.

1. Feel what you're feeling. Don't push it away. Allow the feelings up. Let them see the light of day or the darkness of night. Resist the urge to judge your feelings or judge yourself for having them. Just allow your feelings to be. This way your feelings become your ally, not a hidden entity inside that you have to deny or push away. By feeling what's there, you let your emotions become a doorway to deeper self-knowledge.

Dan, a father of two, shared this story: "My parents both died of cancer within two weeks of each other. September 11th was like that for me. I was grieving for both. The way I dealt with it was to absorb myself in my grief and let the feelings surface. What came up were not only images of my own parents, but images of people grieving around the world." Dan was then able to let go and move on—this time with a greater acceptance of his parents' deaths.

Clinical social worker Virginia Abu Bakr says, "We live in a society that fosters the concept of disposable pain. People look at pain as something they need to get rid of right away. Yet when we can learn to be with our pain, we are brought closer to our source, our deepest authenticity." Pain can be one of life's most powerful teachers—embrace its lessons.

There are a variety of ways to do this. Journaling can be a wonderful catalyst for letting your feelings rise to the surface. Sometimes in the process of writing, things get revealed that you didn't even know were there. Free writing without a specific direction teases feelings out. It's like an invitation to what's been hiding to come up and make friends with you. This may sound strange—to think of making friends with fear and dread—but it's the only way to move forward. Trying to relegate them to a hidden corner only makes them stronger.

Here's a poem that poured out on the pages of my journal on September 22, 2001:

Several weeks ago
before the great divide of time
I walked along quiet streets
with the naive notion that somehow those of us

who'd once predicted
injustice would surely threaten peace
were wrong.

And on that day
complacent faces peered out of closed windows,
twenty-something mini moguls spent quick fortunes,
and women got their nails done.
Countless kids sat glazed in front of TV screens,
everyone stuck behind a glass wall,
numbed by illusions of safety, perhaps not caring anyway
That people not so far away
scraped for a meal, and rebel forces
in unnamed mountains
planned our deaths.

Now through lingering clouds of smoke
and TV screens radiating death images
we wonder why
but don't look back
long enough to ask.

Writing this poem and others enabled me to let out the fears and questions that were haunting me. Each time I discharged something onto the pages of my journal, it was one less thing I had to walk around with rambling in the caverns of my mind.

Journaling works this way. Once the thoughts and feelings are up, out, and on paper, you no longer have to carry them around. Let your journal hold the burden of your fears so your mind doesn't have to do it.

Other things you can do to bring feelings to the surface are:

- Talking to a friend
- Crying—perfectly acceptable for people of any age and gender
- Going for a ride in the car by yourself and yelling or singing at the top of your lungs

- Deep breathing
- Doing artwork of any kind
- Playing music or listening to it
- Going to movies that tap into your emotions
- Singing or dancing
- Exercising

A word about crying. Dr. Frank H. Boehm, author of *Doctors Cry Too,* commented on how healthy it was for the nation when New York city firemen broke down and cried as they were being interviewed on television after September 11th. He noted how they cried our collective grief in their openness and bravery, and said, "Now that male crying is in the open, maybe there will be less hiding. That would be good for all of us, since psychologists tell us that men who are allowed to show their feelings in times of stress are less likely to act them out in violent and aggressive behavior. . . . Tears can reveal strength, not weakness; compassion, not fear; maturity, not loss of control" (*New York Times,* December 5, 2001).

Crying is a powerful way to let feelings up, enabling them to dissolve instead of staying static and frozen like a chunk of ice in a dark stream.

When our feelings are exposed to light, they loosen, shift, and begin to dissipate. This is an ongoing process. Deep and difficult emotions don't just melt away all at once. They require our continued willingness to let them rise to the surface layer by layer. Each time a layer dissolves, the grip of hurt, sorrow, fear, or pain lessens too.

EXERCISE: Have your notebook handy. Close your eyes. Breathe deeply. Let your feelings speak to you. What are your holding on to? What feelings need to see the light of day? Invite your feelings up and write about whatever is there. It may be something from this moment, or something from the past. Whatever it is, breathe into it, and let it be. Write down whatever comes to mind. Let your thoughts and feelings flow uncensored. Be careful not to judge what comes up. By honoring your feelings, you honor yourself.

Also, you might want to keep a log of your emotions over a specific period of time, say, a weekend. Every hour jot down what you're feeling. This will help you see that over a short span of time you actually feel many things, and those feelings can change. Bad feelings don't have to remain static. As a high school nurse tells her depressed students, "It's a road hump. You'll pass over it."

2. Name the feeling. Is it fear, anguish, resentment, frustration, anger? Is it loss, grief, or despair? Allow the feeling to be, and identify what it is. Sometimes we have to look below the surface of one feeling to find what's really at the core. Some people get caught up in anger, but if they look deeper, what's really there is fear. We live in a society that has put such a stigma on feeling bad, we often try to ignore what's happening inside us. It's as though our feelings have been nameless orphans that no one wants to claim. "If it feels bad, make it go away," is the mind-set we have been living with.

But now the events of our world are forcing us to take another look. It's time to adopt those orphans wandering around in the recesses of our psyches. It's time we honor them and give them a name. And when we do, we'll start healing on a deeper level than ever before.

EXERCISE: Continue writing from where you left off in the last exercise. Can you name your feelings? Maybe you can relate them to a color, mood, or place. Allow yourself to free-associate. Your feelings may bring you back to another time. If they do, allow their wisdom to guide you to wherever you need to be. Trust this wisdom to lead you to a place of healing.

3. Be with your feelings. This doesn't mean "dwelling." What it does mean is accepting what you feel and doing what you can to soothe it. Picture getting a cut on your finger and trying to ignore it. Picture going about your daily business pretending you feel no pain. Before long, the cut's infected.

Repressing feelings is like this. Think about people you know. I used to work with a woman who was perpetually sad. She always had a pained look on her face, and her body seemed slightly hunched forward, as though she was protecting something. She was. She was protecting her pain. And every time you asked her how she was doing, she said, "Fine," with a forced smile. How much effort it must have taken her to get through each day.

Being with your feelings means letting them up to the surface, acknowledging them, naming them, and breathing into them. Literally. If we can breathe into our anger, pain, or frustration, we can start to transform it. We can then choose what to do next. When we repress feelings, there's only one choice: to keep pushing them down. The person with the cut carries pain around continuously. But imagine this same person acknowledging the cut and caring for it. Now it can heal.

> **EXERCISE:** Is there a particular feeling you need to be with? Close your eyes, breathe deep, and find out. If an emotion calls your attention, listen to it. Honor it and spend some time with it. This may be like getting to know someone you see every day but never talked to. Allow yourself to just be with the emotion for now.

4. Let the feeling go. Once you've allowed your feelings up, named them, and allowed them to be, you can move forward. This is the time to gently urge yourself away from focusing on the feeling. Bring your attention to other things. The feeling might still be there, but you can gently acknowledge its presence and move ahead.

This process reminds me of a conversation I once had with my sister. She said, "I can't get over how you never seem to be afraid. You write books, you speak to large audiences; I'd be terrified." I looked at her incredulously and said, "You think I'm able to do these things because I'm not afraid? It's not like that at all!" I said. "I'm afraid a lot. The secret is, I just don't let it stop me. It's like my fear is this little animal that I've learned to make friends with. I just pick it up in my arms and take it with me. Sometimes it's quiet, sometimes it's noisy, and sometimes it stays home. If I waited for it to go away before doing anything, I'd be waiting forever."

So many of us miss the opportunity of making friends with our negative feelings. This is our moment to shift, our time to embrace feelings we've harbored and hidden from, because these feelings will ultimately become our allies in coping with whatever comes our way.

Author and Buddhist nun Pema Chodron calls experiencing our most difficult feelings "reaching our limit." This doesn't meaning reaching our limits of sanity; it's actually about reaching the limits that hold us back, beyond which exist peace and wholeness. "When we reach our limit, if we aspire to know that place fully—which is to say that we aspire to neither indulge nor repress—a hardness in us will dissolve. We will be softened by the sheer force of whatever energy arises—the energy of anger, the energy of disappointment, the energy of fear. When it's not solidified in one direction or another, that very energy pierces us to the heart, and it opens us. Reaching our limit is like finding a doorway to sanity . . ." (Chodron, pp. 15–16). Finding a doorway to sanity—that's what it is to honor our feelings and give them life. That's what it is to let go.

This process enables us to become more available to those we love. Kate, the mother of two, said, "I'm not as effective in helping my children cope because I have my own stuff I haven't dealt with." As we engage in the cycle of letting feelings up and letting them go, we become freer, enabling ourselves to better guide our children along their path of healing. As we heal, they heal.

EXERCISE: Here are some things that will help you move on after you've let your feelings rise to the surface:
- Immerse yourself in meaningful work.
- Do something physical like cleaning, laundry, yard work, or exercise.

- Listen to or play music.
- Dance.
- Go outside.
- Talk to a friend.
- Help someone else. This can be the best tonic of all.

HELPING CHILDREN DEAL WITH DIFFICULT EMOTIONS

Visiting an elementary school recently, I was touched by the depth of feeling the children expressed. "Why can't we find ways to live in peace instead of being violent with each other?" asked a fourth-grade boy. "The people of Afghanistan are human beings, too. It makes me feel so sad that we've hurt them." Jessica, a third-grader, said, "War is bad. Our President should talk to the people instead of killing them."

Children are very much aware of events going on in the world, even if they don't verbalize it. Providing opportunities for our children to process what they're experiencing is critical to their healthy emotional growth. James P. Grant, executive director of UNICEF, says: "Helping children express their emotions and externalize their fears and worries is essential to alleviating trauma. Preventing them from sharing their feelings and experiences only pushes the emotional pain deeper and causes problems later."

Here are some things you can do to help your children process and express their emotions:

• *Open up discussion, but don't push.* Your children will let you know how far they want to go. If you're talking about world events and you have fears of your own, admit it, but don't dwell or give too many details. Focus instead on things that are being done to keep us safe and all of the kind and magnanimous acts we have witnessed in the past year.

If your children still have issues about their safety, the best thing you can say is, "I will always keep you safe in every way I can." Then allow your child to speak his or her truth. One father

I talked with said his five-year-old daughter wanted to know who would take care of her if something happened to him and her mom. He calmly reassured her that he and Mommy were safe, but if anything should ever happen to them, Grandma and Grandpa would be there to take care of her. Just knowing she would be taken care of seemed to be enough for his daughter. For older children, deeper discussions may be in order. We'll talk about this more in Chapter 3.

• *Encourage your child to express feelings using different modalities.* If your child isn't comfortable verbalizing feelings, offer him or her the opportunity to write, draw, or engage in dramatic play. Provide your child with related materials. Sometimes a reticent child will talk about something she's drawn or painted; from there feelings may emerge. In the following pages you will find a plethora of activities to help your child express feelings using a variety of modalities and mediums.

• *Listen with an open heart to what your child has to say.* Refrain from judgments, opinions, or pat solutions. Just listen compassionately and reflect back what you heard your child say. This will open doors to communication. We'll go into great detail on this in Chapter 5.

• *Make an extra effort to be close.* Spend more time at the end of the day or before bed just to be there, talk, or listen. Just being there is a statement of comfort. Check in from time to time, and if your instincts tell you your child needs an extra hug or dose of listening, give him what you think he needs. He might not always tell you.

ACTIVITIES TO HELP YOUR CHILDREN EXPRESS FEELINGS

Feelings Popsicle Sticks

This is a variation of an activity guidance counselor Jane Mangino does with her elementary students. Sit down with your children and name every feeling you can think of together. Use markers to write them down on popsicle sticks. Each stick gets a different feeling word. Talk about what each feeling is like. Ask your children to role-play some of the feelings, or to identify them on the faces of people in books and magazines. Make a pocket out of construction paper, oak tag, or old wallpaper so you can hang up the popsicle sticks. From time to time ask your child to choose one that represents her feeling in that moment. As the feeling changes, have your child choose a different stick. Do the same thing yourself. It will help your child understand the range of feelings you experience too.

This activity has three purposes:

- It helps children identify feelings and own the feelings they have.
- It helps children understand that feelings can change, that even bad feelings are impermanent, and that we can do things to change our feelings.
- It helps children tune into the feelings of others, seeing how our behaviors influence how other people feel.

Help your child discover ways they can change negative, painful, or angry feelings. Then, each time they do, ask what worked. Children seven and over can write about this in a journal. Learning how to identify and change feelings is a very important life skill. The next two activities will help children identify their emotions.

Feelings Hearts

Dr. Heidi Kaduson, a play therapist specializing in anger and trauma, suggests this activity to help children of all ages identify emotions. Give your child drawing paper and crayons. Make the following key to help your child correspond feelings with colors:

yellow—happy
red—mad
blue—sad

purple—scared
brown—bored
green—frustrated
gray—worried
black—lost

Have your child draw a heart large enough to fill the entire paper. Next ask your child to fill in the heart using colors that show how she is feeling in this moment. Her heart may contain a mixture of various colors in varied sizes, depending on which feelings are strongest. Now, have your child tell you about the colors she chose and what they represent. You can do this activity along with your child. It's a wonderful way to express and validate feelings. Repeating the activity at different times will help reinforce to your child that feelings can change, and that we all have a wide range of feelings.

Feelings Box

Here is an adaptation of another activity recommended by Dr. Kadusen. Have your child decorate a shoe box. On it write the words "Feelings Box." Using 3 x 5 cards, write some of the following phrases:

I feel happy when . . .
I feel sad when . . .
I feel angry when . . .
I feel hurt when . . .
I feel disappointed when . . .
I feel afraid when . . .
I feel frustrated when . . .
When someone is angry with me, I feel . . .
The best thing for me to do when I am angry is . . . (on other cards substitute for angry sad, hurt, afraid, disappointed, frustrated)
When I keep anger inside, I feel . . . (again substitute sadness, hurt, fear, disappointment, frustration)

I get over feeling angry best when I ... (substitute sad, hurt, afraid, disappointed, frustrated)

Take turns with your children picking cards and filling in the blanks. Use this activity as a jumping-off point for discussion.

Expressing Feelings Through Art

Pablo Picasso once said, "Painting isn't an aesthetic operation; it's a form of magic designed as a mediator between this strange, hostile world and us, a way of seizing the power by giving form to our terrors as well as our desires. When I came to that realization, I knew I had found my way." We, too, can utilize art to help us find our way through powerful emotions. Here's how.

• Have drawing paper and crayons and/or markers available for both you and your child. Do the following warm-up activity together: Close your eyes and breathe in deeply through the nose. Expand your abdomen as you inhale. Hold the breath gently in your lungs, then exhale slowly. Continue breathing slowly and deeply until you are both relaxed. Let images and colors come into your mind. After a few minutes, pick up a crayon or marker and begin drawing. Let whatever emerges flow out of you. Any shape, form, or image is acceptable; your work doesn't have to be realistic or pretty. Just let the forms take shape and see where they lead.

Talk with your child about feelings as they come up. Accept if your child's artwork is angry or fierce. That may be what's inside. One therapist I interviewed talked about children actually taking pencils and ripping holes through their papers. Allow the emotions to express themselves any way they need to. Art is a safe medium for letting this happen.

• Do the above activity to music. Put on any type of music you like, and let the rhythms spark emotions and images for you and your child. Different types of music will complement different moods. If you sense your child might be holding in sadness, find a piece of music that can bring these feelings out. Using this type of creative activity to express what's inside allows feelings to emerge and release.

Try expanding your repertoire of materials. Include paints, colored chalk, or oil pastels. Encourage your child not to predetermine what she going to create. Have the music invite her feelings out. The same goes for you. Your being there and freely engaging in this activity will reinforce your child's sense of safety and openness.

• Creating torn paper designs is an excellent way of releasing anger and stress. Give your child a selection of colored construction paper and some glue. Using one sheet of paper as a base, have your child tear up different colors and glue them onto the paper. The motion of tearing can be creative as well as cathartic. Display whatever your child makes.

Expressing Feelings Through Writing

As I mentioned before, writing is a very powerful tool for unlocking and processing emotions. Megan, a mother I interviewed last fall, talked about how she had been encouraging her children to use writing as a means of dealing with their emotions. After watching the bombing of Afghanistan on television, her eleven-year-old daughter Rachel turned to her and said, "I can't deal with the feelings I'm having right now. I think I have to write."

Listen to the poem Rachel wrote that night:

Last Night

Last night my hopes, they came to me
I dreamt the war was over
The broken hearts all were healed
And spirits all replenished.
I dreamed that every fear was gone
And justice ruled again.

Last night my wishes came to me
I dreamt it never happened
The twin towers, high they stood

> *And lives that were lost still lived*
> *I dreamed that anthrax was unreal*
> *And terror yet unborn.*
>
> *Last night I dreamed my dream.*

Writing can be a powerful catharsis for children. In 1998, the year of Columbine and the war in Kosovo, I worked with elementary students to create a book expressing their deepest concerns. Many children who had trouble verbalizing painful feelings were able to express themselves through writing. If your child is a reluctant writer, have her dictate her words as you type or write them down. We adults don't always realize the depth of fear young children have. Here are excerpts from the writings of seven-, eight-, and nine-year-olds:

From Tommy, age eight:
"If there ever is a bomb threat in my school I know perfectly what to do. We would probably get in a straight line and act like it's a fire drill and we would walk very quietly outside. Even though I can block bombs out of my head I'm still afraid of them."

From David, age nine:
"I don't like the war in Kosovo. I don't like people dying. Killing innocent people in wars is not right. I don't know who started the war. Why?"

From an eight-year-old child whose family had escaped war-torn Africa:
"People started running everywhere because they wanted to get away from the soldiers. We ran inside the house. We were listening to the news. It said that people would kill everybody who is outside. Next they came to my house."

From Mark, age seven:
"I'm afraid that someday someone will come and start shoot-

ing people and may even have me as a target. I think it will happen at the beginning of the year when people are just getting used to their grade."

These words sound shocking coming from such young children, but this is what many of them think about. Provide your child with a journal and encourage her to write. You'll be giving her a life-long tool for self-awareness and healing. In Chapter 3, you'll find more ways you can help reluctant writers get started.

Free Play

Young children most readily express emotions through free play. After September 11th, several parents and primary-grade teachers shared stories of how their children were acting out the destruction of the World Trade Center. One teacher was shocked to see her students building towers with blocks then pretending to have planes knock them down. This is actually a healthy response to traumatic events. Young children may not feel comfortable or even able to verbalize their reactions, so they process them through play. Doing so helps them make sense of difficult or traumatic events. Each time children replay the event, they let go. Allowing for dramatic and other types of play will help your young child deal with emotions that might otherwise stay trapped under the surface. Now, as we see images of September 11th replayed in the media, unprocessed emotions may begin to resurface.

Helping Adolescents Express Feelings

Teens and preteens try to make sense of their worlds through talking, seeking information, and grappling with the larger questions. They are entering an age of more highly defined moral development, and they'll probably need to spend extra time with you discussing what's going on in the world, giving their point of view, and gathering information. Keep the lines of communication open and listen without judgment. Remember, you don't have to agree with what your teen says, but you do need to allow him the right to say it. Doing so helps nurture a sense of acceptance, something critical at any age, and necessary to your child's growth process.

The anniversary of September 11th and the months that follow may bring up feelings that might have lain dormant. Be sensitive and watch for signs. If your teen is more sullen, withdrawn, or irritable than usual, he may need some extra support right now. Also, watch for changes in eating, sleeping, and homework habits.

Be honest with your teen about how you feel, and encourage him to let his more vulnerable emotions up. Sometimes lurking under the exterior of the false bravado we see in so many teens is a deep sense of vulnerability. Make it safe for your teen to express this. More on this in Chapter 3.

BEING SENSITIVE TO YOUR CHILD'S UNIQUE NEEDS

"Christie has been telling me she loves me several times a day," said Laura, the mother of a sixteen-year-old. "She's been in need of more affection lately."

"My son has been making comments that he wishes we could move to Canada. He doesn't feel safe here anymore," said Carol, mother of nine-year-old Todd. Although Todd and Christie are different ages, over the past year they each have had a need for extra reassurance. Meeting these needs as best as you can will help your children cope.

"My eight-year-old son wants to know everything that's going on," said one father. "Yet my eleven-year-old daughter gets upset when she hears us talking about world events. We've solved the problem by talking to our son when our daughter isn't around."

It's more important than ever to be tuned in to our children's unique needs. What works for one child may not work for another. Also keep in mind that difficult events trigger memories of other difficult events. If your child experienced loss or trauma prior to September 11th, be aware that old wounds may have reopened as a result. Also, be aware that as each anniversary of September 11th nears, old fears and vulnerabilities may re-surface.

Be patient and supportive if your child needs to work through old wounds, traumas, or losses like divorce, any death or serious illness, loss of a treasured pet, a move to a new house, going to a new school. Even though some of these are positive, they still in-volve loss of old attachments and routines. Be sensitive to this in your child and in yourself. Any of the activities mentioned earlier can help either of you move through emotions that come up. In the next chapter we'll go into more detail about helping your child heal from traumatic events of any kind.

> **EXERCISE:** Close your eyes, breathe deeply, and ask yourself this question: "Does my child have an old wound that has reopened up over the past year. Do I?" See what reveals itself in the process of writing and reflecting. If something specific comes to you, spend some extra time with your child, offer reassurance, and just plain listen.

DEALING WITH EXTREME LOSS

Many people lost loved ones over the past year. If you are one of them, or if you have suffered losses at other times, there are many things you can do to heal. Pamela Albert, RN, BSN, wrote a won-derful comprehensive article in which she offers insight into the process of grieving ("Grief and Loss in the Workplace," *Med-scape* 11(3):169–73, 2001). Albert says there are three critical things we need to know: "Each loss launches us on an in-escapable course through grief; each loss revives all past losses; and each loss, if fully mourned, can be a vehicle for growth and regeneration."

Albert cautions against trying to ignore our grief or simply re-lease it through talking. Allowing emotions to surface is one of the most fundamental things we can do. Grief therapist Ron Lewis, M.A., concurs. He tells this story of healing about a young client he once helped:

> A seventeen-year-old boy came to me for counseling. He said he felt this deep sadness inside him that he couldn't shake since his grandmother passed away when he was fourteen. His grandmother had been very involved in raising him and he'd been extremely close to her. On the day she died he went into his room and cried and cried. Then he had a thought that if he could go in the bathroom and smile, he might feel better. He looked in the mirror and found that he could smile, but he felt so guilty for doing so that his grief literally froze. He had this overwhelming belief that by smiling on the day his grandmother died, he had betrayed her.
>
> For three years he never talked to anyone about this experience. As he related it to me, I told him that I believed his smile was a good thing—it was his connection to his grandmother's spirit. He immediately started to sob uncontrollably. The grief he'd been carrying around for three years was released and so was the guilt. After finally letting all these emotions come out, my young client told me he felt more alive than he'd felt since his grandmother's death.

As in this young man's case, sometimes our grief gets frozen. Different things can spark it anew, and each is an opportunity for healing. Again, Pam Albert: "We grieve on a recurring basis as we face the commonplace losses that line our lives—be it the loss of an heirloom, a hope, an ideal, a friendship, or a loved one. The course of our lives depends on the ability to make these breaks, to adapt to all losses, and to use change as a vehicle for growth. Losses not fully mourned . . . shadow our lives, sap our energy, and impair our ability to connect. If we are unable to mourn, we stay in the thralls of old issues, out of step with the present, because we are still dancing to tunes from the past."

END THOUGHTS

Expressing emotions is the first step to healing. Once emotions begin to release, they move up and out through the channels of the body. It's important to feel what we feel and nudge our minds to let go. As Dag Hammarskjöld, former Secretary General of the United Nations once said, "Our work for peace must begin within the private world of each of us."

As we engage in this process, we begin to soften and change. This is transformation in action. Difficult times provide us with this golden opportunity. May we honor the vast spectrum of human emotions life provides, allowing each to move us to the next step in our personal evolution. And as we evolve as individuals, may we each contribute to the evolution of peace on earth.

RESOURCES AND BIBLIOGRAPHY

Websites

National Institute of Mental Health
www.nimh.nih.gov
Resources, advice, help. Call this number for immediate assistance: 800-64-PANIC.

American Academy of Child and Adolescent Psychiatry
www.aacap.org
Provides excellent information on emotional and mental health issues for parents of kids of all ages.

Rainbows
www.rainbows.org 800-266-3206
They help people set up peer support groups in churches, synagogues, schools, or social agencies, and supply curricula to people of all ages and religions who are grieving "a death, divorce, or any other painful transition in their family."

The Dougy Center
www.dougy.org/adult_grievchild.html
Assists children, teens, and families coping with the death of a family member. They offer guidebooks on grieving for people of all ages.

GriefNet
www.griefnet.org
Provides e-mail support groups and websites for people who are grieving and a safe environment for kids and parents to find information and ask questions.

Compassionate Friends
www.compassionatefriends.org
A national network that helps parents who have lost a child of any age. Connects parents to each other.

Books and Articles for Parents

Albert, Pamela L. "Grief and Loss in the Workplace." *Medscape* 11(3):169–73, 2001.

Benzwie, Teresa. *A Moving Experience*. Tucson: Zephyr Press 1988. Shows how to connect arts, feelings, and imagination through movement.

Benzwie, Teresa. *More Moving Experiences*. Tucson: Zephyr Press 1995. More activities using movement to express emotions. For parents and teachers.

Borysenko, Joan. *Inner Peace for Busy People*. Carlsbad, Calif.: Hay House, 2001. Fifty-two ways to introduce small changes into your life to help bring greater balance.

Capacchione, Lucia. *The Creative Journal for Children*. Boston: Shambala, 1989. Seventy-two exercises for journal keeping for children to enhance creativity, language skills, and emotional well-being.

Chodron, Pema. *When Things Fall Apart: Heart Advice for Difficult Times*. Boston: Shambala, 1997. Wonderful book by the visionary Buddhist nun. Contains practical, powerful advice on dealing with whatever life puts in our path.

Domar, Alice, and Henry Drecher. *Self-Nurture: Learning to Care for Yourself as Effectively as You Care for Everyone Else.* New York: Penguin, 2001. Honoring ourselves with emotional and spiritual self-care; stress reduction techniques.

Kabat-Zinn, Jon. *Full Catastrophe Living.* New York: Dell, 1991. Healing, destressing, and self-nurturing from one of the top experts in this area.

St. James, Elaine. *Inner Simplicity: 100 Ways to Regain Peace and Nourish Your Soul.* New York: Hyperion, 1995. Simplifying your life, nourishing the mind and spirit, the value of alone-time.

Books for Children

Bohlmeijer, Arno. *Something Very Sorry.* Boston: Houghton Mifflin Co., 1995. Rose and her family are in a car accident. When her mother dies, supportive friends and relatives and a sensitive father help Rose cope. Moving. (Grades 4–8.)

Brown, Laurie Krasny, and Marc Brown. *When Dinosaurs Die: A Guide to Understanding Death.* New York: Little, Brown, 1996. Suggestions for coping with grief, and ways to remember those who are gone. Sensitively presented. (Grades K–2.)

Fox, Paula. *One-Eyed Cat.* New York: Simon & Schuster, 1985. After shooting his air rifle, eleven-year-old Ned suffers emotionally over the consequences of his action. (Grades 5–9.)

Frank, Anne. *Anne Frank: The Diary of Young Girl.* New York: Pocket Books, 1958. In Anne Frank's actual diary she tells her story of attempting to survive the Nazis for two years. It is a story of tolerance as well as anti-Semitism. (Grades 4–6.)

Gellman, Rabbi Marc, and Monsignor Thomas Hartman. *Bad Stuff in the News.* New York: Seastar Books, 2002. Helps older children deal with issues from terrorism to hunger, and explains causes in an understandable way. (Grades 6–12.)

Griffin, Adele. *Rainy Season.* Boston: Houghton Mifflin Co., 1996. Through the story of a troubled girl living on a military base, kids can learn coping skills. Twelve-year old Lane goes through fear, aggression, anxiety, and sadness. (Grades 6–12.)

Jones, Frances, and Fred Chase. *A Circle of Love: The Oklahoma City Bombing Through the Eyes of Our Children*. Oklahoma City: Larry Jones International Ministries, Inc., 1997. Letters from kids to children affected by the Oklahoma City bombing.

Martin, Jacqueline Briggs. *Grandmother Bryant's Pocket*. Boston: Houghton Mifflin Co., 1996. After Sara's dog dies in a fire, she overcomes her grief and nightmares with the help of her grandmother's special pocket that is filled with herbs. (Grades K–3.)

Rapp, Adam. *The Buffalo Tree*. New York: Harper Collins, 1988. A powerful first-person account by a twelve-year-old boy of life in a juvenile detention center. Depicts emotional, socioeconomic, and other factors that contribute to youth crime. (Grades 6–12.)

Roca, Nuria. *Feelings: From Sadness to Happiness*. New York: Barron's Educational Series, Inc., 2001. Adorably illustrated book helps young children identify and deal with a wide range of feelings. Includes activities parents can do with their children. (Preschool–first grade.)

Rodowsky, Colby. *Remembering Mog*. New York: Avon, 1995. Annie's older sister has been murdered. Unable to make decisions about her future, she begins working with a therapist who is able to help her. (Grades 6 and up.)

Spelman, Cornelia Maude. *When I Feel Scared*. Morton Grove, Ill.: Albert Whitman & Co., 2002. Precious book to help young children understand feelings of fear and what to do sbout them. (Preschool–first grade.)

Turner, Barbara J. *A Little Bit of Rob*. Morton Grove, Ill.: Albert Whitman & Co., 1996. Lena's brother Rob has died. When Lena finds Rob's sweatshirt, she and her parents stay up all night sharing memories and tears. (Grades 4–8.)

Chapter 2

Calming and Coping for Parents: Gaining a New Perspective

We create our own hope.

—Laurens Hogebrinn, Dutch Theologian

Lord grant me the serenity to accept the things I cannot change, the courage to change the things I can, and the wisdom to know the difference.

—Saint Francis of Assisi

Over the past year we have been told continuously to get on with our lives and move forward. Yet as we know, the process of healing takes time. We don't just go through a major trauma and bounce back the next day, the next week, or even the next month. This is so individually and as a nation. Healing is a nonlinear process that occurs as we allow feelings to come up, be acknowledged, and transform over time. As you saw in the last chapter, we must honor the process of healing by giving it the attention and patience it requires. Quick fixes don't work. Walking the path to peace means getting our own houses in order first.

For all of us, the past year has been one of many ups and downs. For those who lost a loved one, every birthday, holiday, and anniversary sparks pain anew. All of us are confronted with a common loss—we no longer have a sense of the world as we once knew it. One of the most important questions of our times might be: How do we, nevertheless, create peace and happiness in ourselves and our families, and how do we use what we've been through to create greater peace in our world?

This chapter and those that follow will help you discover insights into the answer.

A NEW PERSPECTIVE

As you and your children move through the processes introduced in Chapter 1, you will begin to let go of some fears and anxieties. Yet as we've seen in the past year, these anxieties never completely go away. We hear dire warnings from our government that another attack may be imminent; we wonder if it's safe to travel by air or if our water supply might be poisoned. A neighbor of mine said just the other night, "Our family is supposed to take a trip to Italy next month. I'm so terrified, I can barely sleep." Another friend said, "My mind went into a kind of a fog on September 11th, and it still hasn't quite come out of it." The fact is, much as we try to go about our "normal" lives, we live in a continual state of disequilibrium.

Mental health counselor Robert Gerzon, author of *Finding Serenity in the Age of Anxiety,* writes, "Terrorism has brought home the reality that our individual lives, our families, our neighborhoods are all at the mercy of a roiling sea of deep global anxiety. As we navigate this exciting yet perilous 21st century, our collective response to the raging anxiety and confusion on our planet may determine whether we descend into a destructive cycle of violence or evolve to a new level of human society" (*UU World,* March–April 2002). You might be wondering: Is it actually possible to maintain a sense of balance when the world seems so insane, and our anxiety is so high?

The answer is yes, if we're willing to do what it takes, and if we're willing to open our eyes. Many people in the world live every day of their lives with far more anxiety than we'll ever know. So many of us have been insulated and cut off from the dire problems that millions face every moment. Judith Lief, writing for *Tricycle* magazine, says, "The U.S. is finally experiencing a small glimmer of what life is like outside its privileged bubble." We've had the dubious dispensation of living in a country compartmentalized from its own problems and the problems of the world—until now. This is our wake-up call. It's time to start understanding what people not as privileged as we live with every day. As Faye Wattleton, advocate for civil rights and women's rights, says, "Let this crisis wake us from our self-absorption."

Were you aware that 27,000 people worldwide die every day of starvation and preventable diseases, and that a high percentage of those who die are children (United Nations figures) Were you aware that even here at home we have a shamefully high number of people living in poverty and hunger? According to America's Second Harvest, "31 million Americans are either going hungry or unsure of where their next meal will come from, and *one in five children—approximately 15 million—in our nation live at or below the poverty line.*"

The National Center for Children in Poverty reported that a large majority of children living in poverty have at least one employed parent. Too many of us have been oblivious to these glaring inequities. September 11th calls us to open our eyes and become part of the solution. And as we do, we accelerate the path to our own healing. When we help others, we heal ourselves, and with enough of us helping, we will begin to heal this fractured world. One of the key roots of war and violence is poverty, yet, according to the United Nations, there are enough resources in the world so no one has to go hungry or die of preventable diseases. Doing something about this is a fundamental marker on the road to peace.

There's actually a lot we can learn from people who have lived through serious deprivation. A certain grace emerges from those who have dealt with suffering. Fontella Cawley is a case in point. This thirty-six-year-old mother of three has overcome poverty and homelessness and now dedicates her life to children. She works full-time for Homefront, an organization that helps homeless people start new lives—the same organization that once helped her. She says, "It's important to give back. If I didn't have anyone to help me, I don't know where I'd be. Even though I was really determined to better myself, having help made all the difference. If I can give the same help to someone else, maybe they can make it too. I bring my children along when I work with kids at night and on weekends so they can also learn to give back."

Fontella urges us not to set ourselves apart and look down upon those who have less. "They're human and they may just need that extra hand. Your encouragement gives them hope and helps them see a light at the end of the tunnel. I would urge everyone to volunteer at least a half hour a week. That might just be enough to help someone pull themselves up. Everybody needs a little love."

Crystol Thompson is another woman who inspires. A twenty-five-year-old mother of three, she overcame homelessness, depression, and three suicide attempts. With the help of caring people, Crystol has managed to turn her life around and now teaches nutrition at Rutgers University.

Like Fontella, her sense of altruism is finely tuned. "Whenever I can, I do things to help people get on their feet. If someone needs a place to stay, I let them stay with me. If they need a ride or something else, I'm there. It's so important to give of yourself. Everybody's here for a purpose, and one of our purposes is to help others."

What's amazing to me is that these women are single moms with full-time jobs, and one of their top priorities is to give back. Time isn't an issue for either of them, even though they're both pursuing advanced degrees on top of everything else. Life has taught them that we need to take care of each other, so they have a completely different perspective on how they use their time. Both of these women are sterling examples of transcendence and hope.

Emmanuel is another. He and his family came here from Liberia in 1999 after his father was killed in a military takeover, and his mother was left alone to raise seven children.

"I go to college full-time, work four days a week; on Sundays

I spend half my day at church, and then I go for tutoring. I have very little time for myself, but that's okay. The money I earn feeds my family."

Emmanuel shakes his head in disbelief at the waste he sees in America. "I don't understand the kids here. How can they spend money on nightclubs when some people have so little?" He added, "It's really easy to save money if you put your mind to it. After I pay my tuition and buy food for my family, I even have enough left over to give my little sister an allowance, and sometimes I can buy myself a pair of pants."

The beautiful thing about Emmanuel is his overwhelming sense of gratitude. Living through war and near starvation has made him see the simplest things as gifts. "I can remember not having any food to eat. We lived at the mercy of people with kind hearts who helped us when they could. There were days we went without food or water. We'd go to the gutter, get some water, and filter it with sand. You wouldn't believe how good it tasted." Even then, gratitude. This from someone who almost died of starvation: "I was so malnourished you could see the bones in my head. The wind could blow you away. The flies would sit on your mouth. I remembered wishing I could die on those days."

One of Emmanuel's greatest frustrations is this: "Some of the basic freedoms and privileges people here have go so unappreciated. I cry within myself when I see it. People here were so shocked by September 11th; in my country we would see people die every day." Yet, above all else, Emmanuel's gratitude shines through. "Now in America I appreciate what life has to offer. I make enough money to feed my family. God is good to me."

When I think about all the children I have seen over the years throwing a fit because their parents wouldn't buy them a toy or candy bar, I wish they could trade one day in Emmanuel's life. And when I think about the many adults who get depressed because they can't lose weight, there's a sadness to the irony.

We must keep people like Emmanuel, Fontella, and Crystol in our consciousness to broaden our perspectives. We are the lucky ones, and we will be most fortunate if September 11th gives us the gift of new eyes to see with, and bigger hearts. Our greatest sense of hope will come when this happens.

STRATEGIES FOR CALMING, COPING, AND HEALING

There are many other people who have used the experience of suffering to become more "golden"—more compassionate, loving, wise, and generous. The Dalai Lama is the epitome. Taken from his parents at the age of two, exiled from his homeland of Tibet as a young man, and shaken by the deaths of thousands of his countrymen, the Dalai Lama has every reason to feel hopeless and bitter. But just the opposite is the case—he is one of the most joyous people alive. He laughs often, smiles profusely, and emanates lightness. Hearing him speak in New York, I was deeply touched by his warmth, humility, and even playfulness. The writer Pico Iyer said it best: "If someone who has seen and lost all that he has seen and lost—forty years waiting to go back to a home that is slowly, systematically, being destroyed—can look at the light in things, what right does any of us have to feel sorry for ourselves? If he can find hope, how can the rest of us not do so?" (*Shambala Sun*, October 2001).

The Dalai Lama has been able to create peace in the midst of chaos by using many tools, some of which you will find in this chapter. Read on to discover ways you can do this too, and use things you have suffered through as a path to greater wisdom.

• *Live in the now.* The first and perhaps most important principle of calming and healing is to stay focused on *this moment.* Leslie, the mother of two young sons, has gone in and out of feelings of anxiety since September 11. Hard as she's tried to conceal them, it's been a struggle. Gesturing toward the wide swath of trees beyond her children's school yard, she said, "I used to be able to look out at the trees and feel happiness, but now I feel like there's a cloud of darkness looming behind them. The future seems so scary." Like many parents, Leslie has fears about her children's safety, not knowing if there might be another attack and where it might take place. Sometimes these feelings seem overwhelming.

"I know what you mean," I told her. "Each time I read the newspaper, I get upset too."

"It's hard to know how to cope," Leslie replied . "I wish there was a place we could move to that was safe, but I don't even know where that would be."

"You're not the only one who feels this way," I reassured her. "So many parents I work with have expressed the same fears."

As we continued talking, I shared with Leslie what's been helping me cope—living in the moment and honoring each one. Projecting fears onto the future adds to anxiety, but staying in the now grounds us in our present experience. Living this way gives us a sense of balance.

I said, "Each time I start projecting into the future, I literally feel my feet on the ground and imagine the earth protecting me and the people I love. I feel the soles of my feet firmly planted on this earth that has always supported and nourished us, and I remind myself that right now—in this moment—things are okay. I also realize that this moment can lead me to greater power within myself. Instead of dwelling on fear, I think about what I can do to make things better. Then my fear actually has a positive effect—it pushes me toward action. The reason I'm involved in the work I do is because I'm so concerned about the kind of world we're leaving to our children. Each time I do something to make the world a little better, I feel more in control."

"Sometimes it's hard to think about making a difference," said Leslie. "I'm just trying to handle each day."

"That part can come next," I said. "For now, just concentrate on staying present to each moment and doing whatever you can to calm yourself. But don't put off making a difference indefinitely, because that may be the most powerful thing you can do to feel better in the long run."

Several weeks later I received this from Leslie:

In trying to get through this game called life, I've realized some things.

Since September 11th, changes have happened in ways I
hadn't even noticed:

Flowers seem more vibrant.

Leaves seem to have taken on more colors than I remember.

Air seems "crisp" not cold.

Hugs last longer. Tighter than before.

The touch of my boys' hands, and bodies feels secure,
warm, new.

The desire to be with my family, more urgent.

With each new morning, I see a new day,

the only day I have, the only day I ever had.

Tomorrow is something we wish for, something we pray
will be,

but, really, tomorrow never exists at all.

Because when tomorrow comes . . . surely it becomes
today.

By grounding herself in the present, Leslie was able to experience the peace of *this* moment. Each time fearful thoughts come
back she would bring herself in to the present. The need to do
this reminds me of something Mark Twain once said: "My life
has been filled with terrible misfortunes—most of which never
happened." Continually bringing herself back to "this moment"
has enabled Leslie to cope better, and once again see the trees and
feel a sense of calmness. As a result, she's able to give her children
a sense of hope from an authentic place within herself.

• *Focus on gratitude.*   Meister Eckhart, the thirteenth-century
mystic and writer, once said, "If the only prayer you say in your entire life is 'Thank you,' that would be enough." What are you thankful for right now? Consider the small things as well as the large.

As I write these words, I glance out the window and see this
beautiful panorama of falling leaves and winding roads dappled
with sunlight. For this I am grateful. I am acutely thankful for my
health, my wonderful family, my cozy home, and even for the
negative experiences of life that have taught me great lessons. I'm

grateful to be writing this book and for the opportunity to make a difference in your life. I am grateful for every today. For me this sense of gratitude has increased tremendously over the past year. Life seems so much more precious now, and I am grateful just to be alive.

People who've endured the most difficult of circumstances like Emmanuel, Fontella, Crystol, and the Dalai Lama resist embitterment by staying finely tuned to the goodness of life. They continuously find the place within that is authentically grateful. I remember seeing a twenty-seven-year-old man being interviewed after the World Trade Center was attacked. Thirty-seven percent of his face and body had been severely burned, forcing him to spend many weeks in the hospital. Yet foremost in his mind was gratitude. He was so happy to be alive, so grateful for his friends and family and for all the people who had helped him that he is now dedicating his life to giving back. He said, "The way people treated me opened my eyes to what's possible if we all really care. It's been a rebirth for me."

Another person who stands out in my mind is Miriam, a Holocaust survivor, who is now nursing her husband through the final stages of cancer. "I practice being grateful for everything that comes my way," she says. "I am thankful for the good and thankful for the bad, because the bad things I experience could actually be worse. Living this way helps me keep life in perspective."

Exercise: Have your notebook at your side. Close your eyes and breathe deeply. Do this a few times until you feel relaxed. Now ask yourself this question: For what am I grateful? Reflect on this for a little while, then open your eyes and start writing. List everything you can, large and small. Add to your list daily. As many times as you can throughout the day, whisper a silent prayer of thanks.

• *Regard each moment with a sense of reverence.* The events of September 11th gave us a gift: we saw, perhaps for the first time, that life is finite, and each moment cannot be guaranteed.

Knowing this calls us to live with an immediacy we may have never experienced before.

But now, a year later, do we still have this sense of life's preciousness, or have we fallen back into our old ways of thinking? Are we still honoring life the way we did a year ago or have we already forgotten lessons learned?

I remember how in the weeks after September 11th, the many acts of kindness and heroism by rescue workers at Ground Zero inspired people to be more caring and helpful. Even on the highways people were more patient; they weren't cutting each other off as much. On the streets, strangers were making eye contact. Even on the subways in New York, there was more kindness and connection. I remember the story of a woman who was sitting on the subway crying, and strangers coming over to see if she was okay. Now, we seem to be allowing the compassionate part of us to fall back into dormancy.

Even some of the violent movies held back from release after September 11th are now on the screens. The worst example of war has given us the greatest opportunity for peace, but we are missing the opportunity to keep living life as the precious gift it is.

Yet as we saw after September 11th, each time we express kindness, generosity, compassion, and service, we honor life. This is a minute-by-minute challenge. It requires living with the constant consciousness that no moment is guaranteed. Ask yourself this question: How can I better honor each of the moments I have been given?

Exercise: Breathe deeply several times, get quiet, then write about ways you may be dishonoring life . On a separate page, write about ways you honor life. You might consider ways you open your mind and heart, use your creativity, share your talents, help others, express kindness, show compassion. How else do you honor life?

Now answer this question: In what *new* ways do you want to honor life? Write about this on a new sheet of paper that you can hang up and use as a call to action. Post it in a place where you can see it every day.

Nurturing the Mind

It's hard not to let our thoughts run away with us sometimes. Maggie, the mother of three, summed it up: "I want to stay on top of the news so I know what's going on, but then my mind starts running wild. Sometimes I'll watch the news before I go to bed, and that's it for a good night's sleep." Dire warnings, increased violence in the Middle East, threats of bioterrorism, nuclear weapons—hearing about any of these can set our minds racing.

One of the most important things we can do to preserve our mental health is to strongly curtail the amount of news we take in. I actually started instituting days where I declare a full moratorium on news. What I quickly discovered was that the news would still be there the next day, and if something really important happened, someone would let me know. My state of mind on the no-news days has been noticeably calmer.

There are a number of other ways we can soothe our minds and cut down on anxiety. Clarissa Pinkola Estés, Ph.D., author and specialist in post-trauma management, suggests the following.

• *Don't linger on negative thoughts.* Estes says, "Refuse to dwell on what psychically depletes you of hope, contentment, and ease." As soon as negative thoughts threaten to overtake you, very deliberately shift your focus. Tell the negative thoughts "No" using a very firm internal voice and put your focus on something that calms you—music, exercise, nature, gratitude. What else?

> EXERCISE: Take out several pieces of paper and write down every negative thought you can think of. Include the "what-ifs"—all the things you fear but try not to think about. Consider the pages you are writing on as a mental garbage dump. Let it all out and don't stop until you've gotten to the bottom. You'll be surprised by what's in there. Once you're finished, tear the papers up into little tiny pieces. Then either burn them in a safe place or flush

them down the toilet. When I did this, I took a small stainless steel pot out to my backyard and burned my list. Watching my worries go up in smoke was very cathartic. Doing this will help your unhinge all the gunk lodged in the recesses of your mind.

• *Do what strengthens you.* Things that make you feel peaceful also give you strength. What strengthens you? Is it being outdoors, working on a project, reading, cooking, gardening, doing something fun with your spouse or children? Whatever it is, do it more often. Doing what strengthens you needs to become an ongoing priority in your life. For me it is exercise and yoga. I no longer look at either of these as a luxury; I see them as necessary for my physical and mental well-being. If it's a choice between straightening the house or yoga, I'll choose yoga. Honoring my priority gives me more energy for the important things in life: my family, my work, and my peace of mind.

EXERCISE: What strengthens you and makes you feel more peaceful? If you're not sure, brainstorm some ideas. The best way to do this is by giving yourself no more than two to three minutes to write down as many ideas as you can *without censoring any of them*. Let whatever pours out of your mind land on the paper. Allow this process to furnish the ideas rather than trying to "think" them. Pick a few things on your list to start doing now. Honor yourself this way.

• *Don't believe you can't cope.* By weathering storms and dealing with difficulty, we become more alive and compassionate. The Buddhists believe that suffering strengthens what is most human in us and makes us more whole, like a rough-edged stone that's been polished into a diamond. Each time we suffer through a difficult time of our lives, our capacity for wisdom and sensitivity increases. Our souls become more seasoned, and we are better able to understand the suffering of others.

Know that you have within you all the resources you need to cope with whatever comes your way. Each time the voice of doubt or negativity comes up, let it pass, and bring your mind back to your place of strength.

> **EXERCISE:** Think of times in the past when you've had to cope with difficult circumstances. What did you do? What thoughts, actions, decisions, or connections helped you? Write about this and choose some of your old coping strategies to use whenever difficult situations arise.

• *Tune in to your "inner voice."* We each have a place inside us that knows what to do under all circumstances. It's a place of insight, wisdom, and the highest self. Trust your intuitive voice. It may be your greatest guide during challenging times. I often urge parents I work with to go to this place when they are not sure how to handle a particular problem with their child.

Elyse was concerned about her child's nightmares. When I encouraged her to go to her "wise place," she realized that her seven-year-old son, Jason, was dreaming the fears he'd been accumulating over the past year. Several parents of his schoolmates had been killed in the World Trade Center attacks, and even though it was months later, Jason had lingering fears about his own safety and the safety of his parents. By tuning in to her inner voice, Elyse realized that through his nightmares, Jason was releasing anxieties that were beneath the surface. Now Elyse was better prepared to help Jason deal with the fears that populated his dreams.

In the next chapter we will go into a lot of detail about what you can do to help your children deal with nightmares and other residues of trauma.

> **EXERCISE:** Go to a quiet spot. Have your notebook at your side. Close your eyes and take some slow deep breaths. Expand your abdomen with each intake of breath and allow it to go deep into your body. Let any thoughts you have pass through your mind. Just keep returning your focus to the breath. Do this for a few minutes, then invite your "wise self" into your consciousness. Trust any

images, words, or feelings that come to you, and write them down.

Once you've done this a few times, you can expand this exercise by asking your "wise self" a question and then waiting to see what answer is revealed. This is what helped Elyse understand the nature of Jason's nightmares. Trust the voice of your "wise self" and remember that we hear this voice only when we are quiet enough to listen. Give yourself some silence and solitude so the voice of your intuition doesn't get drowned out in the fray.

Nurturing the Body

In times of stress, taking extra care of our physical well-being is a must. Basics like proper rest, healthy foods, and exercise can make the difference between being able to cope and feeling overwhelmed. Don't short-change yourself on any of these. We know all too well the effects of hunger and lack of sleep. Just taking care of these basics can buffer you against the burden of added stress.

Practice extreme self-care. When you feel good, you have more patience to give to the people you love. When you're overwhelmed, tension seeps into the atmosphere, affecting everything and everyone.

Too often sleep and healthy eating are the first things to go in times of stress. Notice your own patterns. Do you become wakeful at night when you're under stress, or do you find yourself craving more sleep? Do you lose your appetite, or do you use food as a crutch? Doing either takes its toll on our immune system and adds to the tension we already feel, so it's critical to find ways to minimize the tension that throws us off balance. What follows are a variety of ways you can nurture your body in times of stress.

Deep Breathing

This is my favorite tension-tamer—one that's available anytime anywhere. Try it now. Breathe in deeply through the nose, expanding your abdomen as you do. Let the air go all the way down, imagining it going past your lungs and into the abdomen itself. Hold the breath in there for a little while, then release it slowly through the nose. Continue doing this at least three times. Try adding a soothing visualization. Close your eyes and picture a place you've been where you felt happy, peaceful, and safe. Picture every detail, and as you do, try to recall the scents and sounds of that place. If extraneous thoughts intrude, just let them go, and bring your focus back to your peaceful place.

Do this whenever you feel tired, stressed, angry, or fearful. It really works. The oxygen calms the body and energizes the mind. The visualization intensifies the calming effect. I've even done this on a crowded train and it's helped me feel calmer and more prepared for what I had to do next.

Physical Exercise

A natural elixir, always available, and free. Get out and take a walk, go for a jog, do some calisthenics, or lift some weights (soup cans can make ideal weights, by the way). You don't have to join a gym or engage a personal trainer; you just have to move your body for at least thirty minutes at a clip. According to *Mental Health Weekly* (November 5, 2001, "Chemical May Explain Exercise's Benefit"), "A naturally produced chemical may play a part in explaining why exercise acts as an antidepressant." When researchers studied people who exercised, they discovered a 77 percent increase in something called *phenylacetic acid,* a substance which is low in depressed people. Combined with the release of endorphins that exercise triggers, it's clear that this should go on your list of wellness essentials.

"Exercise is my salvation," says Ralph, a father of two. "Regardless of what's going on in my life or in the world, if I get out and exercise, I come back in a completely different frame of mind." Doing exercise not only helps *you,* it provides valuable role modeling for your children. Both of my grown sons are avid exercisers, having watched me and their dad exercise since they were young. You can exercise as a family too. Take a walk after dinner when the weather is nice, or even when it's not. If it's rain-ing, open up an umbrella and go for a walk. Your kids will love it, and they'll get the double benefit of being in nature while they get some exercise.

It doesn't matter what exercise you choose, just find a way to integrate it into your life on a regular basis. Leading stress expert Dr. Paul Rosch says, "Just making a commitment to follow any regimen that you have confidence in often provides a feeling of control, that in itself, can provide significant stress reduction benefits."

EXERCISE: Do you already exercise? If so, how often? If not, when can you begin? Set a goal to exercise at least thirty minutes three times a week. Fast walking is an excellent exercise, so if you're short on time or cash, consider doing at least this. Consider bringing your kids. Movement and fresh air can shift moods quickly.

Remember, too, that forming a new habit takes thirty days. If you commit to making exercise a part of your life, by weaving it into your schedule over a thirty-day period, the habit will take hold. Once this happens, the rest is easy.

Nurturing the Spirit

The Greek ideal of body, mind, and spirit speaks to the balance that helps us feel whole. One positive outcome of the events of the past year has been a rekindling of spirit. In many ways we've been strengthened and inspired by images of people coming together to pray, to honor those who passed, to learn more about each other's faiths, to help. Theologian Matthew Fox urges us to nurture our spirits by expressing care for others and reaching out to make a difference: "The lesson is not to waste our lives, not to waste our opportunities, our precious gifts, our strengths, whatever they may be. . . . So service and compassion become the lessons. This is at the heart of everything because this is the fullness of our humanity" (from *Bridges* quarterly magazine, summer 2001). Each time we contribute to another person or the world around us, we strengthen our own spirits.

Nurturing the spirit through contribution is so necessary in times of stress. Helen Keller once said, "Faith is the strength by which a shattered world shall emerge into the light." Faith and service go together. Yes, our faith has been tested over the past year, but we reclaim it each time we involve ourselves in acts of compassion and helping. Faith fueled the spirits of Gandhi, Martin Luther King, Mother Teresa, Nelson Mandela, Desmond Tutu, and so many other "regular" people who've transcended insurmountable circumstances and changed the world in large and small ways. They express their faith not only through religious and spiritual practices, but by making the world a better place. This is what the collective spirit of the universe calls us to do right now.

Meditation/visualization

Meditation and visualization can be deeply calming, healing, and empowering. When we meditate, we clear our minds of extraneous thoughts and focus on the breath, a phrase, or an image. When unwanted thoughts come in, we let them pass, instead of keeping our attention on them. Meditation can be done in as little as five minutes, and as long as sixty or more. If you're short on time and have the desire to meditate, go to a quiet spot even for just a few minutes and try it.

I meditate every day. In fact, this practice has been a key ingredient for writing this book. Here's how I do it: I've set aside a shelf in my office where I've put several candles, pictures of my family, and some shells and stones from special places we've been. It's an altar of sorts and it brings a sense of sacredness to the space where I do my work. Before I begin writing, I light the candles and sit before them either in a chair or on some pillows. I close my eyes and say a little prayer to set the intention of my meditation. Then I start breathing slowly and deeply, and I bring a peaceful image into my mind. It's usually a picture of a place I've been to where I've experienced feelings of calmness, like the ocean or mountains. I focus on this image and imagine every detail. If extraneous thoughts come up—which they always do—I bring my focus back to the image and to my breath. I might change the image and let it expand. Or sometimes it changes by itself. Eventually the image falls away and I focus on the breath.

I continue breathing slowly and deeply, opening myself to receive whatever wisdom and guidance I need. As I continue, my body and mind become more and more relaxed. It's like the feeling you get right before falling asleep. I usually don't meditate for long periods of time—sometimes only five or ten minutes. But doing this in even short segments helps, giving me greater energy, focus, and calmness.

There are actually many different ways of meditating. Some people just focus on the breath; others focus on a sound. You can even look at the flame of a candle, close your eyes, and let the image of the light take you into meditation. One caution, though—getting to a place of calmness doesn't happen right away. It took me months before I got there. The body and mind have to adjust. If you find yourself restless or your mind wandering, don't give up. The benefits are really worth the discipline.

Researchers at UCLA have quantified some specific benefits of meditation in people who suffered from a variety of ailments: "Patients with hypertension who meditated regularly reduced their blood pressure and widened their arteries. Risk of heart attack was reduced by 11% and risk of stroke by 15%. Regarding chronic pain relief, meditation helped diminish pain symptoms in 85% of chronic pain sufferers listed" (*Women's Day,* October 9, 2001).

Visualization is similar. It's best to use a tape if you're going to do a guided visualization, or have someone who can read the visualization to you. In the following pages you will find several you can use and even put on tape.

Try doing these at the end of a busy day or, if you have time, first thing in the morning. Lie down in a quiet place or sit comfortably in a chair. Then listen, relax, let go, and enjoy.

• The Stream •

Close your eyes and take in a slow deep breath through the nose. Bring your breath all the way down, imagining it can reach into your stomach. Gently expand your abdomen as you breathe in. Hold the breath there for a moment and slowly release it. Now take another slow deep breath in, expand your stomach, and slowly exhale. One more time: breathe slowly in, and slowly out.

Continue breathing slowly and deeply. Pretend your mind is a movie screen. Nothing is on it except for the color blue. Imagine the screen dissolving into the sky, a wide clear, luminous sky. Look around. There is a beautiful forest beckoning you toward it. Walk into the forest. As you pass through the trees, notice a clearing where the sun shines radiantly on everything in sight.

Before you is a rippling stream with water so clear you can see down to the bottom. Take your shoes off and put your feet into the water. It's fresh and cool. Linger at the edge of the stream and feel the sun warming the top of your head,

> your shoulders,
> your arms,
> your body,
> your legs.

Lean back and lie down on the grassy edge of the stream. Feel a light breeze gently caress your skin. As you lie there, listen to the sounds around you:

> rippling water,
> soft breezes,
> gently rustling leaves,
> bird songs.

Smell the moistness of the soil, freshness of the air, scent of the trees, honeysuckle. You are filled with a sense of calmness. In this moment, everything in your world is right. You are at peace.

Rest here a little longer and let this serene moment course

through your entire body. Let it settle into a place inside that you will bring with you wherever you go.

When you open your eyes, you will feel refreshed, happy, and relaxed.

Now, open your eyes and smile. It's good to be alive.

• Wise Self •

Close your eyes and take a slow deep breath in through the nose. Bring your breath all the way down as though it can reach into your stomach. Gently expand your abdomen as you breathe in. Hold the breath there for a moment and slowly release it. Now take another slow deep breath in, expand your stomach, and slowly exhale. One more time: breathe slowly in, and slowly out.

Continue breathing slowly and deeply. Pretend your mind is a blank movie screen. It is pale gold. Invite onto the screen an image of your wise self. You may see this image as a person or perhaps something else. Invite the details of your wise self to sharpen and clarify.

Now invite your wise self to walk over to you and sit down. Picture you joining with your wise self in conversation. Ask your wise self a question and see what is revealed. It may be a feeling, a sensation, or a thought. Whatever comes to you in this moment is a reflection of your innate internal wisdom.

Continue talking to your wise self, and see what other insights emerge. Trust whatever comes up. The highest part of you is revealing itself to your conscious mind. Trust the love and wisdom of your high self. It is there to guide you in any way you need.

Invite your wise self to make his or her presence known to you whenever you have a question or problem. Let your wise self know that you will always welcome his or her presence. Now, thank your wise self for whatever insights have been revealed.

When you open your eyes, you will feel relaxed, confident, wise, secure, and at peace. You will bring these qualities with you throughout your day. Now, open your eyes. Welcome to a new day.

Prayer

People who pray find comfort and solace, but the benefits go beyond this. An article in the May 2001 *Reader's Digest* reported several interesting findings about the power of prayer:

- In a 1995 study, Dartmouth Medical School researchers found that patients who found comfort in their faith had a three times better chance of surviving six months after surgery than patients for whom faith provided little comfort.
- Researchers at Duke University studied 4,000 seniors in 1999. They found that those who attended a house of worship suffered less depression and anxiety than those who didn't.
- Dr. Herbert Benson of Harvard Medical School reported that prayer and meditation can lower the effects of psychological stress, including high blood pressure and lowering of the immune system.

Religious scholar Karen Armstrong says, "Faith is something you work at day to day, hour to hour." She emphasizes that we can't just expect faith to be there if we're not willing to do our part of the deal. We have no guarantees that our prayers will work, but offering our words to God or whatever higher power we believe in is perhaps enough.

Sometimes our prayers are answered in ways we don't even know, or in ways that are revealed to us years later. This is what happened to me. When I was growing up, my mother suffered from a serious mental illness. Every night as a child I would lie in bed and pray for her to get better, but year after year my prayers went unanswered. I started to feel like God had abandoned me, that he answered certain people's prayers, but not mine. But for some reason I still kept praying.

Years later, I talked about this issue with a wise mentor. What she told me stayed with me for the rest of my life: God never did abandon me; he just chose to answer my prayers in a different way—by helping me get through, by helping me survive circumstances that could overwhelm any child. And that was the most important thing of all.

Hearing this was like a lightbulb going on. God really *had* heard me, but he was listening to the need *underneath* my prayers. And in his listening, he provided me with many gifts that may never have come had my mother been well: the gift of compassion, the gift of acceptance, and the gift of service. God had never abandoned me after all. In fact he blessed me with unexpected riches.

Those who lost loved ones on September 11th or at any other time have had their faith shaken to the core. One young woman I spoke to who lost her fiancé in the World Trade Center attacks has questioned her belief in God ever since. On the other hand, for Pam Whicher, who lost her husband in the 1995 Oklahoma City bombings, her experience of mourning has taken her to a place of faith. Listen to her advice to people who lost a loved one on September 11th: "You will mourn, not only for your murdered loved one, but for your life, the innocent pre bombing world you once knew. But I tell you also that it will be OK. Because you will someday forge a new life, one that can be richer because you will have come through fire and survived" (*New York Times,* December 23, 2001).

Faith calls us to believe that the fire our nation survived will bring us closer to something better. Perhaps it is that we must honor our inherent connections and know that we were placed on this earth to love each other and live in peace. This may be the highest call of every faith—one we must all answer now.

Nature

Nature may be one of our most underused tools for calming and healing. Try this next time you feel stressed: Stop everything and walk out the door. Look at the sky, feel the air, listen for sounds of nature—birds singing, leaves rustling , wind moving, sand shifting. On your skin feel the sensation of warmth, coolness, humidity, or whatever is present in your particular part of the world. Let the elements of nature reconnect you to the earth and to yourself. Now, especially, we must treasure this precious earth that we have so taken for granted.

When you can't step out your door, go to a window and look at the sky. Know that whatever problems you may be dealing with will ultimately shift and change, just like patterns of clouds that continually reconfigure. Know, too, that the sky is always there for you to cast your eyes upon, like a blessed friend reminding us of the infinite power of nature. Get your children in the habit of doing this on a regular basis. Help them make it a part of their lives.

When I taught elementary school, each year I would do a unit on the moon and stars. One of the homework assignments was for my students to go outside every night for a month and observe the moon. I'd ask them each to write down not only what they saw, but what they experienced as they stood before the vast expense of night.

Through the writings of my students I saw how the simple act of gazing at the night sky connected them to the universe and to something deep within themselves. Try this individually or as a family. It is another powerful way of using the elements of nature and the universe as a tool for healing.

> **EXERCISE:** Tonight when it gets dark, go outside with your children and stand beneath the majestic expanse of the night sky. Encourage your children to talk about what they notice and what they feel. Share your own thoughts with them. Imagine other families in the far reaches of the world, looking up at the sun or moon right now. Send them your blessings.

Surrounding Ourselves With Beauty and Meaning

Often it is the simple things that touch our spirits and uplift us, be they a vibrant piece of art, an elegantly written poem, dance, music, or our children's drawings. Surrounding ourselves with any of these adds beauty and depth to our lives. In our overly commercialized society we often forget the importance of simple aesthetic pleasures, none of which have to cost much.

Simple things of beauty and meaning can be so uplifting. My sister collects shells and stones that she keeps in a clear jar in her living room. A mom I know displays her children's artwork in beautiful frames throughout the house. So many things of beauty are available to us when our eyes and hearts are open.

> **EXERCISE:** What inspires you? Art, music, dance, crafts? Is there a low-cost way you can bring more of these into your life? Can you or your children create something to display in your home? Children's artwork is so vibrant. What have they made that begs to be framed? How can you increase the personal aesthetic of your life? Close your eyes, breathe deeply, and see what reveals itself to you. Jot down any insights in your notebook. Then follow up on at least one.

Live By Your Highest Priorities

"My family is the most important thing in the world to me, but I'm so fragmented by work and other obligations that the time left for them is filled with stress and tension. I find myself yelling all the time, and it really upsets me." Sharon voiced the words many parents feel. We want to have it all and do it all, and in the process we sometimes sacrifice what is most important. These uncertain times call us to honor our highest priorities now more than ever.

"I had rules that governed my working life before Sept. 11," *New York Times* journalist and mother Lisa Belkin wrote. "Looking back, they all included the word 'try.' I will 'try' not to work over the weekend. I will 'try' not to have dinner meetings two nights in a row. I will 'try' not to travel when my husband does. When the twin towers fell, I eliminated that conditional 'try' and started concentrating on 'will' or 'won't' instead" ("Rules Change Along With Psyches" *New York Times,* November 21, 2001).

What new "wills" and "won'ts" do you have? Rachel, the

mother of three, discovered some new priorities after September 11th. "I'm allowing myself to do things I thought I couldn't make time for before. I hadn't read a book in months, but last week I picked up a book I'd had on the shelf for ages and actually started reading it. Also, after ten years, I've taken out my guitar again. Hearing me play is great for my kids too. It brings a sense of lightness into our home. I'm realizing you can't put things off forever. If I've been wanting to do something, I'm going to do it now."

Jen, another mother of three, realized she had gotten so swept up in her children's schedules that she had lost touch with her most important priorities. "I made the decision to pull back on some of the kids' activities. I was driving them around so much we never had any decent time together. I was stressed, they were stressed, and this added to the tension we were already feeling." Since September 11th, she has decided to pull back. "Now, each child has one after-school activity that I have to take them to, and we all have down-time in the evening. Doing this has made a huge difference in the way we relate to each other."

If you're worried that pulling back on your children's activities will put them at a disadvantage, don't. Harvard University released a statement this year that an overabundance of activities doesn't necessarily make for a more attractive candidate. Enabling a child to develop inner resources, imaginative capacity, and the ability to reflect are far more important than constantly being barraged by structured activities. Being overscheduled can actually get in the way of your child's creative capacity and emotional well-being.

Now ask yourself these questions: Are you and your family enslaved by a rigid schedule that provides no breathing space? Are you living your highest priorities? If not, what keeps you from living them? The exercise below will help you find out.

EXERCISE: Have your notebook at your side and close your eyes. Inhale some slow deep breaths through the nose, expanding your abdomen as you do. Hold the breath in gently for a moment, then exhale slowly. Repeat this several times until you feel relaxed. Then ask yourself this question: "What are my most important priorities—the ones I feel deepest in my heart?" Reflect on this for a few moments.

Write down whatever comes to you. Now close your eyes again and ask yourself this question: "Am I living my highest priorities, and if I'm not, what's in the way?" Breathe slowly and deeply and allow whatever is there to come up. Write about this too.

Now ask yourself one more question: "What can I change that will enable me to live congruently with my true priorities?" Here's where suspension of disbelief comes in. The first voice in your head will probably say, "I'm trapped. There's no way I can change things." Let go of this reaction; it won't serve you. Now, look again, and be creative. Is there some subtle shift you can make? Is there something you can add or subtract from your life that will enable you to honor your priorities more?

Stay with this question for a while and allow the answer to reveal itself. The solution you are seeking may take time to unfold. Just keep staying with the question and return to your notebook to reflect upon whatever comes up. When you discover a solution (which you will if you stick with this), please drop me an e-mail and tell me what it is. You'll find my e-mail address at the end of the book.

Make a Difference

I can't stress enough how important this is in making our lives meaningful and healing the world around us. Of the hundreds of people I have interviewed for this book, one theme keeps coming up over and over again—people who are out there making a difference have more hope. They have a greater connection to their own goodness, power, and purpose. They remind me of words the mystic poet Kabir once said: "Something inside of me has reached to the place where the world is breathing." That's what happens when we contribute. We step into the place where the world is breathing, rather than being trapped in our own little corner.

Regardless of age, ability, or socioeconomic status, people who are out there making a difference have a more hopeful, empowered outlook. Sarah is eleven. She has been involved in community service activities all her life. Listen to what she has to say: "I know things are scary right now but I think I'll be fine as long as I keep looking out for everybody and helping make things better. It's like you're helping the world out. Even if it's something not so big, like going to a shelter and giving people food, you're still helping and that really does make a difference."

Janice, the mother of two, told me about how she's given herself a greater sense of control since September 11th by helping organize a resource center that offers free counseling to people in her community who were affected by the World Trade Center attacks. Janice's involvement in this project has given her the sense that regular people really can make a difference. "I don't feel as frightened now," she said. "Being involved gives me sense of hope."

As you read on, you'll come across stories about people of all ages and walks of life who are healing by helping. Doing this yourself may be the most important thing you can do. There is an urgency for all of us be involved, and heal the earth by helping others. Yes, we're all busy, but think of this—there are twenty-eight thousand people in our world who die every day from hunger and hunger-related diseases. That's over nine times the amount of people who died in the World Trade Center. And what's worse, this is preventable. How can we allow ourselves to be so busy that we enable this to continue?

If you're inspired to start right now, go to Resources and Bibliography at the end of Chapter 7. You'll find a list of organizations that would be thrilled to have your help, and they'll tell you exactly what you can do. Reach in to that place where the world is breathing.

END THOUGHTS

Frank Ostaseski, founder of the Zen Hospice Project, works with people at the end of life. He has learned many valuable lessons over the years from those he has helped. Ostaseski says the two questions people tend to ask most as their lives are coming to an end are: "Am I loved?" and "Did I love well?" The quality of the love they have given and received is what matters more than anything else. All the other things people strive for in their lives—success, wealth, material objects—pale in comparison. This may be the most important thing to remember on the road to peace, hope, and healing.

RESOURCES AND BIBLIOGRAPHY

Websites

Beliefnet
www.beliefnet.com
   Meets spiritual needs through readings, meditations, and insightful writings by the worlds top experts on spirituality.

Internet Mental Health
www.mentalhealth.com
   A free encyclopedia of mental health information and resources for people of all ages.

Books and Articles for Parents

Breathnach, Sarah Ban. *Simple Abundance*. New York: Warner Books, 1995.
A daybook of thoughts, quotes, and suggestions for a peaceful, harmonious life.

Brussat, Fredrick and Mary Ann. *Spiritual Literacy: Reading the Sacred in Everyday Life*. New York: Touchstone, 1996.
Wonderful collection of readings and ideas on finding the sacredness in life.

Dalai Lama and Howard C. Cutler. *The Art of Happiness.* New York: Putnam Publishing Group, 1998.
One of the world's most renowned thinkers tells how serenity and inner peace can be attained by all of us.

Dalai Lama. *An Open Heart.* New York: Little, Brown & Co., 2001.
A simple guide to finding and sharing compassion and happiness.

Estes, Clarissa Pinkola. *Women Who Run With the Wolves.* New York: Ballantine Books, 1996.
Antholgy of folklore, fairytales, and dream symbols to help restore women's intuitive abilities.

Flanigan, Beverly. *Forgiving Yourself: A Step-By-Step Guide to Making Peace With Your Mistakes and Getting On With Your Life.* Foster City, Calif.: IDG Books Worldwide, 1996.
Letting go of guilt and forgiving oneself in order heal relationships, gain inner peace, live more freely, and honor the self.

Fox, Matthew. "From Despair to Hope, from Grief to Creativity, a Spiritual Response to September 11th." *Bridges,* summer 2001, vol. 12, no. 2.

Gerzon, Robert. *Finding Serenity in an Age of Anxiety.* New York: Bantam Books, Inc., 1998.
Techniques to help you "make anxiety work for you, not against you."

Hanh, Thich Nhat. *Peace Is Every Step.* New York: Bantam, 1991.
A beautiful, easy-to-read book of practical ways we can make our lives more peaceful. Brilliant in its simplicity.

Peck, M. Scott. *The Road Less Travelled.* New York: Touchstone, 1978.
A classic. Helps build a deeper understanding of self and others. Nurtures peacefulness in our relationships.

Vanzant, Iyanla. *Faith in the Valley: Lessons for Women on the Journey to Peace.* New York: Simon & Schuster, 1996.
Tells the reader how to deal with low points in life and seek inner peace.

Chapter 3

Calming and Coping Strategies for Children

Children are love made visible.

—Anonymous

Our loving presence is the first thing that makes our children feel safe. And when we feel calm, we have a calming effect on them. Doing the activities in the preceding chapter will help you develop a calmer place inside yourself. Forced calmness doesn't work; children see right through it. Raising peaceful children requires us to be peaceful at the source, because we are the well from which they drink.

Even children of the youngest ages can sense our stress. Radha, the mother of three, shared this story with me:

My husband worked at the World Trade Center. On September 11th he was one of the lucky ones—he got out. But during the hours before he reached us we were numb with fear. When he arrived home safely I was filled with a sense of gratitude and relief. Yet, in spite of it, something strange happened—my month-old baby immediately stopped nursing. From that day on he would not return to the breast. Even though my husband was safe and our lives seemly intact, my baby was picking up the stress beneath the surface. Young as he was, he knew.

The impact of living in a world where war and terrorism have come into our living rooms has touched our children more than we may realize. In a *New York Times* article, "A Sisterhood of Grief" (December 23, 2001), Edward T. Linenthal writes about the link between the Oklahoma City bombing and the World Trade Center attacks, stressing how the push toward closure is simplistic and perhaps even damaging. "The ripple effect of the bombing in Oklahoma City was devastating, but the scope of its impact still will not be known for years. Preschool children who watched images of the ruins of the Federal Building on television in the days after the bombing often thought a new building had been blown up each time they saw it. For years, these children kicked the walls of buildings they went into to make sure they would not fall." Linenthal wondered how the repeated images of the planes crashing into the World Trade Center and constant references to anthrax and other forms of bioterrorism would leave their mark on the psyches of our children. And now we must take care not to let our children be enveloped by those images once again as the commemoration of these events is played out in the media.

Children have been affected in ways we might see for a long time. Depending on your child's underlying emotional stability, reactions will vary. The anniversary of September 11th, for some, will open old wounds. As an elementary guidance counselor told me, throughout the school year following the attacks, many children who were emotionally vulnerable experienced recurrences of grief or trauma relating to past events. For some, grief that was unexpressed before came rising to the surface in episodes of anger and rage. According to the National Institutes for Mental Health, "Grief over the loss of a loved one, teacher, friend, or pet . . . may be reawakened by reminders such as media reports or the anniversary of the death."

"Some of my students are just plain out of sorts," a second-grade teacher told me many months after September 11th. "I have two who burst into tears at the slightest provocation, and another who stares out the window in a daze. For each of these children, these behaviors are new. Yet when I ask them what's the matter, they force a smile and say 'nothing.' "

This type of behavior is not atypical for six- to nine-year-olds. Developmentally, they're old enough to be aware of what's happening in the world, but are often reticent to talk about it. In their minds, talking about what scares them makes it more real. Also, some children of this age want to protect the adults in their lives from upsetting thoughts.

According to a study done by the National Center for Post-Traumatic Stress Disorder (PTSD), school-aged youth are the ones most likely to be affected by traumatic events. How much they're affected depends on a number of factors, including proximity to the event, personal involvement, and prior traumas. Renowned child expert Dr. T. Berry Brazelton explained that children reacted to September 11th in specific age-related ways. According to journalist Marion McParland, Dr. Brazleton said that "three- to six-year-olds generally wanted to know why it happened, asking questions like, "Was it because the people were bad?" Six- to twelve-year-olds wanted to know how it happened, asking questions like "How do we protect ourselves?" And twelve- to twenty-year-olds wanted to know what it meant. They reacted with statements such as "We're living in a new world, not the one to which we were looking forward." Dr. Brazelton also said, "Parents and teachers are the models children watch. Parents can teach resilience by how they respond, how they handle anger and fears, and how they behave as members of society. We have to be resilient ourselves. Let your children know that you're going to do the best you can to keep them safe and to keep yourself safe."

Remember, too, that every child is an individual, and your child's responses might not fit into a prescribed dictum. Being sensitive to the nuances of your child's words and behaviors is the best way you can determine if the stress of world events has taken a greater toll than you might have suspected.

SYMPTOMS OF STRESS AND TRAUMA IN CHILDREN

Don't think that just because your children aren't talking about their fears they don't have any. Even children who have been shielded from the news can't help but pick up things on the playground or even passing a newsstand. Sometimes between children's TV shows there are news flashes that sound terrifying: "Shopping mall bombed in Israel." "Chances of another attack in the United States." "Can we survive bioterrorism?" All of these ideas have seeped into the national consciousness, and our children are absorbing them. Listen to some of their words:

"Sometimes I'm scared," confided thirteen-year-old Frank. "My dad was going to go to France. I didn't want him to go on the plane. I was so relieved when he canceled the trip."

Five-year-old Hannah expressed feelings of fear also. "When you do a war, what if the other side wins? What would happen to us?"

Eight-year-old Ben said, "It's not a very good time. There's war in Afghanistan and there's war in the world. I don't like the bombings."

"I'm scared the Taliban might come to New Jersey someday," eleven-year-old Jeffrey shared. "Maybe they'll decide to bomb McGuire Air Force Base."

"It's sad that all these crimes are being done all around the world. It makes me feel so bad that all these awful things are happening," said twelve-year-old Andrew. "I find it scary."

Fifteen-year-old Amy said: "I feel unsafe to know that people are dying all over the place. It's frightening to think about."

Six-year-old Leigh said, "I hope there's not a World War III. I don't want to have to go and fight."

Nine-year-old Tess gets upset every time she sees reports of war on television. "It feels like it will never be peaceful again. I'm worried the world may come to an end."

In the January 2002 issue of the *New York Times* "Education Life," Leslie Berger talked about "new levels of student anxiety and depression" in college students. Along with the fallout of

September 11th, societal factors are sending them into therapy in greater numbers. "The classic concerns—leaving home, fitting in, forming relationships, doing well, finding the right career—have been complicated by more split families, more lifestyle choices, the alienating effects of technology, constant bombardment of information, a shrinking economy and mounting academic pressure." In the same article Rubin Kaufman, director of the counseling center at SUNY-Purchase, said, "We are drowning here."

Young people of all ages are more vulnerable than ever to the effects of stress.

If you think your child might be suffering from reactions to stress or trauma of any kind, here are some signs to be aware of:

Ages 3 to 5

- Physical complaints such as stomachaches and headaches
- Fearfulness and feelings of not being safe
- Stranger or separation anxiety
- *Compulsively* "playing out" the source of trauma; e.g., building towers with blocks and crashing them down
- Avoidance of situations that may or may not be related to the trauma
- Sleep disturbances
- Loss of acquired developmental skills (like dressing oneself)
- Frequent crying

Ages 6 to 10

- Physical complaints and concerns about their health
- Anxiety and fearfulness
- Compulsive reenactment of the trauma through play or drawing
- "Omen formation"—believing that warning signs predicted the trauma, and a tendency to be hyperalert in order to recognize new warning signs.
- Preoccupation with how the crisis could have been solved or averted
- Sleep problems

Preadolescence and Adolescence

- Nightmares and flashbacks, difficulty sleeping, and feeling detached or estranged
- Impulsive and aggressive behaviors
- overpreoccupation with other concerns unrelated to the trauma
- rebelliousness and antisocial behaviors
- risk-taking behaviors

Teens can normally be rebellious, even a little aggressive, but if this becomes excessive, it's time to seek professional intervention. If your teen starts engaging in promiscuous behavior, starts dabbling in drugs, or using alcohol, all these are danger signals. Also, any extreme changes in behavior—eating, sleeping, recreation, homework, or activities with friends.

The National Center for Post Traumatic Stress Disorder encourages parents to be alert to other changes in children of all ages. If your child was directly affected by the trauma of September 11th or any other, he or she may experience symptoms such as feelings of isolation, poor self-esteem, difficulty in trusting others, acting-out behaviors, and problems with school performance. If your child develops syndromes that weren't present before, like attention-deficit/hyperactivity disorder, oppositional defiant disorder, and conduct disorder, they could be related to the trauma he or she experienced. In any of these cases, it is important to seek professional help. Therapeutic intervention has been highly effective in helping children heal from the effects of trauma.

There are lots of things you can do in your own home to help your child calm, cope, and heal. Now let's take a look at what they are.

HELPING CHILDREN COPE WITH STRESS

First let's look at a general breakdown of age-related strategies for helping children cope. After that, we'll look at a wide range of creative activities you can do at home with children of all ages.

Ages 3 to 5

Children of this age need plenty of reassurance that they are safe, but make sure it's authentic. Avoid statements like, "We will never have another terrorist attack again," but you can say, "I am here for you and I'll always protect you in every way I can. And when you're at school (or day-care), your teachers are keeping you safe." Taking your children to visit the local police and fire department so they can talk directly with the people who work there can be very reassuring too.

For young children, Dr. Perri Klass, pediatrician and author of *Love and Modern Medicine,* says, "It's alright to make the promise you can't keep for sure: 'I'll be here to take care of you tomorrow and every day.' " She says, "Even 5-year-olds understand that everyone dies sometime and will be comforted if you simply say, 'I have every intention of being here until you're old. I'm going to be very careful about what I do' " (*Parenting,* December–January 2002).

Let your children know it's okay to feel afraid or sad if that's how they are feeling. Soothe them during these times rather than trying to talk them out of their feelings. Validating how your child feels is essential. Initiate discussion, but don't push. Open the door gently and encourage your child without being intrusive.

Try sitting down on the edge of your child's bed at night before she goes to sleep. Cuddle up together and then say something like, "I'm just wondering how you've been feeling about all the stuff that's been going on in the world lately." Or, "I'm just checking in. Anything you'd like to talk about?" Let your child take the lead from there.

Encourage play that allows your child to act out some of the things he's afraid of. Playing fireman or police officer is a healthy way to do this. This is how young children try to make sense of what we've lived through. As long as this type of play doesn't become obsessive, it's a good outlet.

As we talked about earlier, encouraging your child to draw or paint whatever is on his mind is very healing. You'll find lots of way to help her do this later in the chapter.

Listen and reflect back whatever your child has to say. Sometimes this can be hard, because, as parents, we often want to fix the problem. But by listening and empathizing, we allow our child a safe space to reveal what he really feels. When five-year-old Tad told his mom he was afraid to fly, she encouraged him to talk about it. Here's their conversation:

TAD: I don't want to go to Disney World for vacation.
MOM: Why not?
TAD: I'm afraid bad people will come on the plane and hurt us.
MOM: So you're afraid that we'll get hurt if we fly.
TAD: Look what happened to all those people who were on the planes the hijackers took!
MOM: You're afraid hijackers might come on our plane?
TAD: Yes. I don't want us to die.

By just plain listening Mom allowed Tad to get his fears out on the table. Then she was able to give reassurances like, "I know how scary it is to fly right now. I was a little nervous too. But then I thought about all the planes that fly safely every day, and all the people traveling on them. In fact, our neighbor Tom flies several times a month for his job, and he's gotten home safely every time. I know the airlines are taking extra measures keep all their passengers safe."

Mom didn't try to talk Tad out of his feelings. Instead, she listened, reflected back, and offered assurances that were authentic. After that, Tad wasn't as nervous about their trip.

Ages 6 to 10

Children this age may avoid discussing painful feelings. Be open and encourage them to open up to you. Dr. Janine S. Shelby of UCLA Medical Center developed this wonderful activity to help children express feelings—make a personalized book with your child's name on the cover. On each of four pages write the following:

- Page 1—This is Sara. Something happened that was very scary. (Sara draws her picture on this page.)
- Page 2—Sara doesn't want to talk about it. Here's what would happen if she did. (Here the child writes or draws a related picture.)
- Page 3—If Sara starts talking about how she feels, this could happen too.
  —She would feel worse.
  —Mom and Dad wouldn't like hearing how she's really feeling.
  —Something else might happen.
  (Help your child check off the appropriate choice and write about it further.)
- Page 4—If Sara decides to talk about what's on her mind, I wonder how she might end up feeling? (Here draw a happy face and a sad face. Have your child circle one. then she can explain why she feels the way she does.)
  (Adapted from "Brief Therapy With Traumatized Children," by Janine S. Shelby.)

Other things that help children of this age are:

- Deep breathing and visualization
- Positive self-statements like, "I am safe and well and so is my family."
- Altruism, reaching out to help others. Guidance counselor Jane Mangino says: "After kids have expressed their feelings, the thing that helps them the most is taking action." When children help others, it removes their own feelings of helplessness.

I have used many of these strategies for years with children of all ages and they are extremely effective. Take the time to teach your child each of the steps above and you will be giving them a life-long tool for calming and destressing. The younger you start, the better. You can actually start doing this as part of a bedtime ritual with children as young as four.

Preadolescents and Adolescents

Here are some strategies that work with this age group:

- Discussing fears openly with an empathetic listener
- Deep breathing
- Visualization and relaxation techniques like the ones you will find later in this chapter
- Positive self-statements like, "I am safe and well."
- Altruism, reaching out to help others. This is particularly helpful for kids of this age. Allowing them to translate fears into positive action gives them a healthy vehicle for healing. There's a wonderful website you can go to for ideas on how your teen can help. It's called TeenHoopla. Their website is: http://ala8.ala.org/teenhoopla/activism.html

  Here your teen can access a wide range of helping activities from homelessness to saving the rain forest. If your child expresses feelings of hopelessness about the world, have him look here. It will show him that people really can make a difference, especially people his age.

Sometimes just being there with your teen in a safe and loving setting is enough to help him open up. Or by gently asking questions about other parts of his life and listening without judgment. Our intent listening is the best way to get our teens to talk more. When we show authentic interest, and validate what they say without interrupting or interjecting our opinions, they usually end up sharing more. More on this in Chapter 5.

Physical affection also opens channels to communication. Many kids in their teens still like to be cuddled when they're alone with us. The kind of closeness that hugs bring out can help a teen feel safe to open up.

CALMING ACTIVITIES FOR CHILDREN OF ALL AGES

Dealing With Fears and Nightmares

Alan Siegel, coauthor of *Dreams and Nightmares,* suggests the following creative steps to help children overcome the effects of nightmares.

• Give your child emotional and physical reassurance. Siegel writes that the first step to calming your child's anxiety is by "welcoming the dream." Provide a safe environment for your child to talk about his nightmare openly and without judgment.

• Help your child imagine a different ending of his dream. Siegel calls this "rescripting." Brainstorm together a better way for the dream to end. Then have your child draw, write, or act out the new ending. "Rescripting is like assertiveness training for the imagination," Siegel writes. "Ominous dream monsters, demons, and werewolves can be tricked and trapped, tamed and leashed, given time-outs, bossed around, and generally made less intimidating."

"With parental assistance, the child with nightmares can be taught to revolt and throw off the yoke of dream oppression by using magical means such as fairy dust, a wizard's wand, Star Trek 'Phasers,' special incantations and spells, or other handy tools of the imagination." This creative practice can help children with problem solving in other areas of their lives too.

• Now the child is ready to rehearse how he's going to handle the nightmare if it comes back again. Siegel advises having your children "create their own repertoire of Magical Tools." Think of specific things they can do to get rid of the monsters, witches, or bad guys in his dreams. Be as creative as possible and actually put what your child needs next to his bed like a special spray to dissolve a monster, or a pretend sword to ward off an evil sorcerer. Use your imaginations and fire away against the demons of night!

By the way, many experts advise that following a nightmare, it's best not to get into your child's bed or allow him to sleep in yours. According to the Department of Pediatrics of Arkansas

Children's Hospital, this gives your child the message that he can't recover from a nightmare without you. Remember not to downplay the nightmare or tell your children "It was just a bad dream." To your child, the nightmare was very real and very scary. Denying this can make him feel unsupported.

Calming Nighttime Rituals

Tense times can cause sleep problems in children of all ages. Greta, the mother of ten-year-old Terry, shared how she's been helping her son calm himself at night:

> My son has always had difficulty falling asleep. Lately it's gotten worse. We've developed some wonderful rituals that have really helped. First I give him warm milk, a source of tryptophane which helps induce sleep. We choose a good book to read together. Then I snuggle up in his bed and turn the lights low so he can drift off to sleep at the end of the story.
>
> We also hug and say how much we love each other, and sometimes we talk for a while after the story. On some nights instead of reading a book I tell him stories from my childhood. This is particularly calming for him. He loves hearing about things I did as a little girl and what his grandparents were like when they were younger.
>
> Our routine has been very comforting for Terry and it's helped him fall asleep even when he's been anxious during the day.

Don's eleven-year-old daughter, Randy, also tends to be anxious at night and often has trouble falling asleep. "We've done guided imagery with our daughter when she can't calm herself down. It helps her relax and drift off to sleep with soothing images. On some nights I'll say, 'Imagine yourself an ice cream cone on a hot day. Imagine yourself melting in the sun.' Sometimes I'll use the image of warm water. I'll start at her toes and have her imagine the water working its way through her body, relaxing each part. I think the calming sound of my voice also helps. She likes knowing I'm by her side when she's anxious. And through guided imagery she's learning how to help herself feel calm even when I'm not there."

Another couple I worked with had difficulty getting their two boys to sleep at night. What helped was creating a calm, quiet environment in their home during the hour before bedtime. Adjusting the level of activity, lowering the lights, and modulating noise helped lull their children to a calmer place. Putting on quiet, soothing music in their rooms also helped.

If your child is anxious or tense, any of these will create a soothing atmosphere. Also, keep your voice low, and slow your movements. Rushing at bedtime only heightens the tension. Slowing down and speaking low can infuse your nighttime routine with peacefulness and calm.

Guided Visualization

As we saw in the last chapter, visualizations are a wonderful way to soothe the mind and body and feed the spirit. Children of all ages can benefit from this practice. Visualization will give your child a tool for self-soothing and provide images that she can continue to picture when you're not there. Once your child has learned how to utilize her imagination in this way, she'll have a skill she can use for the rest of her life.

Here are some visualizations you can use with kids of all ages. Have your child lie down, then turn the lights low and read to her in your most soothing voice. Linger between sentences from time to time to enable your child's mind to fully picture each part.

• The Mountain •

Close your eyes and take a nice slow deep breath in through the nose. Bring the air all the way down into your stomach. Gently stretch out your stomach like a balloon as you breathe in. Slowly release the breath and let your stomach deflate. Now take another slow deep breath in, expand your stomach, and slowly release it. One more time: breathe slowly in, and slowly out.

Continue breathing slowly and deeply. Keeping your eyes shut, pretend there is a blank movie screen. Nothing is on it except for the color blue. Now bring on to your screen a tall, beautiful mountain covered with green grass and flowers. Walk onto the screen of your mind and start walking up a path along the mountain.

The air is clear and crisp—feel it blow gently through your hair.

The scent of flowers is sweet—breathe it in, and the sun shines bright—feel it on your skin.

With each step up the mountain, you feel calmer and lighter. You feel like you can almost float up the mountain.

You arrive at the top and it is illuminated with the light of the sun. Stand at the top of the mountain and look down. You are protected here. Grass and flowers surround you and the sun warms your entire body. Look around and see the healthy green earth below. Look up and see the clouds, sun, and sky above. Breathe in all this light and beauty and bring it to a deep place in your heart. Feel the beauty and peacefulness of this moment fill you completely.

Now you are ready to walk back down the mountain. Pick some flowers to bring with you on the walk down. They are red, yellow, purple, orange, and blue. Their stems are bright green. Smell the flowers as you walk down the path of the mountain. (You can use some lavender essential oils here. Put a drop on a tissue and let your child inhale the scent while keeping his eyes closed.)

Each step feels light and free. You arrive at the bottom peaceful, happy, and calm.

Bedtime: You are tired from your walk. You find a soft bed of grass to lie down upon and go to sleep. Your eyes are heavy; your heart is full. Sleep well, my love, and have peaceful dreams.

Alternate ending: You are energized by your walk. You feel happy, confident, and ready to face the world. Everyone you meet today will make you feel like smiling. Extend peace and calmness to all of them.

• The Waterfall •

by Joan Sichel

Put your hands in your lap or at your sides. Join your thumb to your middle finger, making the letter "O." Breathe in deeply and imagine that your stomach is a balloon filling with air. Now breathe out and imagine the air is leaving your stomach. Breathe in again, and breathe out. One more time, in and out.

Now close your eyes and keep breathing deeply and slowly.

Relax your feet.

Relax your legs.

Relax your arms.

Relax your body.

Relax all your muscles.

Relax you neck and head.

Relax your mouth and tongue.

Take another slow deep breath in and out. Now imagine you have a third eye—right in the middle of your forehead. This eye has the power to see an invisible path that is right in front of you. Take a step down your path as you breathe slowly and relax. Take another step, feeling even more relaxed. Take a third step and feel the calmest you have ever been. Walk along your path. At the end is a waterfall. Touch the water and feel its drops on your skin. *Become* the waterfall. Imagine yourself flowing down then dissolving into ten thousand drops. Now feel yourself landing in the gentle arms of a sunlit pond.

Look, a child is floating in the water. It's you! Enter your body and feel the sunlight on your face as you float. Stay there for a while and feel yourself floating on the gentle waters. Breathe in and breathe out deeply and slowly.

Now you're ready to leave the pond. As you stand, you feel a pebble beneath your foot. It is smooth and cool. Pick it up and put it in your pocket. Wherever you go, your pebble will remind you of the love, safety, and peace you feel right now. (Note: After this visualization, give your child a pebble to keep.)

All you'll ever have to do is touch your pocket and you will feel this calmness again. (Allow your child a few moments to savor the calmness of this moment.)

Keeping your eyes closed, touch your pocket, and silently give thanks. Stretch your hands to the sky and give thanks to everything that is good.

Lower your arms. Send peace and hope to someone in your family,

to your neighbor,
to someone in your school,
to someone from another country,
to all the leaders of the world,
to the earth, air, and water,
and to all living things.

Now picture yourself standing taller and prouder than ever before. Open your eyes (or drift off into a peaceful sleep).

Note: If your child has never seen a waterfall before, show her a picture of one before beginning this visualization.

• The Star •

Close your eyes and take a nice slow deep breath in through the nose. Bring it all the way down into your stomach. Gently expand your stomach like a balloon as you breathe in. Slowly release the breath and let your stomach shrink. Now take another slow deep breath in, expand your stomach, and slowly release it. One more time: breathe slowly in, and slowly out.

Continue breathing slowly and deeply. Pretend your mind is a movie screen. Nothing is on it except for the color blue, dark blue, the color of night. Bring onto your screen a bright, twinkling star. It sparkles like a hundred diamonds. Walk onto the screen of your mind and look up at the star. You want to touch it, but it is too far away.

Raise your arms higher to reach toward the star. Feel yourself lifting up into the sky. You begin to fly. You are weightless. Each time you move your arms, they lift you higher into the sky. You feel safe and light. The light from the star guides your way. Fly toward it, and see the light become more sparkly and bright. Pass through a mass of sparkles. A light above draws you closer and closer.

Now you arrive at the star itself. It is luminous and radiant. Reach out and touch it. The light goes straight to your heart and warms you from the inside out. Rest on the star for a little while. Soak in the calm feeling the light gives you. It is the calmest feeling you have ever had. Look at the sky, stars, and heavens. Let the light continue to fill you.

Now you are ready to return home. Once again you are lifted up and begin to fly. Look back at the star and continue to feel its radiance as you fly away. The radiance is now inside of you. Fly back to your home and gently land in your warm. cozy bed. You are calm, peaceful, and filled with light inside.

Bedtime ending: You feel so relaxed and ready for sleep. Close your eyes and let the light of the star lull you into a peaceful sleep filled with beautiful dreams. Good night.

Alternate ending: You feel calm and alert. Take the peace and calmness you feel right now into your day. Let the light inside you bring kindness and love to everyone you meet. Today will be the best day ever.

• The Beach •

(For Bedtime)

Close your eyes and take a nice slow deep breath in through the nose. Bring your breath all the way down into your stomach. Gently expand your stomach like a balloon as you breathe in. Slowly release the breath and let your stomach shrink. Now take another slow deep breath in, expand your stomach, and slowly release it. One more time: Breathe slowly in, and slowly out.

Continue breathing slowly and deeply. With your eyes closed. Pretend your mind is a movie screen. Nothing is on it except for the color blue, light blue. Now the blue becomes a big, full sky on a summer day. The sky is filled with fluffy white clouds and a shining yellow sun. Beneath the sky is the beach.

Walk onto the beach and feel the sand under your feet. It is soft and warm between your toes. Look out toward the ocean. The waves are very calm. Watch them roll in and roll out, in and out. Each time a wave rolls back to sea, it leaves a shiny imprint on the sand. Touch the cool, wet sand.

Now let water cover your feet. It feels cool and refreshing. Put your hands in the water and feel the droplets of a wave splash your body. Now walk into the water and let a tiny wave lift you up. You are floating. Another wave comes along and lifts you higher. Your body moves with the gentle motion of the water. And as you float, you feel each wave rolling under you,

lifting you up

and lowering you gently down.

The water feels warm and soothing.

The sun shines on your face and arms.

You hear the sounds of seagulls,

you smell the salty water.

You feel a deep sense of peace as you float on the waves.

You return to the shore. There is a soft white quilt on the sand. Lie down on the quilt. Cover yourself with one end and cuddle into the softness. Rest on the beach and let the breeze calm you even more. Close your eyes and drift into a gentle sleep where you will enter the world of beautiful dreams. Good night.

Movement Activities

Movement can also be healing, cathartic, and fun. Often our inhibitions cause us to shy away from movement activities, which is a shame, because there's such transformative power here. Think of how great you felt the last time you danced. Watch people on a dance floor; they're usually smiling and vibrant. We deprive ourselves of these vital feelings when we neglect to include movement in our usual repertoire of activities.

Therapist, author, and movement specialist Dr. Teresa Benzwie works with people of all ages, helping them reconnect to themselves and others through motions. She says, "Creative movement as a modality helps us gain knowledge through the body. . . .

connecting to ourselves in the deepest, most direct ways." Below are adaptations of two calming activities she uses with people of all ages:

Gentle Sway

You can either do this as a family or with one child at a time. If you do it as a family, you'll need to partner up in sets of two. One partner sits comfortably on the floor or in a chair and closes his eyes. The other partner stands behind him. She gently takes her partner's head in her hands and very slowly moves it around in the most nurturing way possible. Every movement should be filled with love, care, and gentleness. Continue doing this for about two minutes. Then release you partner's head and gently lift one arm, roll it, and move it around lovingly and gently. Then very slowly, put the arm down and lift the other. Take about two minutes for each arm. You can stroke your partner's head and arms too. Wind up with a short backrub. Then switch places. Follow this up with a hug and some conversation about how you each felt giving and receiving this kind of nurturing.

Mirroring

I remember doing this partner activity years ago and being absolutely transfixed by it. Put on some slow, quiet music. When I did it, we used the music of Pachelbel. Choose one partner to lead, the other to follow. Sit facing each other on the floor and hold your hands up about one inch from each other's as though they were pressed against a pane of glass. Make sure your hands don't touch. In rhythm to the music, the leader moves her hands and the follower mirrors the exact movements. The movements can be large, small, circular, or linear, as long as they are slow and rhythmic. The head and shoulders can be added. After about two to three minutes, switch. Continue switching back and forth for about ten minutes. This activity is very calming, soothing, and connecting.

Art

Using clay or play dough, have your children model shapes and objects. Pounding clay is a good anger-releasing activity. Rolling and shaping clay can also be very soothing. Encourage your children to create abstract or realistic forms of different shapes and sizes. Talk about them afterward and see what emerges.

If you're brave, fingerpaints are a wonderful medium for catharsis and calming. The colors and textures of the paints can be very visceral and the feel of smooth paint on your fingers very soothing. Cover your kitchen table with an old plastic tablecloth or several layers of newspapers and let your children finger paint to their hearts' content. If you're really brave, join them.

Creating collages is another creative way to calm. Help you children gather old magazines with colorful pictures, colored paper, objects of different kinds that can be glued onto a piece of construction paper or cardboard (Styrofoam bits, yarn, toothpicks, old postcards, wrapping paper remnants, anything shiny). Put out scissors and glue, and have your children create shapes and forms with a variety of materials. Collages can be any size or shape, and they can be accessorized with markers, glitter, sequins, and more.

If you have lost someone close to you, you can help your child make a memory collage of that person using photographs and objects. This is not only a great catharsis, but a beautiful way to honor the person you loved.

Writing

As I mentioned earlier, writing can be a powerful medium for expressing feelings. It's also a tool for calming, enabling your child to recall happy experiences, work through difficult ones, and develop deeper self-knowledge.

In the entry below, a young girl struggles to understand herself through her writing. These words are from the diary of Anne Frank:

> I hope I shall be able to confide in you completely, as I have never been able to do in anyone before, and I hope that you will be a great support and comfort to me.

I have two things to confess to you today, which will take a long time. But I must tell someone and you are the best one to tell, as I know that, come what may, you always keep a secret.

I want to go on living even after my death! And therefore I am grateful to God for giving me this gift, this possibility of developing myself and my writing, of expressing all that is in me.

Expressing all that is in us—writing enables this. It can help children of all ages work through so many things that confront them in life, including grief and loss. Listen to this excerpt from a story by six-year-old Ketan:

"I had a bird that I used to feed. One day he died. I was so sad. We buried my bird. I loved him so much."

In *The Creative Journal for Children,* author Lucia Capacchione suggests the following ways to get your children started using writing as a tool for living:

• Encourage your child to start off by drawing if she's not comfortable writing. She can use abstract lines or scribbles to represent her feelings or she can draw something more realistic. Have her do a self-portrait. Reassure her that her journal is just for her and that you'll never look at anything she writes or draws unless she asks you to.

• Until your child's writing starts to flow on its own, suggest topics for journal entries. Capacchione suggests starting your child off with a letter to herself. Encourage her to include all the things she likes about herself and things that have special meaning in her life.

In the next entry she can describe her day, her family, or her life in an autobiographical sense. Every page can be accompanied by pictures. Some children like to glue things into their journals: photos, ticket stubs, pictures of things they like. Any of these can be a jumping-off point for writing.

• Encourage your child to move on to feelings after she's become comfortable with the journal process. If you journal yourself, you might want to share excerpts of what you've written.

Sharing your writing with your child can spark her thoughts and help her feel safe expressing them, even if only for herself.

• If your child gets stuck coming up with ideas to write about, you can suggest these as prompts:

My Best Friend
My Family
Heroes
Blessings in My Life
Favorite Things
Likes and Dislikes
Memories
Special Birthdays
How I'd Like to Change the World
Three Wishes
When I Grow Up

Poetry

There are so many wonderful books of children's poetry, some of which are listed at the end of this chapter. A good children's librarian can suggest more. Try reading poetry with your child, letting its rhythms lull and soothe you. *The Place My Words Are Looking For,* by Paul Janeczko, is a wonderful book to start with. It is a short anthology of wonderful poetry that's very accessible to adults and children alike. Here are a few excerpts from poems it contains.

From "A Little Girl's Poem," by Gwendlyn Brooks:

> *Life is for me and is shining!*
> *Inside me I*
> *feel stars and sun and bells singing.*
>
> *There are children in the world*
> *all around me and beyond me—*
> *here, and beyond the big waters . . .*
>
> *I want the children to live and to laugh.*
> *I want them to sit with their mothers*

> *and fathers*
> *and have happy cocoa together . . .*

Or this by Cynthia Rylant on her estranged father's death. From "Forgotten":

> *Mom came home one day*
> *and said my father had died.*
> *Her eyes all red.*
> *Crying for some stranger.*
> *Couldn't think of anything to do,*
> *so I walked around Beaver*
> *telling the kids and feeling important.*
> *Nobody else's dad had died.*

Poems like these express something deep and alive inside children. Often when they've been exposed to poetry that's meaningful to them, children start writing poems on their own, discovering another life-long medium for self-expression and healing:

Listen to these powerful lines from a poem by ten-year-old Annie:

> *First a secure knot.*
> *Me at one end,*
> *my dad at the other. Slowly*
> *something is cutting away at the knot and*
> *it finally breaks.*

And these by Melinda Whicher, whose father was killed in the Oklahoma City bombing:

> *And I discover a dark and lonely place*
> *where no person should have to go*
> *And I claw my way out the best I can.*

For some children, poetry can be their salvation. I remember students I worked with who had great difficulty in many academic areas, developing passion for poetry. It reached into an unexplored part of their psyches and allowed them to express feelings that would have otherwise lain dormant.

END THOUGHTS

The most awe-inspiring quality of the human spirit is its resilience. I remember watching a documentary about the lost boys of Sudan. War had taken everything from them—their parents, their homes, their siblings, and even access to food and water. Yet somehow they survived. Many of them found each other, and together they navigated the desert terrain to refugee camps, where they were finally given the basics for survival. Alone, emaciated, and apart from their loved ones, these young men somehow managed to hang on to hope. They wanted a better life and would do anything in their power to create it. A humanitarian organization brought a group of the lost boys to the United States so they could start a new life. When asked how they had managed to maintain hope, they spoke about the deep faith that kept them going. Even though they had lost everything else, they held on to the spiritual part of themselves, and that made all the difference.

The lost boys of the Sudan triumphed in spite of it all, and their resilience was almost incomprehensible. They are a living tribute to the fact that human beings are gifted with possibility. As we embark on the path to peace, we must remember that this is so for all of us.

RESOURCES AND BIBLIOGRAPHY

Websites

KidsPeace
www.kidspeace.org
    Provides mental health treatment programs, crisis intervention, and education initiatives. Helps families help kids avoid and over-

come crisis and violence. "Healing," their on-line magazine, can be ordered at: healing@kidspeace.org.

Stone Soup
www. Stonesoup.com
   Stories and writing activities for children. Excellent site.

Books and Articles for Adults

Brooks, Barbara, and Paula M. Siegel. *The Scared Child: Helping Kids Overcome Traumatic Events*. New York: Wiley, 1996.

Capacchione, Lucia. *The Creative Journal for Children: A Guide for Parents, Teachers, and Counselors*. Boston: Shambala, 1989.
Seventy-two writing and drawing activities to express emotions, build self-esteem, and foster creativity.

Kaduson, Heidi, and Charles E. Schaefer. *Short-Term Play Therapy*. New York: Guilford, 2000.
Compilation of writings from leading play therapists on helping children of all ages through emotional difficulties.

"Practice Parameters for the Assessment and Treatment of Children and Adolescents With Post-Traumatic Stress Disorder," *Journal of the American Academy of Child and Adolescent Psychiatry*, 37:10 supplement, October 1998. The National Center for PTSD.

Shelby, Janine S."Brief Therapy With Traumatized Children: A Developmental Perspective." *Short Term Play Therapy*, 2000.

Siegel, Alan, and Kelly Bulkeley. *Dreams and Nightmares*. New York: Random House's Three Rivers Press, 1998.
Creative solutions for helping children with nightmares.

Unicef. *I Dream of Peace*. New York: HarperCollins, 1994. Preface by Maurice Sendak.
Moving anthology of poetry and drawings by children from the former Yugoslavia.

Books for Children

Adoff, Arnold, ed. *I Am the Darker Brother*. New York: Macmillan, 1968.
Wonderful anthology of poetry by black poets.

Berry, Joy Wilt. *Let's Talk About Feeling Angry*. New York: Scholastic, Inc., 1996.
Part of the "Let's Talk About" series, which deals with all the feelings childen experience. Explains how to handle even the toughest situations and emotions in a clear, simple language. (Grades K–2.)

Bunting, Eve. *Smoky Night*. New York: Harcourt, 1994.
Daniel learns about violence and concilliation when riots go on in his neighborhood. This is a 1995 Caldecott Medal winner. (Grades K–3.)

Clifton, Lucille. *Everett Anderson's Year*. New York: Holt, 1974.
Poems for younger African-American children.

Cohn, Janice. *Why Did It Happen: Helping Children Cope in a Violent World*. New York: Wm. Morrow, 1994.
A little boy becomes fearful and angry when his friend, the grocer, is injured during a robbery.

Dunning, Stephen, et al., eds. *Reflections on a Gift of Watermelon, Pickle, and Other Modern Verse*. Glenview, Ill.: Scott Foresman, 1966.
For teens and preteens, a wonderful anothology of poetry.

Frank, Anne. *The Diary of a Young Girl*. New York: Doubleday, 1967.
Anne Frank's orignal writings during the Holocaust. (Grades 6–12.)

Gardiner, Barbara, and Jane Aaron. *When I'm Angry*. New York: Golden Books, 1998.
Children learn how to deal with anger. Includes a parents' guide in a question-and-answer format. (Grades K–2.)

Grant, Cynthia D. *Mary Wolf*. New York: Simon & Schuster/ Atheneum, 1995.
Depicts the mental instability that difficult circumstances can bring out in a family, and what can happen when a gun is introduced. (Grades 6–12.)

Hoberman, Mary Ann. *Fathers, Mothers, Sisters, Brothers: A Collection of Family Poems*. New York: Little, Brown, 1993.
Poems about all different kinds of families. Includes multicultural illustrations. (Grades K–2.)

Janeczko, Paul. *The Place My Words Are Looking For*. New York: Macmillan, 1990. A wonderful anthology of poems and thoughts from thirty-nine leading poets. A book for parents and kids to share.

Park, Barbara. *Mick Harte Was Here*. New York: Knopf, 1995.
When Phoebe's brother Mick dies in a bicycle accident where he wasn't wearing a helmet, Phoebe's friend, Zoe, helps her cope with the loss. Humor helps lighten the story.

Spinelli, Jerry, *Stargirl*. New York: Knopf, 2000.
The story of a high school student who is very different from everyone else. Addresses the need to conform and the effects of compassion. (Grades 5–12.)

Spinelli, Jerry. *Wringer*. New York: HarperCollins, 1998.
Palmer dreads having to kill a pigeon on his tenth birthday—an act deemed necessary by his bullying friends. Palmer struggles to honor his conscience and stand up to his friends. (Grades 3–8.)

Wolfelt, Alan D. *Healing Your Grieving Heart for Teens*. Fort Collins, Colo.: Companion Press, 2001.
Practical suggestions and comforting words. There is a companion book for younger children by the same author.

PART II

CREATING
PEACE AT HOME

Chapter 4

Creating Peace in the Family

If we are to reach real peace in the world
we shall have to begin with children.

—Mahatma Gandhi

If there is right in the soul,
there will be beauty in the person,
If there is beauty in the person,
there will be harmony in the home;
If there is harmony in the home,
There will be order in the nation;
If there is order in the nation,
There will be peace in the world.

—Lao Tzu

Home is the place that most nurtures us, the safe haven we go to at the end of a stressful day. Home is the one place in the world where we can be exactly who we are. And if we work to make it this way, home can be a place of love and peace, one that nurtures anyone who walks through our door. In times of stress and sorrow, this can make all the difference in the world.

Mother Teresa once said, "Spread love everywhere you go:

First of all in your own house. . . . let no one ever come to you without leaving better and happier." No matter what goes on in the outside world, we have the power to do this and to be "better and happier" for our efforts. Imagine your home as the place where peace in the larger world actually begins. Every world leader was once a child, and the values they grew up with in their homes inform the belief systems and the decisions they make as adults. Imagine the skills and values you teach your children today being carried into the future and used in boardrooms, laboratories, construction sites, hospitals, schools, and the halls of government. Imagine your children as the leaders of tomorrow, because they are. Everything you teach them will have a direct impact on the future.

I remember saying this in a workshop and a mother who was having problems with her son said, "Oh, no, I'm not doing so well with my own child, I shudder to think I could be screwing up the rest of the world too!" If you're feeling that way, please don't. Just as I told this mother, we all make mistakes—none of us is perfect. I made many mistakes when I was raising my boys, and they still turned out great. Trust that your mistakes will have far less impact than the love you give and all the good things you do. And realize, too, that if there are things you need to change, you have the ability to do that now. Every day is an opportunity for growth.

PEACE STARTS WITH YOU

The seeds of peace are planted first when we honor our own needs—acknowledging emotions, nurturing ourselves when we need nurturing, calming ourselves when we're afraid. When we give ourselves what we need, we allow the seeds of peace to take root. Only then can these seeds grow, thrive, and spread to those around us. A plant deprived of water cannot germinate. But nurtured by the sun and nourished with rain, the plant will thrive, producing seeds of its own. Hundreds of seedlings can grow from a tiny plant. So it is with us. By taking care of our own needs, we can spread countless seeds of peace to those we love and those we come in contact with.

Peace in the larger world begins with each of us, and now the quest for peace is being put to the test. Every word we speak, every deed we perform, radiates out and affects others. Philosopher and psychologist William James once said, "The greatest discovery of my generation is that human beings can alter their lives by altering their attitudes of mind." We have the power to do this—to alter our attitudes, and to reframe the way we see ourselves in relationship to the world. We are an integral cog in the wheel of peace. Our attitudes, beliefs, words, and actions have an impact far beyond what we realize, sometimes even when we don't know it.

I remember one day driving to work, feeling totally wiped out. I decided to stop for a cup of coffee at a little convenience store along the way. I went to the self-service counter, poured some coffee, and was about to take the first sip as I handed a Middle-Eastern man behind the counter a twenty-dollar bill. "Sorry, I have no change," he told me, and my heart dropped as the image of having to leave that longed-for cup of coffee on the counter flashed into my mind. "It's okay," he said with a smile, "have it for free." I remember feeling almost overwhelmed by his response. This sweet man in a convenience store offered me more than a free cup of coffee; he offered me a little dose of kindness. His gesture, small as it was, made my day. And as I went about my work, I felt the residue of this man's kindness passing on to the people I interacted with. Without even knowing it, his actions affected many others.

Kind actions have that kind of ripple affect. We each have the ability to generate respect, compassion, acceptance, kindness—or not. The choice is up to us in every minute, and it starts right in our own workplaces, schools, and homes.

The first thing you can do to start creating more peace in your home is to model peace. Our children watch and watch us for cues as to how they should behave. When we deal with conflict in aggressive or disrespectful ways, we see the same behaviors in them. Conversely, when we can manage our anger and handle our conflicts respectfully, our children generally follow suit. As a parent you have much more power than you realize. *You* are the most important role model in your children's lives. Listen to these words from Quinn, an independent, free-spirited sixteen-year-old with solid values and a soaring spirit: "I've learned by my mom's example to do what's right. She trusts me enough to let me make my own decisions. I completely respect her. She negotiates with me instead of just telling me what to do. She helps me understand her reasoning. I want to do what she asks because I love her so much. You do things out of the heart."

This is what many of us want with our children—not that we're going to negotiate every little thing, but that there's mutual respect and a willingness to compromise, a meshing of hearts. Every step you take toward creating a peaceful home makes this more possible.

PEACEFUL PARENTING

Life has provided us with this wonderful laboratory called family. Family is where we are first challenged to live the skills of peace-making through our actions, not just our thoughts.

Marie, the mother of four, said, "Family is the place where it's hardest to do this. Everyone knows how to push my buttons. With friends and colleagues at work, it's different. I'm more de-tached." Family is our place of deepest connection, so doesn't it make sense that family is also the place where we experience our greatest extremes of love, anger, sorrow, frustration, joy, disap-pointment, and pride—the full spectrum of emotions? And ulti-mately, if we allow it, family can be the place where we discover how to deal with these emotions and come to a place of peace. When we embrace the life-changing opportunity family provides, we become more finely tuned, gaining greater depth, compassion, and wholeness. And when this happens at home, we can then bring all of these qualities out into the world, making it, ideally, a more peaceful place for us all.

Please remember, however, that peaceful parenting is not a

panacea. Your children will still fight sometimes, and on bad days you'll still "lose it." Like Lauren, the mother of two little boys, said, "On the days when Brady's hurling himself on the floor for the tenth time, I really find out what I'm made of." Lauren has been practicing the keys to peaceful parenting that you are about to read, and on most days, Brady keeps himself off the floor, but this doesn't happen one hundred percent of the time. And on the bad days, Lauren retrieves her grounding by taking a step back, breathing deeply, and reminding herself of what she's committed to instead of letting herself get sucked into Brady's tirades. She knows that peaceful parenting is a path you walk even when you come to detours.

It's like tending a garden. We might be out there every day, but we'll still get some bugs, and rabbits may still nibble on our lettuce. Our efforts don't guarantee perfection. But isn't it great to watch our plants grow and thrive, even if they aren't perfect? Allow the keys that follow to be like sunlight that nourishes your garden. And know that what you plant enriches the world.

One more thing: Peaceful parenting requires true intentionality, just as peace in the world does. As we see in the papers every day, peace doesn't happen spontaneously. Like maintaining good health and a fertile mind, peace is something we have to work at. Just expecting it to happen out of nowhere is unrealistic. It's a skill that must be nurtured on every level—within ourselves, our families, our communities, and the world. Home is the place where this starts.

Here is a highly effective system you can use to teach peacemaking or any other value you hold in high esteem.

The Most Effective Teaching Framework You'll Ever Use

To teach your children any important skill or value, follow these steps:

- Model it. If you don't do it, they won't either. As I said before, your modeling is the most powerful teaching tool you've got.

- Teach it. Children need to be *taught* the virtues, values, attitudes, and behaviors we most cherish. *Be intentional.* Don't just assume that because something is important to you, your children will automatically absorb it.
- Expect it. Be crystal clear about your expectations when it comes to the most important values and behaviors you want to see in your children. Be specific in spelling things out, and stand tall in sticking by what's most important.
- Reinforce it. Always compliment your children when you see them doing what you want. This is the most fundamental way of getting them to repeat positive behaviors.

The Keys to Peaceful Parenting

1. Make your home a place of kind words. Unkind words can pollute the atmosphere in your home. They spark conflict, injure self-esteem, and undermine relationships. Once again, our role modeling is key. Make a commitment to eliminate put-downs of any kind. Always remember that put-downs create tension and cause anger, even when spoken in jest. They have no place in your home.

Each time I work with teachers, the first concern I hear is: "The kids are so cruel to each other. They hurl insults and sarcasm, and alienate kids who are different." It breaks my heart every time I hear this. Did you know that approximately 160,000 children a day miss school for fear of how they'll be treated by their peers? (National Education Association statistic.) And a poll conducted by *Child* magazine reported that 88 percent of the 2,000 adults polled thought kids didn't treat others with respect.

Put-downs are rife in our homes too. The National PTA did a study revealing that the average parent makes eighteen negative comments a day for every positive comment made to their children. You can help turn this tide by staying acutely aware of what you say, not only to your children, but to your spouse, your friends, and even to yourself. Words have power, and what we speak we'll eventually hear back from our kids. Dr. Maurice Elias, coauthor of *Raising Emotionally Intelligent Teen-agers,* says, "It's not enough to be smart. Being kind is critical. Adults must lead the way."

We must also take care to counterbalance what we're hearing in the news. Labels like "evil-doers" are emotionally loaded and give kids the feeling that if someone hurts you, it's okay to see them as inherently evil. Doing this, in a way, absolves us of our own responsibility and makes us forget that in the majority of conflicts, both parties have done something to contribute to the problem—including the one our country is engaged in now. Certainly we cannot allow the acts of September 11th to go unpunished, nor should we blame ourselves for what happened, but we must not oversimplify the situation and believe these acts were solely motivated by the evilness of the perpetrators. Violent acts are not perpetrated in a vacuum. If we want to prevent this kind of thing from happening again, we must seek to understand the complex causes.

Using hate-filled language brings on more hatred. It creates a descending spiral of vengeful acts, followed by more hateful language, followed by increasingly more violent acts. Yes, it's appropriate to express anger, but not with labels like the ones we've been hearing. "I'm heartsick and angry about what's been going on in the world," one mother told her teen, "and I can only wonder what we might have done to bring about such wrath." Her teen replied, "You're acting like we got what we deserved!" "No," her mother replied, "no one deserves to have innocent people slaughtered, but we need to understand what motivated that kind of behavior so we prevent it from ever happening again." Hateful words preclude this kind of thinking.

Words of hate and unkindness poison the atmosphere in our world and in our homes. Here's a good rule of thumb for your home someone once told me a long time ago: "Try treating your children like you would a friend who's come to visit." As the writer Jessamyn West said, "A broken bone can heal, but the wound a word opens can fester forever."

Using kind words is a critical step in making your home a

place of peace and teaching that words have the power to both harm and heal.

2. Have clear, fair standards and limits and stick by them. Teaching your children the standards that are most important to you, and *expecting* them to be honored, is another critical step in creating a peaceful home. Harmony isn't possible without clear standards and limits that you're willing to stick by. This doesn't mean autocratic rules and an unwillingness to compromise; what it does mean is deciding what's most important, letting your children know what it is, and following through. Without this, all our well-intentioned directives fall apart.

Emma McLaughlin and Nicola Kraus worked as nannies for wealthy families for seven years and ended up writing a book about it. What they saw in many cases made them sad—a lack of time spent with kids, a lack of intimacy, and a lack of consistent standards. The result, according to Emma: "The children are so angry they want somebody to lash out at. They realize there are no consequences for that behavior." She went on to express deep concern about these children, saying, " . . . they haven't turned out O.K. and that's heartbreaking for us." (*New York Times,* February 7, 2002)

Time, warmth, intimacy, and love are all fundamental to our children's happiness and well-being. So are standards.

When I was raising my kids as a single mom, these were the standards I had for them:

- We treat each other with care and respect.
- We don't hurt each other physically or verbally.
- We listen to Mom and speak to her respectfully, whether or not we agree with what she has to say.
- We are honest.

At our family meetings, when we put together our guidelines for a peaceful family, my children were clear that these standards needed to be interwoven. Being clear on what was important to me helped them understand what I expected from them.

The majority of parents I've worked with who've had trouble disciplining their children admit that they've been inconsistent in conveying what their standards are. They've also been inconsistent in sticking to them. If one of your standards is "There is no physical fighting," you need to be one hundred percent clear that this is nonnegotiable. Then even on bad days when your nerves are shot and you're energy's drained, don't ignore a physical fight. Something I say to every teacher, parent, and principal I work with is this: physical fighting *always* needs a consequence. Physical fighting, like put-downs, has no positive purpose and does *not* belong in your home.

EXERCISE: What standards are most important to you? Reflect on this, and write about it. Brainstorm a list of standards and then choose the top four. As much as possible, frame them in the positive, e.g.: We treat each other with kindness and respect. We work out our differences using words, not fists. We listen when Mom and Dad ask us to do something. Now have a family meeting and tell your children what your standards are.

As I said before, being clear about your standards is critical to your children honoring them. The second critical piece is explaining why these standards are important so your children don't see them as arbitrary. For example, "Physical fighting only makes things worse. Can you imagine if your dad and I belted each other every time we got mad, or if Dad punched his boss each time they had a disagreement? It's important for you to learn how to talk things out, just like Dad and I do."

Also critical is having fair consequences. Some parents find it helpful to sit down with their children at a family meeting and allow them to suggest some consequences along with the ones you think of. Children are a lot harder on themselves than we often expect. One mom said, "My boys suggested they miss TV for a week if they have a physical fight. I thought two nights would be plenty." Children have an innate sense of right and wrong. Including their input helps them become more responsible for their own behavior.

Some parents feel guilty about setting limits. "I work all day," lamented Carol, the mother of three, "and when I come home at night I don't want to be punishing my children, so I let a lot go by." Don't fall into this trap. By having clear, consistent standards and limits, you will ultimately prevent power struggles and extended periods of nagging.

When I was teaching first grade many years ago, I still remember one child turning to a boy who was used to getting his way by badgering his parents, and saying, "Nagging doesn't work with Mrs. Drew so you might as well forget it!" Children learn very quickly not to waste energy nagging and whining when they get no response. By honoring our own standards and sticking by what we say, children start to see that manipulation doesn't get them anywhere.

Our standards and limits create the firm ground that our children walk on. Each time we ignore our own standards it's as if the ground beneath our children's feet opens up and their foundation becomes shaky. Renowned child psychologist Haim Ginnott once said, "Children depend on the adults in their lives to set limits for them until they are old enough to do so for themselves." By consistently setting fair limits and honoring our own standards, we teach our children that the ground they walk on is solid.

Does that mean never compromising? Absolutely not. The trick here is to compromise when *you* think it's the best thing to do, not when your children have worn you down. In fact, it's a good idea to think ahead of time about areas where you are willing to compromise. This is particularly important with teens and preteens, whose growing independence is supported by a balance of compromise and limits.

Where are you comfortable compromising? Choose areas that would in no way impact your child's moral development or safety. Clothing and the condition of their rooms are good places to start. Look for places where you can say "yes" so that your "no's" won't feel like they're constant. When we compromise, we teach our children to do the same.

Positive discipline requires us to walk a fine line between laying down the law and negotiating, sticking to our guns and compromising, being caring and being firm. Remember the exercise we did earlier about the "Wise Self"? This is a good thing to repeat when you're in doubt about which way to go. Try it now:

> **EXERCISE:** What current discipline issue are you dealing with? Close your eyes and take some slow deep breaths. Call your wise self into your consciousness. Invite her to sit down next to you. Now ask her what she thinks you should do about this particular issue. Allow the high place in you to provide insight and direction. When you are finished, write down the insights that were revealed.

3. Catch your children in the act of doing things right. Usually our radar is attuned to what our children are doing wrong, not right. And that's what we tend to comment on most. "Andy, comb your hair. It's a mess!" "Sarah, hurry up and finish your dinner. I can't believe how long you take."

Too often when our children are doing what we want, we heave a sigh of relief and remain silent. Catching our children doing things right is an extremely powerful way of reinforcing the good things they do and building their self-esteem. Remember the statistic I shared with you earlier: the average parent makes eighteen negative comments to one positive. Yet, we're sitting on a gold mine of untapped positive results we can bring about with a minimum of effort.

Each time we sincerely compliment our children on something good they've done, we hold up a mirror to their best selves and allow them to see its reflection. "Carrie, I like the way you cleaned your room. All of your toys are put away and your dirty clothes are in the hamper. Good job!" Expressions of affirmation like this one mean the world to our children and prompt them to repeat positive behaviors.

Just make sure your compliments are deserved and sincere. Find the place in your heart that feels a sense of joy about what your child has done, and affirm her from that place. Doing this has tremendous power. "Alex, I don't tell you this very often, but I'm so proud of the kind of student you are. You work so hard and always try your best. That matters to me more than A's on your report card."

One word of praise holds more weight than a thousand reprimands.

Teach your children to do this for each other, too, not only complimenting positive things, but affirming each other for the wonderful people they *are*. "Jenny, you're such a kind person. You always let me join you when I want to play." "Henry, you're such a good athlete. You run faster than anyone I know." Developing an atmosphere of affirmation is another potent way to create a more loving, peaceful atmosphere in your home. And when you do this, your children take what they've learned out into the world around them.

4. Spend at least fifteen to twenty minutes a day listening to and interacting with each child. Life gets so busy that moments of intimacy and connection get lost. A recent study found that on weekdays, moms who stay home with their kids spend only an average of thirteen minutes a day of exclusive time with each child. For working moms, it was eleven. Our kids need more than this and they're hungry for it.

A second-grade teacher I talked to from a large suburban district expressed deep concerns about how this lack of time was affecting the children she worked with. Listen to what she had to say:

> My students' lives are so frenzied. After school they go from one activity to the next and never seem to have any

down-time. I'm seeing more and more children with attentional issues, and I'm starting to wonder how much all this frenzy is a factor.

I've started doing pie graph charts with parents at conference time so they can see how much time they're actually spending with their children—not time in the car rushing from one thing to the next, but time when they really interact with their children in a meaningful way.

When we put their lives on a chart, dividing up how much time they were spending in school, activities, the car, and doing errands, what was left for quality time was shocking. What I saw was approximately 5 percent. That's all! Something has to change. I fear for the future of our children if this trend keeps up. Parents need to be strong enough to streamline their lives and say "no" to all this overactivity.

What our children need most, especially now, is intimate time with you, talking, interacting, and being listened to. Even if our children aren't expressing it, they are affected on some level by what's going on in the world. Intimate time with you is particularly critical in giving them a sense of security and wholeness.

Parents I've worked with who've begun giving their children individual uninterrupted time, have experienced very significant changes:

- Better communication
- Increased closeness
- Fewer power struggles
- A deeper sense of connection

If you can't spend a minimum of fifteen to twenty minutes with each of your children every day, try alternating days. One mom I know who has four boys switches off with her husband—they each spend individual time with two sons on one night, and the other two on the next. A single father of three I talked to can't always give each child individual time on the nights he has them, so on one night he'll be with two individually, and the next night, one.

Working this out in any way you can will be well worth your time and energy. You'll create moments of trust and love with your child that will stay with him for the rest of his life.

5. Hold regularly scheduled family meetings. Family meetings are a wonderful way to stay connected, work out problems, and be intentional about creating peace in your family. Here's how you can get started.

Begin by telling your family how much you love them and how important they are to you. Follow with something like this: "Wouldn't it be great if we could make our home a place where we get along better?" Talk about this, and see what your children think.

Now ask them this question: "What's your vision of a peaceful home? What would it look like to you?" Talk about this too. Your family meetings will run smoother if you have some guidelines for sharing. Here are a few you I'd like to suggest.

Guidelines for Sharing
- Each person gets a chance to speak.
- When someone is speaking, we focus on that person and listen with an open mind.
- Don't interrupt.
- Be kind, respectful, and accepting even if you don't agree with what someone else has to say.

Take time to have each member of your family share their vision of a peaceful home. Then ask this question: "How can we make this happen?" List suggestions on a chart. Keep it brief and try to include something from each member of the family. Your chart might look something like this:

Guidelines for a Peaceful Family
We agree to:

- Be kind and respectful to each other; we will eliminate put-downs of any kind.
- Work out conflicts without fighting.
- Cool off when we're angry.
- Listen to Mom and Dad.
- Help each other.

What's so powerful about this process is that it gives each family member a voice; children more readily follow rules they've helped to set.

Parents who hold family meetings on a regular basis report that they have a greater sense of cooperation in their homes, and fewer conflicts. Here's how Tony and Jessica addressed a troublesome issue they were faced with through family meetings. As the parents of three, they were concerned about the amount of time their children were spending in front of the TV and knew they needed to cut back. When they brought this up at a family meeting, their children initially balked. So Tony and Jessica, avid TV-watchers themselves, made a commitment to cutting back on their own TV-viewing. They knew that if they wanted their children to change, they had to change first.

With their example to follow, the children agreed to a weekly cutback, decreasing TV time by a half-hour each week, then eventually arriving at one hour a day. To make it fun, the family decided to go to a local arts and crafts shop and pick up a variety of materials that the children could use during their TV cutback time. They also decided to do a toy exchange with a neighboring family, trading toys every few weeks so the children could have a variety of different toys to play with at no extra expense. Jessica decided to rotate the toys and projects every few day to keep things interesting.

By working out this plan, Tony and Jessica's family addressed the problem of too much TV in a way the whole family was willing to accept. On top of that, they were taking valuable steps to nurture their children's creativity and imaginativeness, things that get sacrificed for the price of TV.

By the way, current research shows that Tony and Jessica were on the right track. A recent Stanford University study found that children who spend less time in front of the TV or video games—even nonviolent ones—are 25 percent less aggressive than children who spend over an hour day in these pursuits. Limiting TV/video game time to no more than an hour a day lowers the "aggression rating." According to *Building Moral Intelligence* author Michele Borba, "The average child will have witnessed eight thousand murders by the end of elementary school and two hundred thousand other vivid acts of violence by age eighteen." Here's another another shocking fact Michele gives about TV: "The American Psychological Association estimates that televised violence by itself contributes to as much as 15 percent of all kids' aggressive behaviors."

6. *Listen with all your heart to what your children have to say.* Jim, a single father of three in one of my parenting groups, complained that his eleven-year-old daughter would put up a fuss at bedtime every time the children slept at his house. Jim said, "I don't understand Carrie's problem. I spend time reading to all of them, but she always ends up in a snit." When I asked Jim if he knew why, he was at a loss. He said Carrie always shut down when he tried to broach the subject. So he decided to go home and try again using a different approach. He came back the next week, and we had this conversation:

JIM: I found out what's been getting Carrie so upset. She thinks I'm spending too much time with my son and not enough with her.

ME: How did you get her to open up?

JIM: Instead of telling her how annoyed I was by her fussing I told her how much I loved her and how badly I felt that she got upset every time she came over. I told her I really cared about what was on her mind and wanted to hear what it was.

ME: Then what happened?

JIM: When she started to talk, I just listened. I resisted the impulse to jump in with my own explanations. Like I was thinking that her brother Joey is only five so I have to read to him earlier. Then I read to her sister, and when I finally get to Carrie, I'm tired. Instead of getting into all that, I just let her talk and I found out that she's feeling cheated because I end up spending less time with her. She misses me so much that she looks forward to our time together all week long.

ME: And that's why she fusses when you see her?

JIM: Apparently so. I never thought about it that way before. I thought she was just giving me a hard time.

ME: So what did you decide to do?

JIM: Rotate the times I read to them. She doesn't mind getting into bed a little earlier if it means more time with me. She can stay up in her room after we're through and continue reading on her own. Carrie actually came up with that idea herself.

me: Sounds like you really got to the bottom of it.

JIM: I'm so glad I heard her out. It's like a weight has been lifted.

This is what often happens when we listen with all our hearts. Sometimes just hearing each other out is enough—even when there's no way to resolve an issue. And sometimes your child just needs to be listened to, like Carrie did, and reassured that you love her no matter what.

There's tremendous power in the way we listen, and for this reason Chapter 5 is devoted totally to the art of listening.

7. Manage your anger. Express it in nonaggressive ways and teach your children to do the same. Anger management is one of the most critical skills we can teach to our children. With the high degree of youth violence in our society, knowing how to manage anger can save a life. The first rule according to counselor Cecelia Cardano is this: *Don't meet anger with anger.*

Since September 11th, we have seen too many instances of anger leading to vengefulness. A Muslim man was killed simply for being Muslim, and countless people of Middle Eastern backgrounds have endured prejudice and discrimination. A gentle man I know from Egypt who runs an auto-body shop here in the United States told me his business has suffered considerably in the past year. The township officials who'd originally had him service municipal vehicles took the contract away, telling him they didn't want to deal with "a terrorist."

Anger can cause us to stereotype and generalize in frightening ways. Labeling an entire country or race of people "evil" is in itself an evil act. We all have within us the capacity for good and bad. No one person, race, or country is either of these in full. Allowing our anger to take us down the path of narrowness and prejudice is dangerous and we must take extreme caution not to pass this type of thinking on to our children. Learning how to deal with our own anger is critical.

Listen to the words of Nobel nominee Thich Naht Hanh: "The fire of hatred and violence cannot be extinguished by adding more hatred and violence. . . . The only antidote to violence is compassion." Vengeance brings out more vengeance; seeking to understand is the only way we will ever find peace. This is so in our personal relationships as well as in national events. If you're feeling angry about what our country's been through, talk to a friend, write about it, pound it out on the pavement as you run or jog, scream in the car with your windows closed, but please take extreme care not to allow that anger to turn into hatred or vengeance.

This is exactly what we need to teach our children, and it starts in the small moments of our lives. Here's an example of how one mother is doing this with her child. Natalie Gahrmann, who serves as a "coach" for working parents, has a seven-year-old son who's had a history of anger management problems. Natalie quickly learned that you can't teach a child how to manage anger simply by talking about it. Now she teaches him by her example:

> I take every opportunity to model how to calm down and communicate instead of just react. For example, the other day

in the grocery store the clerk did something that really annoyed me. I said to my son, 'Right now I'm feeling so angry I want to yell at that clerk. But that wouldn't be appropriate; it would just make matters worse.' Then I asked him, 'What else can I do right now?' We talked about how we sometimes want to lash out when we feel angry but that usually makes the other person more angry at us, and then things can get out of control. I asked my son to help me come up with some viable options. We talked about taking deep breaths, walking away, and telling ourselves to calm down. He's learning how to examine options for himself that way. And he's applying them more and more in his life. Watching me has been his most important way of learning.

Anger is actually a healthy emotion. It's what we *do* with our anger that makes it unhealthy, especially when we choose to hurt, exclude, degrade, or hate as the result of our anger. But anger can also teach us valuable lessons. Author Gary Zukav urges us to look inside ourselves when we are angry instead of looking at the person who triggered the anger: "Ask yourself what's being triggered in *you*." So often when we get angry it's about something else: feeling threatened, taken advantage of, or afraid. Zukav urges us to use every angry episode to discover what's inside *ourselves* that has us react.

When Veronica did this recently, it gave her deeper insight into reactions she'd been having all her life. Here's her story:

> A colleague had rudely challenged me on something I said. In that moment what I felt in my body was a huge surge of adrenaline that went straight to my heart. I could actually feel its physical release. My heart started pounding faster and my mind immediately went to defensive thoughts, like, "She's questioning my judgment! She must think she's better than I am!" As my mind went into overdrive, I very deliberately shifted my attention to my body. My heart was still pounding and my breath was more shallow than normal. I was breathing at the top of my chest, rather than deep in my lungs where I usually do. All the while, my thoughts were racing.

My mind wanted to stay in that reactive place, but instead, I asked myself what was being triggered here? Nothing came to me at first, so I started doing some deep breathing. I found that the breath had a hard time getting in. It was as though my chest was closed. I kept trying to breathe through what felt like a physical barrier, but it was so hard. There was one moment when I actually became frightened—as I tried to breathe deeper I felt almost like I was suffocating. That's when something clicked, and I realized I had hit the source of my reaction. I saw that what I most avoided when I had conflicts was *my own anger*. It was something I'd always tried to push down and smother. Always.

Suddenly memories started coming back. I recalled how, as a child, I had been taught that expressing anger was bad, and that *I* was bad if I expressed it. Not wanting to be thought of as "bad," I taught myself how to push down my anger each time it came up. I had literally become afraid of my own anger, as though I had some dark, shameful force inside of me. In that moment, I knew I had finally confronted a pattern that's been with me all my life.

Powerful stuff, and available to all of us when we take the risk of doing what Veronica did—looking inside at what was triggered, rather than focusing on the person who triggered us. You can do a variation of this process with your children. Read on to find out how.

Helping Your Child Manage Anger

Help your child debrief from angry episodes.   At a neutral time when your child has calmed down, talk about what happened. Help your child identify what caused his anger. Then brainstorm acceptable options; e.g. "Next time your brother takes your toy, instead of shouting or hitting, take a breath and think about what else you can do. Come to me and ask for help if you need to." Be 100 percent clear that it's okay to feel angry but it is *absolutely unacceptable* to hurt yourself, others, or property because of the way you feel.

Have your child identify what goes on in his body when he's angry. In order to gain control, we need to be aware of our physical reactions to anger. Help your child describe what happens inside—pounding heart, dry mouth, stomachache, rapid breathing, tense muscles. Anger is fed by these sensations along with negative thoughts we think. When I get angry, the first thing I feel is the quickening of my heart and the flush of my face. Adults and children I've worked with talk about tightening of the shoulders and neck, a knot in the stomach, clenching of the jaw, breathing faster, and more. Let your child know that all of these responses are normal and that it *is* possible to calm down when he feels them. Now go on to the next step.

Teach your child how to cool off. Help her list at least eight things she can do to feel better when she's upset or angry: getting a drink of water, walking out of the room, drawing, writing, listening to music, physical exercise, talking to someone, throwing a ball. Have your child keep her cooling-off list in a visible place she can refer to easily. Keep adding to the list. Let your child know that whenever she feels those angry sensations coming on, she needs to take a break, do something on her cooling-off list, then come back and talk about the problem. When you model this, it'll be easier for your child to see that it's really possible to cool off when you're angry. But doing it takes practice. We're so used to reacting. Discovering that we actually *can* cool off might feel strange at first. The more you do it, the easier it gets. The following step will help.

Teach your child how to "Stop, breathe, chill." The uncomfortable sensations in the body we just talked about are signals to STOP and BREATHE. When we feel angry or threatened, we often breathe shallow and fast, which tends to heighten the tension in our bodies. Our minds start going wild, and we want to leap forward in attack. This is actually rooted in our "reptilian brain," the source of the fight or flight mechanism. Millions of years ago that kind of response might have helped keep us safe from outside threats, but now, it gets us into trouble more than not.

When we go forward into anger, we heighten our own negative reactions and the negative reactions of others, usually making the problem worse. By stopping and breathing for a moment, we give ourselves the chance to back away from our reactions and *choose a response* instead. For example, when Margo's kids hadn't picked up the toys they'd been told to pick up a half-hour ago, she walked into the playroom and felt like screaming. Having done this many times before, Margo knew that screaming would only lead to reactions, excuses, and an ugly confrontation. Instead, she took a deep breath, walked out of the room for a minute, regained her composure, and then walked back in. Her children, completely thrown off guard by her atypical behavior, immediately started picking up their toys. (It doesn't always happen quite this easily!) She looked at them and said, "I'm glad you're finally cleaning up, but next time I want it done when I ask, not a half-hour later. I get really upset when I ask you to do things and you don't listen." Margo's "I message" was clear, assertive, and nonattacking. She took ownership of her feelings and held her kids accountable instead of assigning blame. Had she yelled, her kids would have been resistant. By taking a moment to stop, breathe, and chill, Margo not only regained her composure, she was more effective in making her point. *When we go on the attack, we usually escalate the conflict.* By seeing their mom stop, breathe, and chill, Margo's kids now have an example to follow when they're angry.

Introduce this technique at a family meeting or at some other neutral time. Have your child recall the last time she got angry and ask her to identify the emotions she felt. Help her describe the physical sensations she experiences when she's angry or threatened.

Now have her close her eyes, envision the angry situation, and bring the feelings back. Ask her to picture the word "stop" in large letters, like the ones on a stop sign. Have her say the word in her head, then breathe deeply several times. Now ask her to think of something on her cooling-off list she can do right away to help herself calm down. Have her picture herself doing this next time she gets angry, and have her practice saying the words, "Stop, breathe, chill." Make a sign with these words and hang it up.

Help your child create a calming statement he can make each time he gets angry. Anger is fueled by physical reactions and the thoughts we think. Aggressive thoughts intensify anger; calming statements equalize it. Teach your child to substitute aggressive thoughts with calming ones like "This isn't worth fighting over."

Now have your child envision the angry situation as he repeats his calming statement. *Have him picture himself maintaining control.*

Rehearse. Talk about situations that bring on angry feelings. Have your child visualize using "Stop, breathe, chill" and other strategies on his cooling-off list. Role-play a typical conflict using these techniques.

One caution: if you try all of this with your child, and he continues to express anger inappropriately or excessively, this may be a sign that you need to pursue the guidance of a professional. Especially now, if your child has had anger management issues, they may be more magnified. Your child's excessive or out-of-control anger may be concealing a problem that warrants more attention. If so, take heed. I sought the assistance of a family therapist when my sons were younger and I have been extremely grateful ever since. When we catch problems early and do something about them, we diminish the chances that they will become larger.

Being Willing to Let Go

Sometimes we hold on to anger simply because we want to. We might want to punish the person who made us feel that way. Or we might be feeling out of control in some area of our lives, so we take it out on a loved one. We all do this from time to time, but it's a negative choice that only makes things worse. And it *is* a choice.

It's essential that we choose other ways to channel anger, and teach our children to do the same. Otherwise we set in motion a life-long pattern that can undermine our relationships at home, at work, and in the world.

This was the case with Myrna, now in her sixties. As a child she never got along with her siblings, and she carried this resentment into her adulthood. Even after having children of her own, Myrna rarely welcomed her siblings in her home, and on the rare occasions their paths would cross, she'd have harsh words for all of them. Her daughter, Rose, remembers how difficult it was growing up around such animosity. "Even on the way home from a funeral, my mother would be bad-mouthing her brothers and sisters in the car. It was awful and it was lonely. I never got to know my own cousins." Now that she has her own children, Rose longs for the relationship she might have had with her cousins, aunts, and uncles. Her children don't even know them. Myrna's refusal to let go of anger is now affecting three generations.

Selma, on the other hand, chose a different path. Also in her sixties, Selma, had had difficult relationships with her siblings, too. Yet she made a decision to let bygones be bygones and fully embrace all of them. As a result, Selma's children grew up with a houseful of aunts, uncles, and cousins who warmed their lives. Now, as adults, the family is close and Selma's grandchildren have the love of a large extended family. Through the magnanimous gesture of letting go, Selma, her children, and their children have a richness in their lives that would otherwise have been lost.

The way we deal with anger can have a long-term impact on so many lives. Whether the impact is positive or negative is up to us. Many of us are still angry over the events of September 11th. How could anyone hate us so much that they would be willing to kill all those innocent people? Here's where we must rise to a higher level of consciousness and find a place inside ourselves that seeks understanding, not blame, hatred, or revenge. The following story exemplifies exactly what I'm talking about.

Samar Hamati lived with war at her doorstep for many years

when she was growing up in Lebanon. With her father's help she went through a metamorphosis in her thinking which enabled her to turn her own anger and hatred into understanding. These are her words:

> Growing up in Lebanon, I used to walk between bullets to get to school. Our country was under attack constantly, and as a child I started adopting an attitude of hatred. Why were all these people trying to hurt us and kill us? How could they be so horrible! My anger was eating away at me.
>
> My father was this incredible man who always sought understanding. Even in the face of war, he never lost his ability for compassion. One day my father took me aside and talked to me. He told me that in spite of everything that was going on—all the killing, all the hatred—inside we are all the same. He told me that violence is motivated by fearing each other, and by seeing the people who are our brothers as "the other." My father helped me understand that this sense of "otherness" was a fallacy, and that when brothers fight, hating is not the answer.
>
> He showed me that I must look for the light inside of each person, and understand that we are *all* human—every one of us. His words and actions helped me replace hatred with compassion. I carried this with me for the rest of my life and have taught it to my own children. Even though we have gotten threats from people in this country after September 11th, I still refuse to hate. I know their attitude comes from fear. As much as it hurts, I try to understand. My father helped me see that regardless of what goes on, God is inside all of us. If I can see God in every person I am free.

We must remember the profound wisdom of Samar's words each time we are tempted to hate. As she learned, we must take extreme care not to let our anger turn us into that which we fear most.

Not Getting Hooked by Angry or Negative People

Being around difficult people can sap our energy, yet sometimes it's unavoidable. But if we let them, these people can be our greatest teachers, providing us with an opportunity to find new ways of responding. Serena, the mother of two, works with someone who is extremely negative. She used to be very much affected by this person's behavior. Since discovering how to "unhook," she feels a greater sense of control over her own reactions. Here's what she does:

> I remember that in every moment I can make a choice. When I'm in the presence of someone who is angry or negative, I consciously move into the role of observer. I watch what's going on, but detach myself from it. The other person can do whatever they're doing, but by just observing, I don't allow their words or actions to affect me. I choose to go toward the light in myself and focus on that. This prevents me from being drawn into a negative reaction. Even though I can't control the other person's behavior, I *can* control my reaction to it. By observing and detaching, I keep myself centered. Since I've been doing this, I feel more relaxed, happier. I realize that I don't have to let another person's mood affect my day. It's very freeing.

Serena isn't ignoring or repressing her anger. She acknowledges it's there but refuses to let it take over. Moving into the role of observer makes it easier for her to choose the direction she wants to take, rather than letting the other person's mood make the choice for her.

Kathy has taught a similar process to her children: "When we're out as a family and we see someone being rude or negative, we imagine surrounding them with a cocoon of light. That way we don't get pulled into their angry energy. We send out care instead of more negativity." As a result, Kathy's children are seeing that they have the power to not be affected by negative people. They can choose a different response.

Doing what Serena and Kathy do takes consciousness and discipline that's well worth the effort. It's helped them see that *they* are in control, not someone else. Now they're teaching their children this incredibly important skill. This is exactly what we have to do when our anger about world events surfaces. Instead of allowing ourselves to be pulled deeper into rage and thoughts of revenge, we must unhook, then ask ourselves how we can we can channel the power of our anger into positive actions that will rectify the conditions that lead to violence in the first place. We must look at the bigger picture and see how we are all responsible, both part of the problem and the key to the solution.

EXERCISE: Is there someone or something you need to detach from? Try this. Close your eyes and imagine the light of the sun coming into your body, filling you with strength and calmness. Imagine the light surrounding you like an invisible shield. Now bring into your mind's eye a picture of the person who is difficult. Picture yourself safe and calm behind your shield of light, detached from whatever that person is doing. Imagine yourself calmly watching this person, unaffected by their behavior. If you can, imagine sending light to them and surrounding them with it.

You can use this exercise can at any time. Once you've gotten comfortable doing it by yourself, try it when you are confronted with a difficult person or situation. What you'll find is that by detaching, the right words will come to you if you decide a response is in order. When you come from a place of calmness, the words you need will be there.

Now teach this exercise to your children.

Resolve conflicts respectfully and teach your children to do the same. According to a study by the American Psychological Association, the average American family has a conflict every eight minutes. Conflict may be inevitable, but negative responses to it are not. Coleman McCarthy, director of the Center for Teaching Peace, says, "We are either problem describers or solution finders." We each have to power to become solution finders. And when we do this, incidences of conflict decrease, and resolutions increase.

Why is it more critical than ever that we teach our children how to resolve conflicts? Listen to these recent findings from the 2001 report on youth violence by the Centers for Disease Control: "About 3 out of 10 high school seniors reported having committed a violent act in the past year." In America we have a deplorably easy access to firearms, which has put us at the highest rate of firearm-related deaths among youths in *all of the industrialized world.* The death rate by firearms of American children below age fifteen was five times higher than that of twenty-five other countries *combined.* The CDC says, "Youth violence, although international in scope, is greater in the United States, more likely to involve firearms, and more lethal in its consequences."

According to the Children's' Defense Fund's statistics posted in 2002, "Every Day in America, nine children and youth under twenty die from firearms. And among all industrialized countries, the United States ranks first in military technology and *last* in protecting our children against gun violence." As you read in the Introduction to this book, 3,000 children and teens die every year from gunshot wounds (CDF figures).

Parents, if you want to do something right now to make a difference, start working on this issue. There are websites at the end of this chapter that will tell you how you can help.

The other thing we can start doing right now is teaching our children conflict resolution skills at home. Ron Laws of the Anti-Violence Partnership of Philadelphia has been working with schools in his area for the past seven years. He says, "Violence is a learned behavior. I believe the major cause among kids is a lack of the skills necessary to combat the negative forces out there. Combatting violence starts with caring parents. We also need caring energetic, knowledgeable adults in key places—particularly our schools—to provide necessary support in teaching nonviolent alternatives."

The good news is that schools throughout the country have

already begun doing this. One elementary principal I work with described the results he's been seeing since his school has made a commitment to seeking peaceful solutions to conflicts: "The atmosphere has really changed. Kids feel better about themselves when they can talk things out instead of fighting. Before, they thought the only way to deal with conflict was to fight, name-call, or walk away mad. Now they have a way to arrive at an equitable solution. All parents should learn this system."

Below are Win/Win Guidelines and the Rules for Win/Win, a system for resolving conflicts that's being used successfully in homes and schools nationally. Post them in your home and teach them to your children.

The Win/Win Guidelines

1. Take time to cool off.
2. Take turns talking it out using "I" messages.
3. Each person restates what they heard the other person say.
4. Take responsibility for your role in the problem.
5. Brainstorm solutions together, and choose one that satisfies both people.
6. Affirm, forgive, or thank each other.

Rules for Win/Win

We agree to do the following:

1. Tell the truth.
2. Treat each other with respect.
3. Attack the problem, not the person.
4. Wait for our turn to speak. No interrupting.
5. Be willing to compromise.

Introduce these steps to your children at a family meeting and role-play them ahead of time to help you both get comfortable with the process. The steps below explain how to do this.

Teaching Your Children the Win/Win Guidelines

Step 1. Take time to cool off. Don't skip this step. Conflicts can't be solved in the face of hot emotions. Take a step back, breathe deep, and gain some emotional distance before trying to talk things out. Doing this helps you create the opportunity to choose your response rather than just react. The same thing holds true for your children. Have them walk away and cool off before attempting to get them to talk. Earlier in this chapter we talked about ways you can help your children learn to cool off. Now try the exercise below for yourself:

> **EXERCISE:** Brainstorm ten things that make you feel better when you're hot under the collar. Consider some of the following: Breathing deeply while making a calming statement, looking at the sky, clearing your desk or straightening up, splashing cold water on your face, writing in a journal, or taking a quick walk and then coming back to talk about the problem. Some people need physical release, while others need something quiet and cerebral. Determine what works for you, then use it next time you get angry. If you haven't already, do the same with your children.

Step 2. Take turns talking it out using "I messages." When each person has cooled off sufficiently, it's time to talk about the problem. "I messages" help us express our feelings without attacking or blaming. By starting from "I," we take responsibility for the way we perceive the problem instead of placing blame. In contrast, "you messages" put people on the defensive and close doors to communication. A statement like, "You're so inconsiderate! You never clean up after yourself," will escalate the conflict. Listen to the difference when stating the problem in the form of an "I message": "I'm annoyed because I thought we agreed you'd clean up your toys when you're finished with them. Please do it now."

When you deliver an "I" statement, be careful not to undermine your words by including put-downs, guilt-trips, sarcasm, or negative body language. It's important to come from a place inside that's noncombative and willing to compromise. Get rid of the residue anger by cooling off. And if you're still angry, take some more time before talking the problem over. That goes for the person you're talking to also. If either of you is too angry to drop the sarcasm or digs, stop talking and come back later. When you work through your conflict, remember this: *It's us against the problem, not us against each other.*

> **EXERCISE:** Think about the last time you got angry. What "I message" could you have delivered? Write it down. Is there anyone you're angry with now? Write down a few "I messages" you can use.
>   Now think of some common conflicts you have with your children. Write down an "I message" you can use in each situation. Plan to use them next time the need arises.

Step 3. Each person restates what they heard the other person say. When we listen to what the other person says and paraphrase what we heard, we convey that we're open. Reflective listening shows that we care enough to hear out the other person, rather than just focus on our own point of view. Doing this shows respect and helps resolve conflicts. It also fosters empathy. Jeff describes how doing this helped his wife and teenaged daughter resolve a conflict:

> When I walked in the kitchen Erica and her were mom were in a shouting match. In the past I might have shouted for them to stop, only to have been drawn into the fray. Instead I took a deep breath, gathered my thoughts, and chose my words carefully. I calmly asked if they each could tell me what had happened. As they did, I reflected back what they said.

I said, "So, Erica, you're angry because your mom told you that you had to be home by ten o'clock and all your friends are allowed to stay out till eleven?" Erica nodded her head. Then I looked at my wife and said, "And you're concerned because it's a weeknight and Erica already has trouble getting up on school days?' She nodded too. Then I asked them if they could suggest some fair solutions to the problem. They each started coming up with ideas and listening to what the other had to say. Before long, they were actually able to reach a compromise, something I wouldn't have imagined when I first walked in the kitchen.

Reflective listening works that way. When one person listens, the other often follows suit.

> **EXERCISE:** The next time you talk to your child, try reflecting back what he says. You can start with the words, "I heard you say . . . ," or "So, it sounds like . . ." Practice doing this in nonconflict situations first. It may feel a little awkward, but the more you do it, the more natural it begins to feel.

Step 4. Take responsibility for your role in the problem. In the majority of conflicts, *both* parties have some degree of responsibility for what went wrong. However, most of us tend to blame rather than looking at our own role in the problem. When we take responsibility, we shift the conflict into an entirely different gear, one where resolution is possible.

Ellen talked about how taking responsibility helped avert a major falling-out with her husband:

> We were getting ready to go to a family gathering, and as usual I was running late. When my husband Richard spotted me changing my outfit for the third time, he completely lost it. At the sound of his voice, I lost it too, and then we were on our way to a major battle.
> But this time, instead of going into my defensive posture I

walked away for a few minutes, took some deep breaths, and got my bearings. When I walked back into the room, I was able to hear Richard out. He told me that he was so frustrated at having to wait for me whenever we went out. He talked about punctuality as something he highly valued. As I listened, a funny thing happened: I realized he was right. I *did* need to get a handle on my habitual lateness. He's so used to my digging in my heels whenever we have a fight that I thought he was going to pass out when I actually took responsibility and apologized. My apology sparked his, and we ended up having a great day together, something that would have been impossible had we gone along our usual course.

EXERCISE: Think about the last conflict you had. Can you see where you may have been responsible in some way? Reflect on this and write about it in your notebook. If an insight reveals itself to you regarding your role in a conflict, consider making amends with the other person. Doing this is especially powerful when we have conflicts with our children. It gives them the courage to take responsibility too.

Step 5. Brainstorm solutions and come up with one that satisfies both people. The key to resolving conflicts is the willingness to seek compromises. Resolving conflicts is a creative act and there are *many* solutions to a single problem.

Corrine described how her first-grade students started having fewer conflicts when they learned how to brainstorm solutions:

My kids were constantly getting into arguments over crayons, erasers, toys, you name it. After introducing peacemaking, my students started finding ways to solve their problems. The other day during recess when Jacob and Collin both grabbed the fire engine, I took them aside and asked if they could come up with four ways to solve the problem. They thought about it and then suggested taking turns, sharing, getting another truck from the toy chest, and doing a different activity.

This is the kind of thinking I'm seeing more and more. Brainstorming has opened my children's minds to a wider range of possibilities. I wish parents would do more of this with their children at home.

Next time you have a conflict, ask your partner to join you in trying to come up with a variety of solutions. Then choose one that works for both of you. Teach this to your children and encourage them to generate a range of solutions for their conflicts. Knowing how to do this will help them in every walk of life.

Step 6. Affirm, forgive, or thank each other.   A handshake, hug, or kind word gives closure to the resolution of conflicts. Forgiveness is the highest form of closure. Minister Fredrick Buechner says, "When you forgive somebody . . . you're spared the dismal corrosion of bitterness and wounded pride. For both parties, forgiveness means the freedom again to be at peace inside their own skins and to be glad in each other's presence."

Just saying thank you at the end of a conflict, or acknowledging the person for working things out, sends a message of conciliation and gratitude. We preserve our relationships this way, strengthening our connections and working through problems that arise.

What a legacy we can leave to our children when we teach and model forgiveness. Roz, the mother of four grown children, shared this wonderful story about the impact of forgiveness on a friend's life.

A close friend told Roz that his much-loved daughter had chosen to marry someone he not approve of. As a result he severed their relationship. This decision caused deep heartache for both of them.

Roz looked at her friend and said, "You took a detour down the wrong road. You can take another road back, one that will repair the relationship." Heeding Roz's wise counsel, her friend put his grievances aside, forgave his daughter, and made amends with her. The huge weight of holding on to anger and withholding love was lifted. The relief in both father and daughter was overwhelming.

We can all learn from the wisdom of this story. Sometimes we make decisions in anger and then hold steadfast to them, even if we are wrong. Precious time and energy are wasted when we try to "be right." This father was on the road to sacrificing his relationship with the person he treasured most in life, all for the sake of being right. How fruitless this would have been. What deep suffering they both would have endured at the loss of their relationship. By mending fences, this man learned the most important lesson of all: When we choose to forgive, everyone wins.

We are now seeing global ramifications of this. The Truth and Reconciliation Council in South Africa has enabled that country to begin the process of healing its shattered soul. The result— more equitable government, a dramatic decrease in conflict, and an improved economy. South Africa's diplomatic relationships with other countries have also flourished in the process. When we forgive, we all profit—even in the international arena.

It's important to start teaching forgiveness and conflict resolution from the time your children are young. Three years old is a good time to start.

Listen to this story about how a conflict was resolved between a five- and a ten-year-old:

> My brother Sammy really got me mad. After my birthday party he started cutting off the ribbons on my helium balloons. I was furious! Instead of going after him like I used to, I went upstairs, cooled off, and came back when I felt calmer. I gave him an "I message." I said, "I'm really upset about what you did to my balloons. You wouldn't like it if I did that to something of yours!" I said it in a such respectful way my brother was shocked. He'd expected me to hit him. Instead I told him what was on my mind. And I didn't call him names either.
>
> He looked at me and said, "I'm really sorry. I'll fix your balloons. Would you help me?"

Think of your own life. Who are you in conflict with? Picture applying this system to work things out. Think of the impact on all your relationships. As Gandhi once said, "We must be the change we wish to see in others." Peace starts with each of us. Next time you are in conflict, take the first step.

> **EXERCISE:** Post the Win/Win Guidelines in your home. Have a family meeting and teach them to your children. Role-play some old conflicts together or use some imaginary scenarios. Practicing will help you all feel more comfortable using this system next time an actual conflict arises. You don't have to use every step every time. Just make sure to cool off, speak in "I messages," and brainstorm solutions. The key is to be respectful and listen to each other. Try this next time you have a conflict of your own.

END THOUGHTS

Creating a peaceful home can help counterbalance the divisiveness and violence in our world. When we create a peaceful atmosphere in our home, we provide our children with an alternative reality to what they are exposed to in the news, on TV, and even at school. A child who grows up with respect, acceptance, compassion, and altruism gains strength to face the world and to possibly even change it.

Your home is the place where you groom your children for the future. Think about this: Every world leader alive today was somebody's child. What they learned from their parents growing up influences the way they govern.

What you teach in your home will shape how your children live their lives as adults and interact in the world. As a nine-year-old child said to me, "I wish people all over would learn peacemaking in their homes and schools. Then maybe we would never have to fight any more wars."

Imagine children everywhere, starting with your own, learning the ways of peace so that future generations might seek to understand one another rather than resorting to violence. Imagine children in all parts of the world learning how to manage conflicts, large and small. Imagine children everywhere knowing that it will take *all* of us to create a just and peaceful world. Imagine what the world could be like. Imagine.

RESOURCES AND BIBLIOGRAPHY

Websites

Family Life First
www.familylife1st.org
   Helps parents build communities where family life "is an honored and celebrated priority." Tells parents how they can create this.

Family Education
familyeducation.com
   Provides learning and information resources personalized to help parents, teachers, and students of all ages.

Schwab Learning
www.SchwabLearning.org
   Informative website for parents of children with learning differences. Has articles, resources, parent support groups, advice from experts.

Centers for Disease Control and Prevention
www.cdc.gov
   Click on "Youth Risk Behavior" to get the most up-to-date statistics and information on youth violence, alcohol and other drug use, and more.

Million Mom March
www.MillionMomMarch.org
   Works to prevent gun violence. Find out how you can help.

Books for Parents

Carter, Leslie, et al. *The Anger Workbook*. Nashville, Tenn.: Thomas Nelson, 1992.
Interactive program helps identify the best ways to handle anger and eliminate the myths that perpetuate it.

Eastman, Meg, and Sydney Craft Roze. *Taming the Dragon in Your Child: Solutions for Breaking the Cycle of Family Anger*. New York: Wiley, 1994.
Dealing constructively with children's anger from temper tantrums and pouting to sarcasm and sibling rivalry.

McKay, Matthew, et al. *When Anger Hurts Your Kids: A Parent's Guide*. Oakland, CA: New Harbinger Publications, 1996.
Explains why parents get angry, how children are affected, and how to gain control.

Paul, Henry A. *When Kids Are Mad, Not Bad: A Guide to Recognizing and Handling Your Child's Anger*. New York: Penguin-Putnam, 1998.
Handling tantrums, hostility, sarcasm, depression, and more in a loving, constructive way.

Tavris, Carol. *Anger: The Misunderstood Emotion*. New York: Simon and Schuster, 1982.
Anger triggers,their roots, and what to do about them.

Weisinger, Hendrie. *Anger at Work*. New York: William Morrow, 1995.
Practical strategies for dealing with anger.

Whitehouse, Elaine, and Warwick Pudney. *A Volcano in My Tummy: Helping Children to Handle Anger*. Gabriola Island, B.C., Canada: New Society Publishers, 1998.
Full of stories and easy-to-use games and exercises to use with your children.

Zukov, Gary and Linda Francis. *Heart of the Soul*. New York: The Free Press, 2001.

Developing the emotional awareness central to spiritual development.

Books for Children

Blumenthal, Deborah. *The Chocolate Covered Cookie Tantrum.* New York: Houghton Mifflin, 1999.
Sophie finds out that throwing a tantrum will not get her what she wants. (Grades K–2.)

Everitt, Betsy. *Mean Soup.* New York: Harcourt Brace, 1995.
Horace has had a very, very bad day and is feeling grumpy. His mother helps him find a cure. (Grades K–2.)

Lindgren, Astrid. *Lotta on Troublemaker Street.* New York: Macmillan, 1984.
Lotta has a bad temper. After running away she gains insight into a conflict. (Grades 2–6.)

Mayer, Mercer. *I Was So Mad.* New York: Golden Books, 1985.
A young child tries a variety of ways to let go of anger. (Grades K–2.)

Merrill, Jean. *The Pushcart War.* New York: Atheneum, 1987.
Conflict on the streets of New York and how it gets solved. (Grades 2–6.)

Minarik, Else Holmelund. *No Fighting, No Biting.* New York: HarperCollins, 1978.
Rosa and Will hear the story of two alligators who argue until they meet a big hungry alligator. (Grades K–2.)

Moser, Adolph. *Don't Rant and Rave on Wednesdays!: The Children's Anger-Control Book.* Kansas City, Mo.: Landmark Editions, 1994.
Children find out how to control anger and express feelings appropriately. (Grades K–6.)

Naylor, Phyllis. *King of the Playground.* New York: Atheneum, 1991.
A little boy gets bullied and learns how to deal with the problem. (Grades K–2.)

Simor, Norma. *I Was So Mad!* Morton Grove, Ill.: Albert Whitman, 1991.
A look at situations that make children angry including sibling ri-

valry, annoyance with parents, school problems, and more. (Grades K–2.)

Udry, Janice May. *Let's Be Enemies*. New York: HarperCollins, 1961. When John sees James as bossy, he decides that they are enemies. They eventually become friends again. (Grades K–2.)

Van Leeuwen, Jean. *Amanda Pig on Her Own*. New York: Puffin Books, 1994.
Amanda has to solve some problems, deal with angry feelings, and meet other challenges when she is by herself. (Grades K–3.)

Waber, Bernard. *But Names Will Never Hurt Me*. Boston: Houghton Mifflin, 1994.
A little girl with the unlikely name of Alison Wonderland deals with teasing. (Grades K–2.)

Walker, Alice. *Finding the Green Stone*. San Diego: Harcourt Brace Jovanovich, 1997.
Johnny loses both his green stone and his sense of joy after talking mean to the people in his life. As a result he learns some important and life-changing lessons. (Grades 2–4.)

Walter, Nancy, and V. Lin Patfield. *Seemor's Flight to Freedom*. Rosemount, Minn.: Nan Publishing, 1996.
Poignant story of a nearsighted seagull's struggle with anger; includes questions for discussion between parents and children. (Grades K–2.)

Wells, Rosemary. *Benjamin and Tulip*. New York: Dial Books, 1977. Tulip beats up Benjamin. They eventually come to a truce. (Grades K–2.)

Zolotow, Charlotte. *The Quarreling Book*. NY: Harper & Row, 1982.
A chain reaction of angry feelings occurs when Dad forgets to kiss Mom goodbye in the morning. (Grades K–2.)

Chapter 5

Listening and Communicating With Power

Nature gave us one tongue and two ears so we could hear twice as much as we speak.

—Epictetus

When you listen, the integrity and wholeness in others moves closer. Your attention strengthens it . . . In your presence, they can more easily inhabit that in them which is beyond their limitations.

—Rachel Naomi Remen

Moshe Dayan, former Israeli Minister of Defense, once said, "If you want to make peace, you don't talk to your friends. You talk to your enemies." But how often do we do this? Imagine how much violence could be prevented if people were willing to sit down and listen to those with whom they were engaged in conflict.

Peace activist Gene Knudsen Hoffman has been doing this for years. She has worked on issues of peace, negotiations, and disarmament in international diplomacy. Knudsen devised a process called "compassionate listening" which has been used between Israelis and Palestinians in an attempt to create peace. During seven visits to the Middle East, Hoffman talked to people from all walks of life and twice met with Yassir Arafat. She urged people on both sides to listen with discernment. That means to listen for the subtleties, nuances, and things that might be obscured. In "An Enemy Is One Whose Story We Have Not Heard," she cautions people to let go of their own agendas and listen to gain understanding of one's opponent and insight into his needs and motivations:

> We must listen and listen and listen. We must listen for the Truth in our opponent, and we must acknowledge it. After we have listened long enough, openly enough, and with the desire to really hear, we may be given the opportunity to speak our truth. We may even have the opportunity to be heard. For no one and no one side is the sole repository of Truth. But each of us has a spark of it within. Perhaps, with compassion as our guide, that spark in each of us can become a glow, and then perhaps a light, and we will watch one another in awe as we become illuminated. And then, perhaps, this spark, this glow, this light will become the enlightening energy of love that will save all of us.

This process starts right in our own homes. We foster peace through the act of listening. Every time you "listen with all your heart," you give your children the greatest gift of all: a sense of being honored and validated, something that is needed on every level of human relationships. In these times of uncertainty, it is more important than ever to listen deeply, accepting what is in the hearts and minds of people we interact with.

When we listen to our children, we must remember that we are teaching the next generation how to make peace. As we engage in the reciprocal dance of speaking and listening, we need to listen openly and speak honestly. Denying our own feelings or theirs sends a message to our children that it's not okay to feel what you feel. When we speak and listen from the heart, we give our children permission to do the same, thereby honoring who they are. The reverse can happen when we are closed. Listen to John' story:

I grew up in the sixties and clearly remember the Cuban Missile crisis. I knew my parents were afraid, but they never talked about it. I could see it in their faces, I could feel it in their presence. Yet nothing was ever discussed. I remember feeling terrified, and going to bed each night wondering if we were going to be attacked.

I never told my parents. I thought it might make them feel worse, so I just kept all my fears inside. Finally, when I was an adult and had children of my own, I told my parents how frightened I had been as a kid. They were shocked. They didn't realize how much I'd been paying attention to what was going on. They didn't understand I could feel their fear. And, as much as they meant well, they didn't know that by their not talking, I felt like I needed to keep my fears inside.

Children *do* pay attention. They take in far more than we give them credit for, and they need a safe place to express what they feel. Know that they are noticing. Know, too, that they depend on our honesty to validate their perceptions of reality. There's nothing worse for a child than feeling like he must deny his deepest feelings because of tacit messages he receives.

A cautionary note here: It's important to be as honest as you can while not going overboard. Trisha Thompson, writing for *Parenting* magazine (December–January 2002), realized her emotional response to September 11th had gone too far when her children stared at her in stunned silence. Wishing she had kept her reaction more in check, she said, "When you're concerned or upset about what's going on in the world, there's no need to share the anxiety-producing details, and it's best to stay calm. But don't be concerned if your child sees you tear up. Some things really are worth crying over."

A balance of honesty and reassurance works best. You can talk about things you do to help yourself feel better, like talking to someone, giving and receiving hugs, listening to music, writing in a journal. Each time our children open up and reveal themselves is an opportunity to help them cope. Better to encourage them to talk about what's on their minds than to assume that just because they don't bring it up, nothing's bothering them. Award-winning author-illustrator Maurice Sendak wrote eloquently on this in the anthology, *I Dream of Peace:*

> The children know. They have always known. But we choose to think otherwise; it hurts to know the children know. The children see. If we obfuscate, they will not see. Thus we conspire to keep them from knowing and seeing. And if we insist, then, the children, to please us, will make believe they do not know, they do not see. Children make that sacrifice for our sake—to keep us pacified. They are remarkably patient, loving, and all-forgiving. It is a sad comedy: the children knowing and pretending they don't know to protect us from knowing they know.

I saw this firsthand when I visited an elementary school last fall. The teachers I spoke with reassured me that the kids were doing fine in the wake of September 11th. "They're too young to really be concerned about what's going on in the world. It doesn't touch their lives," was something I heard a number of times. Yet when I went into classrooms and asked the children how they were feeling about what's been happening in the world, hands shot up and fears poured out. "I'm afraid of smallpox," said one boy. "What if terrorists come over here and try to make us all sick?" Another child said, "The airlines aren't being careful enough. They let my mom on a plane last week with a nail file in her suitcase. What if someone gets on with a knife?" The fallout of what we experienced in 2001 may reverberate for years to come. Thoughts and fears triggered by pictures, sounds, and memories can resurface well into the future. Be aware; listen to the subtle nuances of your child's questions and conversations, and keep the lines of communication open.

VALIDATING FEELINGS THROUGH REFLECTIVE LISTENING

A very powerful way to help our children feel understood is through active or reflective listening. This is the process of listening for the feelings *beneath* the words and paraphrasing what we hear. Clinical psychologist Dr. Larry Nadig says in his article "Tips on Effective Listening":

> There is a real distinction between merely *hearing the words* and really *listening for the message*. When we listen effectively we understand what the person is thinking and/or feeling from the other person's own perspective. It is as if we were standing in the other person's shoes, seeing through his/her eyes and listening through the person's ears. Our own viewpoint may be different and we may not necessarily agree with the person, but as we listen, we understand from the other's perspective. To listen effectively, we must be actively involved in the communication process, and not just listening passively.

Whether your child is expressing fears, engaged in a conflict, or talking about her day, reflective listening is a powerful tool for helping her feel understood. Here's an example:

WARREN: Leo is such a jerk. I wish I had a different brother!
DAD: Sounds like you're really angry with him.
WARREN: He just walked in my room without asking and took my favorite CD!
DAD: That must have really annoyed you.
WARREN: He never asks when he borrows anything and then if I say anything he calls me names!
DAD: You feel like he's not respecting you?
WARREN: He's not. He thinks that just 'cause he's older he can do anything he wants!
DAD: Is there some way I can help you solve this problem?
WARREN: Yeah, you can tell him sit down and listen to me instead of just walking away when I try to talk to him.

Through reflective listening Dad helped Warren get his anger off his chest and think about a possible way to solve the problem. Dad suspended his own judgments and listened to the feelings beneath the words.

Now take a look at how the scenario might have gone if Dad had been reactive:

WARREN: Leo is such a jerk. I wish I had a different brother!

DAD: Don't call your brother names. It's not right.

WARREN: Well, he calls me names! Why can't I call him names?

DAD: Because I said so and I'm your father. Plus he's your brother and brothers are supposed to try to get along.

WARREN: (*sarcastically*) That's a joke! Why don't you tell *him* that!

DAD: Watch your tone of voice, young man. More talk like that and you'll be grounded.

WARREN: (*stomping off*) Go ahead! You never care about how I feel anyway!

When we fail to listen with sensitivity, we create resentments, hurt feelings, and power struggles, particularly when our children reach preadolescence and the teen years. During this time of growing autonomy, our children have a deep need to be heard. As they work out their relationships to themselves and the world, our willingness to hear them out validates their self-worth and strengthens the bonds we have with them. A study done in 1999 surveyed ninety thousand teens to find out what helped prevent drug and alcohol abuse and teen pregnancy. The number one factor in prevention was *a feeling of closeness to one's family.*

It's critical to start this process when children are young. Listen to the wise words of elementary guidance counselor Cecelia Cardano:

Parents, teachers and anyone who works with kids need to listen to and validate their children's feelings, now more than ever. Our children know what's going on in the world more than we may realize. In our efforts to protect them we often go into a "fix-it" mode. We might rush to offer solutions or say things like, "you shouldn't worry," or "everything's fine." Kids end up feeling confused or discouraged when we invalidate what they perceive. Instead we need to listen fully to their concerns without interjecting anything. As your child speaks, try saying things like, "Yes, I understand," or "What I hear you say is . . ." or "Is that right?" You can also encourage your child to open up by nodding and giving him or her your full focus. Avoid the impulse to take over the conversation; just *listen, validate, and acknowledge.*

Help your child name the feelings too. Sometimes children aren't aware of what they're feeling right away. The more we listen and validate, the more likely our children's feelings will come to the surface and be identifiable.

We also need to periodically check in with our kids even when they look like they're okay. Say, "I'm just checking in with you. Is there anything you want to talk about?" Then listen quietly and patiently. Hearing them out is the most important thing you can do. It's like peeling the layers of an onion. In time, the core of your child's world will reveal itself through your intent listening.

I have seen this happen over and over again with children as well as adults. By listening intently, worlds open up. I'll never forget the day I was observing a fourth-grade class where the children were talking about what's been going on in the world. The teacher created a very safe environment and she listened with deep compassion as each child spoke. Before long a little girl named Amy raised her hand. She talked about how the events of September 11th had made her start thinking about people in her own life who had died at other times. Even though she was only nine, Amy had lost three close relatives. The teacher continued to listen and reflect back Amy's words as she spoke. It was then that Amy began talking about the tragic nature of her grandfather's death, something she'd been carrying around for a long time but never spoke of. In the environment of being truly listened to, Amy finally felt safe enough to reveal what had been on her mind for years.

When we give children time to share, a safe place in which to do it, and our deepest listening, they open up in ways that are both healing for them and healing for us.

KEYS TO GOOD LISTENING

In this busy frenetic world, we hear things all the time, but how often do we truly listen? Often we block things out, protecting ourselves from the constant barrage of overstimulation we're surrounded with. Sometimes, we even block out our children. As a natural defense we go into a "tune-out" mode. True, we can't listen to everything our children have to say, especially when they pummel us with complaints and demands. But we *do* need to make some time each day for intent listening because this is the core of our deepest connection with our children and it builds bonds of love and trust. Our intent listening even fosters self-esteem and a sense of safety. Psychologist and author Dorothy Corkille Briggs says, "What does a climate of trust say to a child? It says, 'You can count on me to help you meet your needs. I am not perfect but you can depend on my being honest with you. . . . You are safe with me.'"

Deep listening doesn't come easy to many of us. It's something we may need to be very intentional about doing. In fact, it's something we might actually have to practice, in the same way we'd practice learning a foreign language or musical instrument. Here's Abby's story:

> Many years ago I decided I wanted to have richer more fulfilling relationships but I didn't know how, so I started observing those who did. I noticed they all had one thing in common—they were wonderful listeners. And the way they listened made you feel like you were the only person in the world. I always wanted to be around those rare and special people, and I wanted to be one of them.
>
> So I decided to use those wonderful listeners as my role models. I started emulating what they did. When I was with my friends, family, or even casual acquaintances, I would practice listening with the same deep intentionality I'd observed.
>
> At first it was hard. I found myself wanting to interrupt, or tell my own story, or disagree, or give an opinion, or let my

mind drift. But I kept resisting these impulses; instead I put my full focus on whomever I was listening to, treating them like they were the only person in the room. Each time I did, it got a little easier. And then something completely unexpected started happening—*I* was experiencing this great sense of joy each time I listened. This may sound strange but it was like the people I listened to began to shine brighter, illuminating something brighter inside of me.

Before, I used to jump in and cut people off because I was always afraid I wouldn't get a chance to speak. But just the opposite started to happen—people started listening to me more. They started seeking me out more too. It was as though they had been hungry all their lives for what I was giving them: this simple but profound act of listening.

Listening is the most basic way we show respect for others, and the first way we teach good listening to our children is by the way we listen. Think of the impact of this as our children grow up. Since our children are the leaders of tomorrow, the impact of learning how to listen can have long-range, global ramifications. Keep this in mind as you take steps to enhance your listening and model for your kids what they need to learn:

1. Make a commitment to listen more than you speak. The theologian Paul Tillich once said, "The first duty of love is to listen."

Be generous with your listening. Know that you will eventually get your chance to speak because your listening will make people more open to what you have to say.

It's a sad paradox that people often feel they have to interrupt or speak over the voice of others to be heard. What they really need to do is just listen. That's how we best garner the respect of others. Think about it: Whom do you hold in higher esteem—someone who interrupts and doesn't pay attention, or someone who looks you in the eye when you speak and values what you say? When we are truly listened to, we get the message that we are of value, the same message our children get when we listen to them.

EXERCISE: The next time you are with your child, listen more than you speak. If your child doesn't have much to say, then ask him to tell you the best thing that happened all day, and the worst. That should get the ball rolling. Then be very present, make eye contact, nod, encourage your child to go on, but don't say very much yourself. If extraneous thoughts pop into your head, let them go and bring your focus back to your child. See what happens when you do this and write about it in your notebook.

2. Catch yourself when you have the impulse to interrupt. Breathe deeply and let the impulse pass. Ask any child something that bothers him about his parents. The answer is usually, "They don't listen to me." Or, "They're always too busy (or tired, or stressed) to listen to what I have to say." Often when our children start talking, we cut them off or interject our opinion, even when they don't ask for it. Doing this closes the lines of communication. Please don't beat yourself up if you do any of these things. *We all do.* In fact, just the other day when I was with my son I fell into the same trap. Mike is a graduate student, and when I visited him in New York, he looked pale and tired. I immediately went into my "mom" mode. "Are you feeling okay?" I asked, and before he had a chance to respond, I jumped in, "Mike, have you been getting enough rest? Are you taking your vitamins? Maybe you should take some extra vitamin C."

Before long, my son got distant and quiet. When I asked him what was wrong, he said, "Mom, I'm twenty-seven years old and you're still treating me like I don't know how to take care of myself! Plus I'm not sick. I was just out all night partying!"

EXERCISE: Try going through a whole day without interrupting anyone. At the end of the day reflect on the following questions and write about any new insights in your notebook: Was it easy or hard? What kind of responses did you get from the people you listened to? Did you learn something new about yourself or another person? Reflect on all of this.

3. Make the person you are listening to your entire focus. For that moment, let them become the center of your universe. One of the most offensive things I can think of is having a conversation with someone whose eyes are scanning the room. It makes you feel almost invisible. Yet when I talk with someone who makes eye contact and listens intently, I feel uplifted, valued.

Sometimes we have to train our minds to focus on whom we're listening to and what they're saying. Too often our minds are multitasking while someone speaks. We might be making a mental list of what we have to do later, or thinking about something someone else just said. We might be planning what we're going to say next, going through the motions of "listening" to the other person, but really focusing on our own thoughts.

Try listening the other way—suspend your own thoughts and hang on to every word that's being spoken, even if it's something that's not especially interesting to you. Doing this is an act of supreme generosity, a way of honoring the humanity and worth of the other person, be it a casual acquaintance, a friend, your spouse, or your child.

> **EXERCISE:** The next time you are with someone, listen to them as though they are the only person in the world. Clear your mind, let go of your agenda, resist the urge to tell your own story, and just listen with great intentionality. It doesn't matter whom you try this with; it can be your child, your partner, your mother-in-law, or the UPS man. The point is to suspend your own thoughts and listen more deeply than you ever have before. See what happens, and write about the experience of deep listening in your notebook.

4. Avoid the impulse to fix things. When our children share things that are on their minds, they're not necessarily looking for a solution. They're mainly looking to be heard. When we jump in and try to fix, we don't give our children the opportunity to come up with their own solutions. By listening and validating, we enable them to sort things out and see the problem more clearly.

Sometimes a solution that might not have been evident before comes to light. But we need to be patient.

Certainly giving our gentle guidance at appropriate times is necessary, but jumping in and fixing can be counterproductive. As Fran, the mother of three, said, "Part of making something better is being able to see where it broke in the first place. I used to squelch my children's feelings. I'd want to get right to the solution. Now I see how much they need to express their feelings without my jumping in and trying to fix. When I actively listen, they begin to see ways to solve the problem themselves. It may take a little longer, but the solution usually works a lot better when it comes from them."

When we establish a pattern of deep, compassionate listening, our children are apt to become better problem-solvers. They also feel safer in talking to us. Take a look at the contrast between the two scenarios below. Notice how in the first scenario Mom immediately goes into a fix-it mode. Notice how Mom's active listening in the second scenario leads to a far different outcome.

MOM: How was school today?

TAMMY: Bad.

MOM: Why?

TAMMY: Because the teacher's mean. She told me the story I wrote last night was too messy and she made me copy it over.

MOM: That teacher is way too particular! This isn't the first time she's done something like that. I'm calling her to complain.

TAMMY: No, Mom! I don't want you to!

MOM: I think I know a little more about these things than you, Tammy. She had no right to make you redo your story. When I was your age, something like that happened to me, and I'm not going to let you be subjected to the same treatment.

TAMMY: (*near tears now*) No, Mom! it wasn't such a big deal! You don't have to call her! I can take care of it myself.

MOM: Stop fussing, Tammy. I think I know how to handle things like this better than you. Wait till I talk to that woman, getting you all upset like this!

Clearly, the next time Tammy wants to vent, she's not going to go to her mother. In her fervor to "fix" the problem, Tammy's mother didn't listen to her daughter's needs. Let's take a look at how this scenario could have been different:

MOM: How was school today?

TAMMY: Bad.

MOM: Why?

TAMMY: Because the teacher's mean. She told me my story from last night was too messy and she made me copy it over.

MOM: Sounds like you're upset about that.

TAMMY: I am. No one else had to copy their story over. And I had to miss free time so I could do it.

MOM: That must have been frustrating.

TAMMY: It was. I can't help it if I have messy handwriting!

MOM: So you feel that the neatness of your writing is something you can't control?

TAMMY: Well, maybe I could if I went a little slower. But I was in a hurry last night because I wanted to watch my favorite show.

MOM: So you rushed?

TAMMY: (*thinking about it*) I guess I did.

MOM: Is there anything you could do differently next time?

TAMMY: Take it slower. I guess if I started my homework right after dinner, then I would have had more time.

MOM: Good idea, Tammy. Would it help if I reminded you to do that tomorrow night?

TAMMY: Okay. Now that I'm in third grade, I guess I have to be a little more careful with my work.

By validating Tammy's feelings, Mom allowed her to get things off her chest and ultimately see how she was responsible.

In fact, by being listened to, Tammy could actually come up with a solution. This is a lot more empowering for a child than when we come up with a solution for them.

Marian, the mother of two children, ages three and five, told me a wonderful story about how she let her children, young as they were, solve a problem that came up between them. They were walking home from the park, and her three-year-old was in the stroller. Her five-year-old started complaining that he was tired and wanted a ride, but there wasn't enough room for the two of them. They kept bickering back and forth, and finally Marian stopped, sat down on the grass, and started nonchalantly eating an apple. Both of her children looked at her with complete surprise and asked her what she was doing. Marian said, "The two of you seem to have a problem and I think you need to work it out. I'll just relax here while you do." Completely thrown off guard, her five-year-old paused, then looked at her three-year-old and said, "So, what do you think we should do?" As Marian ate her apple, the two of them talked over the problem and came up with a great solution—they would take turns in the stroller. They asked Marian if she would stop at every driveway they passed on the way home so they could switch places. Marian did exactly that, and the walk home was peaceful. She said, "It made my kids feel so grown up to have come up with this great solution. Who said little kids couldn't work out their own problems?"

> **EXERCISE:** Practice active listening. When your child (or anyone else) tells you about a problem they're having, listen intently and paraphrase what you heard them say. You can start with words like "I heard you say . . ." or "Sounds like . . ." or simply nod listen, and say "Really?" or "Is that right?" Be patient and avoid the impulse to fix. If you find yourself chomping at the bit, take some deep breaths and just let the impulse to jump in pass. You are developing a new muscle.

5. Let go of judgments. We judge all the time. We are judging creatures and practically everything we see or hear becomes the object of our assessment. "I like this. I don't like that. This is good. That's bad." Our judgments can create a wedge between us and those we're judging. Very often we don't even have to speak our judgments and they still come through loud and clear. Listen to the conversation I had with Sherry, the mother of a sixteen-year-old:

SHERRY: I'm so upset. My daughter Stacey confided in my sister that I was being too critical. I can't believe she would do that! I'm always so loving and concerned!

ME: Did you say anything that might have hurt her feelings?

SHERRY: No, I'm always very tactful.

ME: Was there anything she might have misconstrued?

SHERRY: Well, maybe. The other day I just made this passing comment about her skin and I asked her if she tried the new oil-reducing soap I'd bought for her.

ME: Were you thinking her skin was too oily?

SHERRY: It *is* too oily. I was only trying to help! She's such a pretty girl, but when she lets herself go, she doesn't look as good as she could. I wish she'd take more of an interest in her appearance.

ME: It sounds like Stacey heard what you were thinking underneath your helpful suggestion.

SHERRY: (*nodding*) And now she's upset with me.

It's hard not to judge. The best we can do is catch ourselves as our judgments come up and not give them any more fuel. Doing so is like the Buddhist practice of "noting." You watch the thought come up and you let it go. Then you watch the next thought come up and let it go. Each time the judgments come up, let them go and replace them with something else. Here's a little statement you can use when you catch yourself judging: "I will stay in the presence of this person's humanity." Because each time we judge, the basic humanity of another is diminished.

Think about how judgments have clouded the perceptions of so many people over the past year—believing that good and evil can be determined in black and white, ignoring the fact that within each of us is the capacity for both good and evil. But when we judge, we forget this. Judging causes us to oversimplify the complex and to short-circuit the type of reflection needed to fully understand another person, situation, or problem.

> **EXERCISE:** Try "noting" your judgments each time they come up. Instead of staying with them and allowing them to snowball, let them go and look for what's decent and good in the person you are judging.

6. *Be willing to enter the other person's world, listening to what they say and encouraging them to say more.* Another of my favorite stories came from Kathleen, a mom in one of my parenting groups. Her eight-year old son, Sam, was basically noncommunicative. Sam had ADD and was recently classified as learning disabled. Being pulled out of his regular class each day for extra help was causing him to be even more insecure and withdrawn.

"I don't know what to do," Kathleen complained, "I take an interest, I ask questions, but he doesn't tell me anything. If I want to find out what happened in school, I feel like I have to ask a neighbor!"

"What interests him the most?" I asked.

"Legos," said Kathleen.

"Then Legos may be your way in," I said.

"But I don't want to hear about Legos," Kathleen responded. "I want to hear about school!"

"You may have to hear about Legos first," I said. "It sounds like that's what's at the center of Sam's universe."

Kathleen had already started spending fifteen to twenty minutes a night of exclusive time with Sam, so I encouraged her to get down on the floor with him during their next time together, join him in building Legos, and just plain listen.

Reluctantly Kathleen went back home and did just that. Sam's conversation was sparse, but Kathleen hung in. The next night they built Legos again, and Sam was a little more talkative. By the third night Sam started opening up. Here's how Kathleen describes it:

Being engaged in building helped Sam calm down and get comfortable in the world he loved best. The conversation started to flow more. Comments would come out about things like his difficulty with math. Then I could say something like, "I had trouble with math, too, when I was your age."

More delicate things started coming up too, like Sam's discomfort with being pulled out every day to go to a special ed. class. Kids like Sam have to navigate school in a whole different way.

As he built his castles and monsters, I could enter his world and broach the subjects that he ordinarily wouldn't talk about. It was a turning point.

By entering Sam's world, Kathleen not only got to hear about school, but she was better able to offer support. Moreover, she was able to validate Sam's unique "voice."

According to Gershen Kaufman, author of *Giving Your Child Voice:*

One of the most important psychological factors in raising a family is giving children "voice." What is "voice"? It is the sense of agency that resides in all of us, that makes us confident that we will be heard, and that we will have impact on our environment. Exceptional parents grant a child a voice equal to theirs the day that child is born. And they respect that voice as much as they respect their own.

How can you give your child "voice"? There are three rules. First, assume that what your child has to say about the world is just as important as what you have to say. Second, assume that you can learn as much from them as they can from you. Third, enter their world through play, activities, discussions: don't require them to enter yours in order to make contact.

EXERCISE: How can you enter your child's world and give him "voice"? Close your eyes, breathe deeply, and reflect on this. Write down any insights that surface. Now, choose a way to honor your child's unique voice.

7. Know that deep listening is one of the greatest gifts you can give. Incorporate it into your life every day. Eleanor's eleven-year-old son Aiden also has ADD. Relationships have been difficult for him over the years, and he hasn't always felt accepted by peers and teachers. Eleanor has made it her mission to validate her son and to listen to him with all her heart. Doing this has made all the difference. Over time Aiden has become successful in school, is making more friends, and has a healthy self-image. No matter what challenges he's had to face in the world, his mother's acceptance and willingness to listen have been constants in his life. The other day Aiden put his arms around Eleanor and said, "Thank you, Mom." When Eleanor asked him what for, Aiden said, "You always listen to what I have to say. You accept me and understand how I feel. You make me feel safe being who I am."

This is the kind of gift we give to our children through our listening. And it's a gift we can give at any time. Be generous with your listening. It will indeed be returned.

WHEN CHILDREN SHARE THINGS THAT ARE HARD FOR US TO HEAR

It's especially important to listen without judgment when our children tell us things that are difficult, upsetting, or we just plain don't agree with. Clinical psychologist Yael Danieli gives this advice on listening to children: "Absolutely, listen to them. Listen to every fantasy. Do not stop them from articulating, even if it makes you anxious."

The following story illustrates this beautifully. See how Nancy, the mother of two, skillfully handles a very delicate situation:

> My eight-year-old son Charlie was acting out in school but refused to tell me what was wrong. One morning the dam broke. Charlie revealed that he was very angry with his father but he wouldn't tell me why. He asked if we could call his dad at the office. When we reached him, I stepped aside and let Charlie unload.

"I'm really angry because you never spend time with me! I feel like you're never around, and when you are, you're busy doing other things." So that's what was underneath Charlie's acting out! I just listened as Charlie got everything off his chest.

When the conversation ended, I had this urge to put my two cents in, but I resisted. I knew it would shut down any further communication. I just looked at Charlie and said, "How are you feeling now?" At first he didn't say anything, so I stood by his side and stroked his arm. In a little while he looked up at me and said, "Daddy doesn't love me."

As much as I wanted to tell him he was wrong I knew I needed to validate what he had just said. I quietly replied, "You don't think Daddy loves you?" Charlie said "yes" and began to cry.

"Why do you feel that way?" I asked.

"Because Daddy's always busy. He promised me he'd help me put together my new train track and he didn't do it, just like all the other things he's promised and hasn't done."

Again I resisted the urge to jump in and say, "But Daddy's working hard so he can make a living and support all of us," but again, I knew my son just needed to be heard.

I reflected back the feelings I heard. "So you're feeling let down and disappointed." Charlie nodded and started pouring out his heart about all the times his dad had let him down.

When he finished, I asked, "What can we do right now to make you feel better?"

He thought about it for a while and said, "Maybe *you* could help me put my tracks together." So I sat down on the floor and and that's just what we did.

That night when my husband got home, we talked. Even though I had inwardly agreed with some of the things my son had said, I took a step back and once again listened. Wes admitted that Charlie was right—he wasn't spending enough time with him. I just listened and avoided the urge to jump in and fix things. Instead I asked, "Is there anything about this problem you can change?"

Wes realized that although he couldn't change the amount of hours he worked, he *could* change what happens when he comes home. He agreed that from now on when he's here, he would be so in body, mind, and spirit. Even if he's doing chores, he could involve Charlie and let him know what he's thinking and feeling. By doing this he'd connect on a far more meaningful level than before.

My husband went in Charlie's room, hugged him, and apologized. Having this problem opened the door for deeper communication and connection. Much as it was hard to listen, I'm so glad I did.

Nancy sees this as an ongoing process. "Communicating is just the beginning. It's something we must continuously engage in and it doesn't always have to be verbal. It's showing up for things that are important to our children, it's the touch of the hand, a pat on the head, a hug. It's being there. It's listening for the feelings beneath the words and actions." By actively listening while her son spoke frankly, Nancy set the stage for open communication with both Charlie and his father. Had she balked when her son spoke about the painful things that were on his mind, this opportunity would have been lost.

> **EXERCISE:** Is there a discussion you are avoiding because things you are uncomfortable about might be spoken? Reflect on this and consider having the conversation anyway. Consider, also, listening more than speaking when you do. Imagine actively listening to the other person and hearing out their point of view, even if it's something you disagree with. See what kinds of outcomes result if you choose to follow through on this idea.

Deep listening is a doorway to the Soul. It allows us to understand the deepest parts of other people—those we love, those we know, and those we seek to make peace with. When we listen without judgment, we come to know each other in profoundly intimate ways. And when we listen with great openness, we teach our children how to listen back to us. This starts when we make eye contact with our babies during infancy, soaking in every sound and gesture, responding to coos and gurgles. It continues when we grasp to understand the meaning of our toddler's baby-talk. It blossoms each time we choose to stop what we're doing and listen to the details of our child's day, even the unimportant ones. We reap the rewards of listening when our children enter adolescence and young adulthood, and accustomed to years of being listened to, they keep on talking.

Bonds of trust and love are nurtured by deep listening and open communication. Remember this the next time you feel too busy to listen. And remember also that if you haven't always taken the time to listen, you can start now. Never underestimate the power of listening. It may indeed be the most critical guidepost on the road to peace.

CREATING PEACE THROUGH LISTENING

In my conversations with experts from around the country, what keeps coming up over and over again is the power that people (like you) have to change the world, and how listening can often be an intregal part of this. Jacqueleline Mathes, director of Research, Foundation for Global Community, an international network working for peace, says, "Solving the problems we're faced with now is a matter of will. Right now we each have the opportunity and responsibility to make choices that will contribute to the continuation of life." She stressed that it is our actions that will make this happen. And this starts with an openness to hearing other people's points of view, no matter how different they are from our own. We must listen with an open mind, an open heart, and the willingness to understand. Without this, the path to peace becomes obscured.

At the beginning of this chapter you read about the author and peace activist Gene Knudsen Hoffman, who has worked all over the world using the process of compassionate listening to help opposing people make peace. Once again, here are her profoundly wise words, from "Listening for Truth":

> I am not talking about listening with the human ear. I am talking about "discernment," which means to perceive some-

thing hidden and obscure. We must listen with our spiritual ear, the one inside, and this is very different from deciding in advance what is right and what is wrong and then seeking to promote our own agenda. We must literally suspend our belief and then listen to learn whether what we hear expands or diminishes our sense of Truth.

Gandhi reminded us that there exists within each person a power, an energy, equal to the force of an atom bomb—a loving power, a caring power, a healing power for peace. I believe it is time for us to release this power in new ways.

Sadly, over the past year, we have been listening less. In an Op-Ed piece in the *New York Times* on February 24, 2002, Robert F. Worth writes about the frightening trend of polarizing ourselves into camps of good and evil rather than trying to understand one another. "When the nation's enemies are used as highly emotional political symbols, it becomes easy to lose touch with the reality of their motives—and thus fail to better understand how to defeat or influence them." He goes on to say that by using the language of hate and phrases like "axis of evil," we have "crystalized so much anti-American sentiment around the world." Many are seeing us as arrogant and unwilling to seek to understand people outside our own country.

Nor are we listening to divergent viewpoints here at home. Minds are expected to be in lock-step, and dissenting thought is looked upon as disloyal and unpatriotic. The result, Worth says, is a rising tide of repression: "The McCarthy years in some ways were eerily similar to the present moment." The tendency to demonize the enemy and hold ourselves up as absolutely pure closes down the kind of open discussion that could lead us to greater insight, deeper understanding, and long-term solutions. When divergent thought is not accepted and the faces of immigrants are looked upon with suspicion, we move farther and farther away from peace. As Gandhi said, "Love among ourselves based on hatred of others breaks down under the slightest pressure. The fact is, such love is never real love. It is an armed peace." We must listen to each other's voices, for an armed peace is no peace at all. It's one that shatters and ignites, like a dried twig in a dying forest. Is this what we want for our children? I think not. It's time for us to listen as we've never listened before, and as we do, the words we hear may ultimately forge a path to peace.

RESOURCES AND BIBLIOGRAPHY

Books for Adults

Briggs, Dorothy Corkille. *Your Child's Self-Esteem*. New York: Doubleday, 1975.
A classic in raising emotionally healthy children. Don't miss it.

Burley-Allen, Madelyn. *Listening: The Forgotten Skill*. New York: John Wiley and Sons, 1995.
Excellent techniques for mastering the essentials of good listening.

Faber, Adele, and Elaine Mazlish. *How to Talk So Kids Will Listen & Listen So Kids Will Talk*. New York: Avon Books, 1982.
Communication skills based on the work of Haim Ginnott. Dialogues, anecdotes, and good sound advice.

Lee, Larry, et al. *Listen Up: How to Improve Relationships, Reduce Stress, and Be More Productive by Using the Power of Listening*. New York: St. Martin's Press, 2000.
Insights into becoming a better listener. Shows how gender differences influence our listening styles.

Nichols, Michael. *The Lost Art of Listening*. New York: The Guilford Press, 1998.
If you're going to read one book on becoming a better listener, read this one. Excellent, well-written, and practical.

Remen, Rachel Naomi. *My Grandfather's Blessings*. New York: Riverhead, 2000.
One of my all-time favorite books. Packed with wisdom, insight, and sensitivity.

Shafir, Rebecca. *The Zen of Listening: Mindful Communication in the Age of Distraction*. Wheaton, Ill.: Theosophical Publishing House, 2000.
Teaches people how to really focus in on what someone else is saying. Provides helpful exercises and activities.

Sullivan, James E. *The Good Listener.* Notre Dame, Ind.: Ave Maria Press, 2000.
A humanistic approach to listening. Helps people be more empathetic with others through active listening.

Tannen, Deborah. *You Just Don't Understand: Women and Men in Conversation.* New York: Random House, 1991.
An acclaimed sociologist tells us why men and women have trouble communicating and what we can do about it.

Van Pelt, Nancy. *How to Talk So Your Mate Will Listen, and Listen So Your Mate Will Talk.* Grand Rapids, Mich.: Baker Books, 1989.
Since modeling is key, find out how to employ listening and communication skills in your relationship with your partner.

Books for Children

Adams, Lisa K. *Dealing With Someone Who Won't Listen.* New York: The Rosen Group, 1998.
A book that tells kids what they can do when someone in their lives doesn't listen to them. (Grades K–4.)

Baylor, Byrd. *The Other Way to Listen.* New York: Simon and Schuster, 1997.
Focuses on the wisdom of listening fully to the world around us. (Grades K–3.)

Conrad, Pamela. *Blue Willow.* New York: Putnam, 1999.
Kung Shi Fair lives on the banks of the Wen River. Her rich father realizes too late that he should have listened to her wishes. (Grades 1–5.)

Cosgrove, Steven. *Gabby.* New York: Putnam, 1986.
Gabby turns people off until she learns the need to be a better listener. (Grades K–4.)

Estrin, Leibel. *The Story of Danny Three Times.* Brooklyn, NY: HaChi Publishers, 1989.
Danny's parents have to say everything to him three times before he will listen. (Grades K–2.)

Hoffman, Gene Knudsen. "An Enemy Is One Whose Story We Have Not Heard." From *Fellowship,* the Journal of the Fellowship of Reconciliation, May–June 1997.

King, Mary Ellen. *A Good Day for Listening*. Harrisburg, Penn.: Morehouse Publishing, 1997.
Theodore the teddy bear is a good listener but his brother is not, so he misses out on a lot of good things. (Grades K–2.)

Lester, Helen. *Listen, Buddy*. New York: Houghton Mifflin, 1997.
A funny story about a bunny who never seems to listen until he realizes the consequences. (Grades K–2.)

Micallef, Mary. *Listening: The Basic Connection*. Carthage, Ill.: Good Apple Inc., 1996.
This nonfiction book gives children basic advice on good listening. (Grades K–6.)

Reardon, Ruth. *Listening to the Littlest*. Norwalk, Conn.: C. R. Gibson Company, 1986.
This book expresses, through the voices of children, the need to learn from them by listening. (Grades K–2.)

Showers, Paul. *The Listening Walk*. New York: HarperCollins, 1993.
Father and daughter go on a listening walk and hear the wonderful sounds around them. (Grades K–2.)

Chapter 6

Nurturing Our Connections: Rituals and Beyond

What we need now more than ever is connection among all people. Whether we're Christian, Muslim, or Jewish, we all want the same things for our children. It is in our connections that we will find more peace.

—Dr. Teresa Benzwie

Now pay attention: If the soul wishes to be effective inside itself, it must gather together all its powers and call them back from all scattered activities.

—Meister Eckhart

The time has come for us to reconnect with ourselves, with others, and with our highest priorities. The events of our world over the past year have brought us face to face with a deep need to move beyond our separateness.

Although we are all inherently interconnected, most of us live fragmented lives, cut off from each other and even from ourselves. For a brief moment in time, after September 11th, we reconnected. People across the country reached out to friends and relatives they hadn't talked to in months. We called up superficial acquaintances to find out if they were okay. I even heard a story of a woman from Canada who got ahold of a New York City phone book and called a stranger to ask if he was all right.

My husband and I were in New York the weekend after the attacks and we met a couple from Arkanas. They said they had to come out to lend support. After September 11th, our connections abounded—at least temporarily.

Now, it seems as if we've gone back to rushing from one activity to the next, filling each moment with things, plans, lists, and obligations instead of what's most important—caring, giving, connecting. Often it seems as if we barely have time to think, breathe, or reflect. Where is the heart in all this frenetic energy? What is the purpose of expending so much of it? Living this way doesn't make us happier, healthier, or more fulfilled. It doesn't give us more positive relationships. Living frenetically actually subtracts from our relationships and peace of mind. It becomes next to impossible to connect with ourselves and each other in this mad rush to accomplish and accumulate. And for what?

The events in our world over the past year have shown us that life is too precious to squander. It's time for things to change. Our souls need feeding and so do our children's. Without nurturing connections, we become thrown off balance.

A young mother I talked with recently expressed a growing sense of disconnection that typifies what so many people seem to experience. "I've lived in the north and I've lived in the south. It's the same all over—people pull back from making connections. When I strike up a conversation with someone I don't know, they look at me funny. I get the feeling they think I must want something. They don't realize I'm just being friendly. Why are people suspicious of that?" In today's fragmented society, people yearn for a sense of connection, but pull away from it at the same time.

Harvard's Dr. Edward M. Hallowell, author of *Connect: 12 Vital Ties That Open Your Heart, Lengthen Your Life, and Deepen Your Soul*, writes about the importance of connecting to others: "I call people to connect, from the heart, as a top priority in their lives. We all need each other! We now have scientific, medical evidence that these connections not only feel good, but are good for us. Indeed, without them we die younger, get sick more easily, and do worse at work or at school."

I truly believe that one of the reasons we have so much suffering in the world is because we fail to see our inherent connections. Too many of us believe that people who are hungry or homeless are part of a separate world. But that's a fallacy—if one of us suffers, we all suffer.

How many of you have ever had a "bag-lady" fantasy, in which you imagine yourself out on the street with nothing to eat, unable to feed your children? I used to have this fear. When I was writing my first book and going through a divorce, I would wake up in the middle of the night with my heart pounding, thinking that if something went wrong, we could lose our house and end up out on the street. I thought I was the only one who entertained these thoughts until I read an article by a famous female writer who said she'd had the same thing! In her article she talked about the bag-lady fantasy being fairly common among women. I sometimes suspect men have it too—they just don't talk about it as much.

But why do we even have this fantasy? Perhaps it's because we don't take care of our own in this society. We allow unthinkable circumstances to exist where families actually *do* end up out on the streets, and children actually *do* go hungry. Yet we shield our eyes and pretend they have no connection to our lives. But they do, and ignoring each others' needs gives us an underlying feeling of insecurity, an almost unconscious thought that maybe the same thing could happen to us.

A mom from Belgium in one of my parenting groups said, "How could it be this way in America? You're the richest country in the world but you have people living on the streets, and you have children with no health care. In Belgium, everyone has a place to live, food to eat, and access to medical care. We take care of our own. Why don't you do that here?"

Why don't we? Instead of taking care of each other, we deny our connections and then suffer for it. Poverty, inequity, and oppression give way to violence. But we still allow each of these to exist. One in five children in America lives in poverty. Our dis-connections allow this to be so.

Now is the time to connect more with ourselves, others, and the world around us. The question is—how do we begin? Read on to find out.

STARTING WITH YOU: RECONNECTION AS A VITAL TIE

Because peace starts with each of us, it's essential that we seek ways to find harmony and balance—to feel connected to our own souls. It is only then that we can connect to others. When we don't take care of ourselves, we lose our grounding and feel over-whelmed. When we're oblivious to our own needs, we're cut off from the needs of others.

That's when a chain reaction begins: We become tense and re-active, the people around us react to our reactions, and before we know it, an invisible current of tension ignites. But we each have the ability to short-circuit this tension-reaction-tension cycle and restore internal balance. Here's how.

Four Ways to Connect With Yourself

• *Stop, breathe, and tune in to what you need.* Ask yourself this question: *Is there something I need right now?* If you possi-bly can, give yourself what you need. I know that might seem out of the realm of possibility sometimes, but think about this—something as seemingly insignificant as a cup of tea, a moment of silence, or a breath of air can shift your mood and nurture your spirit. And when you feel nurtured and grounded, you're better with the people you love. We know this, but we forget.

Putting our own needs aside too often causes us to lose touch with what they are. That's when we end up grouchy, irritable, and short-tempered. It's okay to say to your child, "You'll need a to wait a few minutes for that (juice, attention, socks, a ride).

Mommy needs to do *this* right now." Do whatever might restore your equilibrium, then give her some juice. Your family will be the ultimate beneficiaries of your self-nurturing.

Remember, too—the people we love learn to honor us when they see us honoring ourselves. If you let loved ones treat you like a doormat, they will. Also, our children learn to nurture themselves by watching us.

Carmen, the mother of four, is on the opposite path. She runs herself ragged every day chauffeuring her children, picking up after them, and catering to all their needs. "This is how my mother did it, and I don't know any other way," she says. "Lord knows, I wish I did. I love my kids, but I've forgotten who I am. I know I'm in there somewhere, but I don't even know where to start looking." Carmen admits she's too exhausted to think, and she feels burdened by her life. Her kids are growing more demanding and expect her to cater to their every whim. Carmen is beginning to resent it.

Sound familiar? Yes, parenting *is* demanding, especially when our children are young, but that's all the more reason we must find ways to keep ourselves sane.

• *Ask yourself what is really important.* Sometimes we put extra pressure on ourselves by trying to do it all and do it now. As one mom said, "When I die, if they write on my tombstone, 'Her laundry was always folded and her beds were always made,' will it really matter in the larger picture?" Is there anything you can let go of that doesn't add to the quality of your life? If so, consider doing it. Small shifts can spell big changes in the quality of our lives.

That's exactly what Nora, the mother of two, discovered. Listen to her story:

> Last year I would send my daughter Clara off to kindergarten upset every day. I'd been insisting she let me get every knot out of her long hair before she left the house. I'd comb and she'd cry. Watching her leave the house upset made me feel incredibly guilty.

One day I asked myself if it was really so important that I get all the knots out. Was it worth seeing Clara walk out the door rubbing tears from her eyes? The answer was a resounding "no."

I decided that brushing, not combing, her hair would have to be enough. The underneath knots could stay in till I washed her hair. Then I could get them out with conditioner, and no tears. Her hair looks just as nice, and now she goes to school with a smile on her face.

By making this decision I was honoring what was most important: having a peaceful morning, and my daughter going to school happy. Letting go of my need for perfection made a big difference in the quality of our days.

By reconnecting to her highest priorities and honoring what was most important, Nora shifted her mornings from stressful to calm. Simple decisions can have that kind of power.

• *Build calming rituals into your day.* Deep breathing, envisioning, meditation, finding ways to slow the pace of your day, stopping what you're doing and taking an occasional break—all these calm the body and mind and prevent the stress that leads to conflict. All the suggestions you read about in Chapter 2 will help give you that added sense of calm, and they don't take much time.

Here's another ritual you can do that will help soothe tension at the end of a busy day. Carol soaks in a tub with hot water softened by Epsom salts, and scented with lavender. She lights a candle, puts on soft music, and lets the tension dissolve. She says, "Falling asleep afterwards is a piece of cake. I get so relaxed in the tub I can barely keep my eyes open."

Giving yourself permission to do rituals like this one helps you turn down the volume on your life. The increased peace of mind you experience rubs off on your children. Remember, your kids learn by watching you.

• *Avoid rushing.* Even if you have to get up fifteen minutes earlier each day, take things a little slower. Rushing causes pressure. Pressure causes stress and stress leads to conflict. As one dad of two children, ages six and four observed: "I rush all the time, trying to get the kids ready for the day and out of the house on time, getting to work, having appointments, making phone calls—all that stuff is constant. Then I started to realize something: rushing really doesn't help me accomplish more, it just makes me tense. In fact, I think rushing makes me accomplish less, because when I get really tense, I start making more mistakes. I'm actually defeating my own purpose when I rush."

It seems like everyone lives hurried lives today. Each time we rush, we disconnect from something vital in ourselves. The place to begin changing this pattern is right in our own homes.

CREATING DEEPER CONNECTIONS THROUGH RITUALS

A sense of connection is vital to children at every age and stage. As our children get older and start breaking away, sometimes we forget how much they still need to be connected to us. Dr. William S. Pollack wrote about the importance of connection during adolescence in his article,"Preventing Violence Through Family Connection" (*Brown University Child and Adolescent Behavior Letter,* 2001). He says, "Although we are often taught that adolescents need or want to separate from their families, this is another dangerous, unsubstantiated myth." Pollack urges parents to find ways to strengthen connections to their teens as a way of ensuring their mental and emotional well-being. "Most of our children desperately need their parents, family and extended family—coaches, teachers, ministers, rabbis—to be there for them, stand firm, yet show flexibility and form a living wall of love that they can lean on—and bounce off—regularly. For the adolescent, knowing that they have a loving home and that they can tap into the strength derived from positive family relationships—the 'potency of connection'—is truly the key to making it through adolescence." This potency of connection can also be nurtured through creating meaningful rituals in our lives.

When I've worked with parents of teens, I'm often met by surprise when I suggest that their children might actually still enjoy talking to them. "My daughter thinks everything I say is stupid," said one mom, as the rest of the group nodded their heads in agreement. Yet when they tried the active listening techniques outlined in the last chapter, these same parents discovered that their kids were happy to engage in conversation with them. *What they needed most was to feel listened to and understood.* Don't give up if your teen pushes you away. Keep remembering that beneath that aura of false bravado and independence, your teen needs you now more than ever.

Children of all ages thrive on strong ties to their parents. Connections are mutually nurturing, buffeting you both against harsh events and creating a bond that sustains you. This is where creating meaningful rituals comes in. Meg Cox, author of *The Heart of a Family,* says, "Rituals are comfort food for the soul." Rituals have the flexibility to parallel our changing needs and moods and can help us celebrate happy moments and weather times of difficulty. Even in times of overwhelming sorrow, rituals can provide comfort. Meg told me about the touching ritual that took place in Oklahoma City on the day of the McVeigh verdict. Miraculously, one tree had survived the bombing of the Murrah Building. It was here that loved ones gathered to honor people who had been killed and those who'd survived. Each family member poured water on the roots of this tree in what Meg calls "a ritual of cleansing and rebirth."

Grief Ritual

Rituals can honor the living as well as the dead and can comfort families in grief. An article in the *New York Times* profiling people lost on September 11th talked about a beautiful ritual one mother devised for her three-year-old son whose dad, a broker for Cantor Fitzgerald, was killed in the attacks on the World Trade Center. Every night before bed, she would take her little boy out to the backyard and light a sparkler. He would then run around and yell, "Yea, Daddy." The purpose was to "send up a star to Daddy." Doing this helped them both heal. How lucky this little boy is that, despite his mom's grief, she's had the heart and creativity to come up with a ritual that would allow him to both honor his father and shout out his love.

Tea Time

When Joan, the mother of two teenaged girls, lost her much-loved mother-in-law, she created a ritual that kept her legacy alive and strengthened the connection to her daughters. Joan's mother-in-law had left them a beautiful tea set. A long-time lover of tea, Joan decided to use the set with her girls on a regular basis instead of just displaying it on a shelf. When she sensed her girls had something on their minds Joan would say, "Tea time," and they would gather together over Grandma's beautiful tea set, drink tea, and talk. This has been a great way for Joan to keep the lines of communication open with her daughters as they move through adolescence.

Over the years Joan and her girls started collecting beautiful cups to add to Grandma's tea set. This has expanded into shopping trips in which they search for cups together. Continuing their tea time ritual has strengthened the bond between them, and kept alive their connection to their grandmother.

Talk Time

Anxiety and tension have increased in many children over the past year. We can help alleviate this by incorporating soothing rituals like the following one that Kathy does with her eleven-year-old son.

Since Matt's been little, she's been doing the same ritual. She sits on the edge of his bed, and they talk together every night before he goes to sleep. Often this is when Matt reveals things that are on his mind, but haven't come up through the course of the day. The warmth and security of this familiar ritual makes him feel safe to open up.

That's exactly what happened at the start of sixth grade. Matt came home from school one day sullen and quiet. Kathy asked

Matt what was wrong but he wasn't ready to talk. Days went by and Matt remained silent. Finally, one night during "talk time," Matt began to cry. Apparently, his class had been assigned a project that he had taken his own creative approach on, but when he saw what the other kids had produced, his own project seemed inferior. Always an overachiever, Matt was devastated. Kathy quickly realized that the parents of the other children in the class had put some of their own work into their children's projects. Since Matt had done his independently, it looked like a kid's project, as it should. Once Matt opened up, Kathy was able to help him see that his work was just as worthy as the other kids', perhaps even more so, because it was uniquely his own.

The ritual of "talk time" enabled this to happen. "I'm so grateful I've kept this up, even though Matt's getting older," Kathy said. "I can see how much our time together means to him."

Now, with the events of the world as scary as they have been, it would be a good idea for all of us to make "talk time" a regular ritual. Our kids might not open up during the normal course of the day about what's lingering in the back of their minds, but during that safe, warm time preceding sleep, fears and insecurities are more apt to come out. Remember, uncertain times bring out old hurts and magnify new ones. Talk time is a wonderful opportunity for children to be soothed by the person who loves them most in the world.

Peace Shield Ritual

Clinical social worker Virginia Abu Bakr uses a variety of rituals with the children she counsels. She says that rituals have been instrumental in helping her children cope with difficult situations and heal from hurts. When she works with kids who are feeling angry or threatened, she helps them create an invisible "peace shield" around them.

"I have them close their eyes and think of something that makes them happy," Virginia says. Then they imagine locking in the good feeling. I have them envision the energy of peace gathering around them and actually forming an invisible shield. As they're picturing this, I spray a mist of soothing lavender around them to permanently lock in the power of their peace shield."

By the time the children open their eyes, they feel calmer and less affected by the incident that triggered their anger. Virginia encourages children to take their peace shields with them wherever they go. When they feel the need for protection, calmness, or detachment from anger, they focus on the image of their peace shield. Learning this has enabled Virginia's children—many of whom live with volatility and despair every day of their lives—to unhook from anger and hurts that otherwise might overwhelm them. "Having this technique gives my kids a feeling of control. They might not be able to change the circumstances in their lives, but they can *do* something about the way they react to them."

Try doing the peace shield ritual with your children. In fact, try it yourself.

A Ritual for Children Who Are Adopted

Special situations call for special rituals. Meg Cox told me this wonderful story about a ritual her friend Lucy created for her adopted daughter from Guatemala.

Lucy's daughter had a lot of issues around her birthday. She wondered, "How could my real mother give me up and who is she?" Lucy said, "I don't know who your mother is, but I know she's thinking about you too. Look out the window and find a star. Look at that star and talk to your mother. She's probably looking up at the sky right now wondering about you too. Tell her anything you need her to know." Now Lucy's daughter performs this ritual every year on her birthday, and even in between. Doing it has helped her forge an internal connection with her birth mother.

To follow this up, Lucy and her husband took their daughter and son, who is also adopted, back to Guatemala when they were a little older. Although they couldn't find their birth parents, they could find the orphanage and the people who cared for their daughter. For their son, they found the foster mother who'd taken care of him for seven months. The children walked away feeling that "there's a whole other circle of people who love me, know me, care about me, and they will always be there. I will be able to go back to see them." Whenever they look up at the stars, they think of all these people now.

Loving Rituals for Little Ones

Meg recommends doing daily rituals as well as special rituals. "That's where kids get their sense of security. Children need things they can depend on." She told me about a wonderful ritual she devised when she started sending her son to day camp—a place he did not want to go. "We'd take camp chairs, sit in the driveway, read, and talk. It was about creating a fun send-off that would influence his thinking and give him good feelings to associate with camp. When he'd come home, I'd have his favorite toys in different places around the yard. His beanie baby would be on a tree branch, a teddy bear would be on a rock, stuffed lizards along the driveway."

Max's stuffed animals have become a source of several rituals in Meg's household. When Max was a baby, Meg took individual photographs of each of his stuffed animals and made a little scrapbook by putting each picture in a sandwich bag, punching holes in the top, and attaching them with metal rings. She called it "Max's Menagerie." That led to the ritual of Max and Mom sitting together to look at the pictures while Max named each one. On Max's birthday, she lined the porch with stuffed animals, and when he walked inside, there was one on each step and a present at the top.

By the way, Meg does a lovely e-newsletter on family rituals that you can subscribe to for free. You can contact her at megmaxc@aol.com. In a recent issue she shared another beautiful ritual about a mother who made her little daughter a book of photos called "The People Who Love Jenny Book." Several times a week, they sit together and go through the book. Doing this gives Jenny a feeling of being surrounded by the love of many different people.

"Just Family Nights"

Susan Vogt wrote a book called *Just Family Nights,* packed with wonderful activities to foster acceptance, empathy, social justice, spiritual connection, and a sense of responsibility to the larger world. Susan's husband, Jim, administers the Parenting for Peace and Justice Network, a national association of families working for peace and justice in their homes, communities, and the world.

Jim and Susan, the parents of four, have used family rituals to bring to life the values they so strongly believe in. During "just family nights" they would involve their children in activities to heighten their sensitivity to other people and cultures. This helped to profoundly influence the kind of people they've grown up to become and has given them a sense of responsibility to the larger world.

A powerful activity I'd like to recommend from Susan's book is called "Why is There Hunger?" Here's how it works:

If your family is small, invite another family to join you. Cook a one-dish meal, and set your table in the following way to roughly represent the availability of food throughout the world. For 6 percent of the people at your table, create the most elegant table setting you can come up with. This figure represents the United States. For 19 percent of your guests and family, use a simple but adequate place setting. This represents developed countries who have a stronger tendency to conserve resources. For 75 percent of your guests and family, put out plain bowls set on top of newspaper. This figure represents countries of the world where hunger is a major problem. Even though these are rough estimates, they are close enough to give your children a sense of the inequitable distribution of food that exists in the world today.

On corresponding place cards write: the United States, Countries Who Conserve, and Countries With Starving People. Have each member and guest draw straws to see where they will sit. When you serve the food, give the person with the fancy place setting a huge amount, those from countries in the middle range just enough, and those from the poor counties a few mouthfuls. Say a prayer for all the hungry people of the world, then begin eating. Let everyone express their reactions, and see if they come up with solutions, such as sharing food. Afterward, see if there are ways you'd like to help address the issue of hunger. At the end of this chapter are organizations you can contact.

By the way, here are some facts about hunger from Oxfam International that you ought to know: 793 million people worldwide suffer from chronic hunger. Every 3.6 seconds, someone dies from hunger and other preventable causes, 27,000 people a day.

Let your children know that hunger does exist in the United States, to a far greater extent than many of us realize. Although the majority of Americans have far more food than they need, 23.3 million people in our country sought emergency food assistance during 2001. This figure from America's Second Harvest reveals a long term trend. Listen to what else Second Harvest has to say: "Despite a thriving economy in recent years, and reports of welfare reform success stories . . . the USDA recently reported that during the period 1996–1998, some 10 million U.S. households did not have access to enough food to meet their basic needs." America's Second Harvest tells us that this is *not* an inner-city problem, nor a problem of the unemployed. Nearly 40 percent of the households receiving assistance in 2001 included an adult who was working, and 47 percent of emergency food recipients were in suburban and rural areas.

Bringing the issue of hunger to your own table is a very important way of getting your family to think about becoming part of the solution.

Community Service Rituals

Hunger was one of many issues Jim and Susan made their children aware of. They also built an understanding that we must find ongoing ways of contributing to our communities. "We'd go to a park and do clean-up work on a regular basis, and then we'd go out for ice cream to make it fun. We've also worked at the local soup kitchen for more than twelve years. Once every other month, two people from our family would go and volunteer."

If your child resists participating, Jim advises that you "invite, not force," and always end each activity with something fun. Chances are your kids will end up getting enormous value out of their participation, even if they do complain. Jim gives the example of his daughter, Heidi, who often expressed a lot of resistance to their social action activities as a kid, yet when she got a little older, it became clear that her worldview had been profoundly affected. Heidi has volunteered for Habitat for Humanity and is now serving in the Peace Corps in East Africa. One thing she knows for sure is that when she has children of her own, she will do social justice activities with them.

"Country Dinner" Nights

What we value really does influence our children. Kris, the mother of five, has seen this firsthand. She places tremendous value on family closeness, and as a result, her kids do, too. Even though there's a huge age range and the older kids don't live at home, Kris has discovered that family rituals will draw them back.

"When you have kids of multiple ages, connecting becomes invaluable," Kris says. "One of the things we do is our country dinners. One night every week, I try to cook chicken, turnips, stuffing—the works—and make it like a mini-Thanksgiving. It's a time for us to gather without fail." Kris adds, "If I'm really busy, I just make the chicken and something simple. The kids love it anyway because we're all together."

Even though Kris and her husband, Bill, have one child in the Navy and two in college, two of them are close enough geographically to come home each week. The child who is not able to come gets included, too. They call him by phone at the start of the meal and have him do the prayer. Kris says, "We might not be able to have dinner together as often as I'd wish, but we make sure to have our country dinner every week like clockwork."

Wishes and Prayers

A very special ritual spontaneously evolved among Kris and her two daughters. It started when eight-year-old Mariah noticed the hands of the clock at 11:11. This fascinated her, so she looked at Kris and said, "It's 11:11. Let's make a wish." After that, every time the clock said 11:11, they would stop whatever they were doing and make a wish together. Soon Kris's twenty-two-year-old daughter joined in, and before long, wishes evolved into prayers.

In the meantime, Kris's son, who'd been far from the family, began having serious personal problems. Unable to be at his side, Kris was deeply worried about him, and every time 11:11 rolled around, she would send him prayers. "I believed in my heart that the power of prayer would help him overcome what he was struggling with. One day, months into our ritual, Mariah asked me what I'd been praying for. I hesitated, but decided to reveal that all this time I'd been praying for Billy. She looked at me and said, 'Mommy, I've been praying for him, too.' I was floored. I'd thought his problems had escaped her, but she knew anyway, as children often do when we think we're shielding them."

Kris went on, "Recently Billy has managed to overcome the problems he'd been dealing with. He's also realized how extremely irreplaceable your connections are to family, and he's coming back home. Somehow, I believe that our consistent prayers had something to do with it."

Kris's story speaks to a number of connections—the one shared with her daughters each day at 11:11, the link to her son through prayers, and her daily connection to her faith. Did their prayers help Billy heal from his crisis? Who knows? Regardless of the answer, the ritual of prayer gave hope and solace to Kris and Mariah when they needed it, and perhaps even to Billy. Connections like these are necessary and life-affirming, especially in times of stress.

A Divorced Mom Ritual

In an article on family rituals in *Parents* magazine (October 1999), Barbara Biziou talked about a wonderful ritual she created for her son, Jourdan, after her divorce. Barbara's ex-husband had cut himself off from their lives—something that's hard on any child. "To ease the pain," said Barbara, "my son and I began celebrating 'Grandfather's Day' in honor of my dad. We couldn't visit him because he lived on the other side of the country, but we spent hours making cards and gifts to send in the mail. After we finished our projects, we'd go out for a special meal and make a toast to Grandpa." Doing this provided Jourdan with a much-needed sense of connection. Even though Grandpa wasn't there physically, he was there in spirit, and their continued ritual confirmed to Jourdan that he had this loving man in his life.

Donation Day

Barbara has another ritual that all parents should consider doing regularly. She keeps a special jar in her home that she and Jourdan put money into on a regular basis. They declare "Donation Days" throughout the year where they sit down and talk about where they would like to give the money that accumulates. "If kids get into the habit of contributing to the needy," says Barbara, "they'll develop a generosity that will stay with them for life." She suggests having your children write letters to the charities you choose to foster, giving them a greater sense of connection to the people they're helping.

Heritage Day

Here's another wonderful ritual that Barbara recommends. This one involves setting aside special days throughout the year to explore your family's heritage. Using family pictures, globes, maps, and stories of long-gone relatives, you can pass on to your children a sense of their ancestry, something many kids are missing today. My own kids, even though grown, are always fascinated when I come across pictures of their great-grandparents in Russia or Rumania. Now, with so much genealogical information available, you can even start tracing your family's background on the Internet. Cook an ethnic dish on your heritage days, and you'll have a real multicultural experience. Hmm, I wonder if my kids would like borscht?

Speaking of Multicultural Rituals

An interesting website that details a range of Philippine family rituals is www.women.filonline.com. Here, Bernadette Jayne Corrales described a lovely ritual that took place between her mom and dad as she was growing up. "As far back as I can remember, Mom always had the first bite from Dad's plate. Daddy would fork a piece of meat or a bite of fish from his plate and bring it to Mother's mouth and Mom loved it. The ritual seemed to join them in its exclusivity and remind them that they belong to each other."

Even simple rituals like this one can have a great impact. Because of their repetitive nature, rituals form an indelible imprint on our children's memories.

Neighborhood Rituals for the Whole Family

KP Weseloh is a gift to her neighborhood. The mother of four young boys, she places a great value on closeness, community, and connection. Missing the sense of community she grew up with, but pressed for time, KP and her husband, Wayne, devised a neighborhood ritual for every season that could be done almost effortlessly. If you're looking for some ways to form deeper connections in your neighborhood, take a look at the ones below that KP and Wayne have been doing for years:

Spring Ice Cream Social

KP says, "Every May we send out invites to all our neighbors and ask everyone to respond with their favorite brand of ice cream from the local ice cream store. Then we buy a pint for every person. It comes to about sixty to eighty pints altogether, and that's all we serve. So the whole party costs us around a hundred dollars, and all our neighbors have to do is bring a spoon. They love it."

What I adore about this idea is that it's fun, easy, and recreates an era where neighbors join together on someone's lawn. KP and her husband have even taught everyone how to play "kick the can," a game my mother used to play back in the thirties. "We play it almost every night in the summer," says KP. "The kids and even some grown-ups join in. It's become a big thing."

Summer Corn Fest

In August, KP and Wayne do an event similar to their ice cream social, but instead of serving ice cream, they serve corn on the cob. "We get about nine dozen ears of corn, and since August is high season, it only costs a few dollars a dozen. People meet on our lawn and bring their own plates. It's no work at all. Our neighbors usually bring extra stuff and everyone has a great time."

Autumn Ritual

This takes place the day after Thanksgiving and it's a little smaller than the others. KP and Wayne invite twenty to forty good friends, then serve apple cider and donuts for the kids and beer for the adults. Then the whole group walks into town together to watch the lighting of the Christmas tree on the town square and sing carols.

Winter Ritual

Carols are part of another ritual that takes place every year on Christmas Eve "We have a caroling party from six to nine, where I serve soup and bread," says KP. "It's bring your own bowl. I make three or four different soups and a few loaves of bread ahead of time. Everybody gathers around the piano and sings. Someone always plays the guitar too." Again, KP stresses simplicity and connection. "It's all about making it easy for everybody. It's not about what you serve. It's about bringing people together—easily. People just love it. They wonder why no one's ever done it before. It feels like the old-fashioned kind of neighborhood."

One More for the Neighbors

This is a rotating ritual that takes place every Monday night during the summer. Here each family in KP's neighborhood takes turns hosting pot luck dinners. The host usually lights a grill, and whatever people bring gets cooked. As a result of all these rituals, the kids in their neighborhood have a real sense of community. "They know everyone's backyard," KP says. "Kids today don't float from yard to yard like they used to. We create that here." I wish I'd thought of some of these ideas when my kids were growing up!

CONNECTING BEYOND YOUR OWN NEIGHBORHOOD

Many moms I talk to who don't work outside the home have a sense of disconnectedness. Debbie was one of them. Having worked all her life, Debbie decided to leave her job when her first child was born. But what she found was a deep sense of isolation. During the first six months after her son's birth, Debbie says, "I basically hung out in my bathrobe. It was so lonely. There was no one to talk to. I knew other moms were out there—I would see them in the supermarket, but how to find them when I got home was another story. Finally I decided I needed to do something." The result—Debbie created a MOMS club in her area that now serves hundreds of women. Here's how it happened:

> I remembered what it was like when my mother was young—moms would go to the park and they'd meet each other sitting on a bench. Now, it's click your garage door opener, get in your car, and drive somewhere. You never meet anyone. I started looking for ways to recreate the connections I remembered as a child.
>
> That's when I heard about the MOMS Club—an organization where mothers offer other mothers support. I sent away for information and they sent me back a start-up kit. Everything I needed was inside. Another mother decided to join me in starting a group. We told a local reporter about our idea, and she ran an article. The next day the phone started

ringing and it didn't stop for two weeks. I thought "Oh, boy we're on to something!"

The first twenty-five or thirty calls were exciting, but then it became overwhelming. I got about two hundred calls in three weeks. Our first meeting was held in a church and we had over a hundred moms. They were spilling out into the hall! They all felt isolated like I had, and were desperate for social connection. Moms came in from at least eight different towns. Right away we could see one chapter wouldn't be enough. So I asked people who were administrator types to raise their hands, and we met later to get a chapter going in each town. Every chapter took off quickly, and there are between fifty to a hundred moms in each one.

We have playgroups at people's houses, lunch out, and get-togethers in parks and other kid-friendly places. We also do monthly outings to zoos, nature centers, science centers— all local, so we're back in time for naps or picking up older siblings. Once a month we do a moms night out—no kids. There's a book group for our children and a community service component. For this we've adopted a local shelter and homeless organization.

Our Sunshine Committee helps people who get sick or just had a baby. For me, that was one of the most spectacular aspects of the club. It's unbelievable to have a baby and then have ten meals show up at your door-step without even a phone call!

Some of my closest friends are people I've met through the MOMS Club. My children have benefited too. They're growing up with the kids they met in the group. My sense of isolation completely shifted after starting this club. It's helped me connect with other people and gain a sense of community.

If you're interested in starting a MOMS club in your area, go to www.momsclub.org.

Connecting Through the Arts

Marc Chagall once said, "In art as in life, everything is possible." Art can be a creative way to connect with others within and beyond the family. Listen to this wonderful story from art teacher Linda Bradshaw on the power of connecting through the arts:

> Brian was a child who barely spoke. Even thought he was in first grade, he communicated largely through guttural sounds, and in a group he was silent. I decided to include Brian in an art group I had for children in need of emotional support. Realizing that Brian loved to draw but wouldn't communicate on his own, I had to be creative in ways I might encourage him to speak. One of the first things I did was have him visit different people around the school to get ideas for the mural we'd be doing on respect. Brian had to find out what kinds of things to include. Hard as it normally was for him to speak, now that he was on this important mission, Brian overcame his reticence and spoke to the principal and other people in our school. He was actually able to bring back the information we needed.
>
> Once the group began their mural, I told them that if anyone needed a particular color, they would have to use their words to ask, as opposed to just taking a marker, or gesturing toward it. Brian realized that if he wanted the red, he'd have to ask for it. As the group continued to work together, Brian's oral language started to blossom. The mural we ended up with was beautiful. It now hangs over the entrance to our school and has been made into greeting cards.
>
> Through this experience Brian began to speak in other areas of his life. Now he's in fourth grade, and the progress he made at six has carried over. He now communicates normally.

My own family had a lovely art ritual that strengthened the connection we had to one another—all eight of us would gather round the big dining room table and draw or paint together. Often we would sketch each other. I can still remember a lovely pencil sketch my mother did of my father. And in the hallway of their house still hangs a watercolor I painted of my youngest sister when she was two and I, fifteen.

Now that we're adults, my family has a ritual that combines both art and writing. Every Thanksgiving when we're all together, I take out a special book that every member of our family has been contributing to for years now. What was once a blank book now contains words and pictures of what each family member is thankful for. Guests at the table also contribute. This book has become a way of seeing how we have each grown and changed over the years, and it's a record of who we've shared Thanksgivings with. It's quickly becoming another piece of our family's history.

Humor, Laughter, and Fun

Fun? you might be saying right now. *How do I schedule in fun when I don't even have time to go to the bathroom?!!* There's so much we have to do that isn't fun, but that doesn't mean we have to eliminate fun completely. Fun restores balance to life, and in times of stress and uncertainty, balance is essential.

There's a wonderful story in the book *Spiritual Literacy* about how, according to Apache myth, the Creator endowed human beings with special abilities, "to talk, to run, and to look. But he was not satisfied until He also gave them the ability to laugh. Only then did the Creator say, 'Now you are fit to live.' "

We must never get so busy that we forget to create fun and laughter. Here are three simple suggestions for making sure you don't:

• *Set the intention every morning that you will find something to laugh about and someone to laugh with.* Start creating opportunities to make this happen. Bernadette Jayne Corrales, who you met earlier, talked about a humor ritual her family had when she was a teen. Every day her mom would start the morning off by reading the children funny things from the comics. It was her mother's way of bridging the gap between herself and her budding adolescents. Starting the day off with humor was a great way for her to deflect the usual angst that comes up when you're living with teenage children. Humor is actually a great tension reliever no matter what age you are.

• *Look for the humor and ridiculousness in everyday situations.* Once you start looking, you'll see more than you'd ever thought possible. Did you know that in Japan they have laughing clubs? These are clubs that actually schedule daily and weekly episodes of laughter. Can you imagine how much fun that must be? The people in the clubs are also encouraged to find things to laugh about at work and at home. I wish someone would start those clubs here! Doing the work I do can get very serious, so sometimes I have to consciously remind myself to lighten up. Finding someone to laugh with helps give me the energy to continue.

• *Tell jokes.* One year when I was teaching second grade and the standardized tests were rolling around, I decided to relieve the pressure by making time every day to share silly jokes with my students. There are tons of joke books in the library and it was easy to find at least one or two jokes a day. Sometimes we would end up laughing just from the sheer ridiculousness of the jokes— but the point was, we laughed. And right now, with events of our world so serious, humor can be a wonderful ally in keeping our perspective.

CONNECTING YOUR FAMILY TO THE LARGER WORLD

No matter how many people we connect with in our smaller world, we must always remain cognizant of our ever-present unseen connections to the larger world. We are connected, each of us, by the invisible bonds of our common humanity—something we must never forget.

The visualization that follows honors our connections to the larger world. Doing it with your children will reinforce how closely all beings of the earth are connected. Light a candle, get into a relaxed state of mind together, and do some slow deep breathing until you both feel completely calm. Then read the visualization to your child in a slow, rhythmic voice:

• One World •

by Theresa Benzwie

Breathe in slowly. When we breathe out, we will be breathing out good feelings to others.

Slowly breathing in nurturing feelings.

Slowly breathing out loving feelings to each other.

In and out.

With every breath we take, we are filling up the entire room with our positive feelings.

There are so many positive feelings in this room that they can fill up the whole house.

Now everyone in the house can feel our wonderful feelings.

Keep breathing beautiful feelings in and breathing beautiful feelings out. Breathing in and out all the feelings that feel comfortable and warm to you.

Now there are so many pleasant feelings in this house that they are spilling over into the streets and filling up our whole town. The people walking in the street feel them. The people in stores and cars feel them. The cats, dogs, birds, and all of the other animals feel our good feelings right at this moment.

Now there are so many delightful feelings filling up this town that they are spilling over the entire state. The fishes in the water feel our good feelings. People working and people playing feel them right now. There are so many magnificent feelings in our state now that they are spreading to the entire country. Over mountains, through the forests, through the desert, over lakes and rivers everywhere. People throughout our entire country, in their houses or at their jobs, on the street walking or riding, are all feeling wonderful right now. We are spreading beautiful feelings throughout the whole United States.

Now there are so many good feelings throughout the country that these feelings will be able to cross the oceans to Europe, Asia, Africa, and Australia. They will go south to Central and South America and north to Canada. Your good feelings are floating throughout the entire world right now.

People who are fighting will stop because they feel peaceful. Presidents and heads of state throughout the world are feeling loving and want to have peace. Whales and dolphins are playing, lions and tigers and bears are feeling terrific, and the leaf-cutting ants in the rain forest are feeling great. The flowers and trees are feeling bright. All living creatures are feeling glorious right now, because we are sending these feelings to them.

After completing this visualization, you might want to follow it up with an art or movement activity. Your children can act out the images they envisioned, create a mural, or write a story. Integrating the creative process will further connect them to the power of this visualization.

This activity is adopted from Dr. Benzwie's book, *More Moving Experiences* (Tuscon, Ariz.: Zephyr Press, 1996). Many thanks to her for granting permission to reprint it here.

CREATING MIRACLES THROUGH OUR CONNECTIONS

The great Native American sage, Seneca, once said, "Wherever there is a human being, there is an opportunity for kindness." Acts of kindness can connect us to friends, neighbors, family, and even to people we don't know. Being the recipient of an act of kindness from a complete stranger can warm our hearts and sometimes even restore our faith in humanity. This is what happened to Arlene and Len when their son was stricken with kidney disease. Here is Arlene's story:

> Two years ago, my fifteen-year-old son Joshua went into kidney failure. On that day, his name joined the list of close to 50,000 people throughout the United States awaiting a kidney. None were available so Joshua had to be placed on dialysis. Little did we know that this experience would lead us to renewed faith in the goodness of people.
>
> Joshua had to be at the hospital three days a week to re-

ceive treatment. Although he was constantly sick and missed over eighty days of school, his spirits remained high. When other kids on dialysis asked him what he had to smile about, Joshua always told them how important it was to make the best of a bad situation.

Still, I wasn't sure how long he could stay so upbeat. The ordeal of dialysis was draining and he required two surgeries during that time. Joshua also watched a lot of his friends go through painful treatments, and in some cases, develop seizures. Each day he saw adults on dialysis with missing limbs and wondered if someday this could happen to him.

Days turned into weeks, and weeks into months. I began to wonder if there would ever be a kidney for my son. To complicate an already impossible situation, my father was diagnosed with terminal cancer. He ended up spending several weeks in the same hospital as Joshua. But on the day my dad was released, something miraculous happened.

I had hoped to take my parents home, but couldn't leave Joshua's side. The only way for them to get back was to take a taxi. The cab pulled up, and a warm, kind-faced driver greeted my parents. The connection was immediate. During the hour-long drive, my mom began telling the cabdriver, Saj, about leaving her grandson behind in the dialysis center, and the lengthy waiting list for kidneys. Saj listened intently. Suddenly he pulled the taxi to the side, looked at my parents, and said, "I want to help your grandson. I want to give him one of *my* kidneys." My parents were stunned.

Saj gave them his phone number and urged them to have me call.

That night when I heard my mom's voice on the phone she was crying so hard she could barely get the words out: "We've found a kidney for Joshua!" Impossible, I thought. I made her repeat the story three times and hung up the phone in disbelief. This had to be some kind of prank. Who would offer a kidney to a complete stranger?

Even though I had misgivings, I decided to call Saj anyway. My heart was pounding and my mouth was so dry I could barely speak. But when I hung up the phone two hours later, I knew this gentle man was serious—he had lost a son of his own and wanted to give Josh a kidney in his memory.

When we broke the news to Joshua, he was in complete shock. "You mean someone who doesn't know me wants to give me one of his kidneys!" We were all on cloud nine.

Thus began the arduous process of testing that would determine if Saj and Josh were a match. The week of waiting for test results was the longest of our lives. Yet even during the darkest moments of despair over my dad's condition and Joshua's dialysis, my family finally had hope. Saj had given us this gift. No matter what the outcome was to be, his pure act of kindness had changed our lives.

With only three more tests to go, we learned that Saj and Joshua were almost certainly a match. Still in disbelief, Saj came to the dialysis lab to meet Joshua for the first time. Their connection was instantaneous. But days later, we received a call from Children's Hospital—they had located a kidney for Josh, a perfect match.

I immediately called Saj and told him the news. Since we had no way of knowing the final outcome of his last three tests, there was no choice but to take the bird in hand. Saj was thrilled for Josh and offered us his best wishes. It was bittersweet.

It's been six months since Joshua's transplant, and he's healthier than ever. I will never forget the day my parents took a ride in a taxi and met an angel. That chance meeting in a yellow checkered cab brought us the unexpected kindness of an unselfish stranger. His extraordinary gift regenerated our faith. I say a silent prayer for him every night.

With every act of kindness, a little more goodness is added to the world. Extraordinary acts like the one Saj performed are life-changing. But even offering a hand, a word of praise, or a smile can be very powerful. Think about how good it feels when someone goes out of their way to help you. Think about how good your child feels each time a teacher or coach acknowledges him for something he's good at or something he's accomplished. Think about your partner—when we give special kindnesses, our relationship thrives. And huge gifts of kindness, like Saj's, can alter our perception of the world forever. They infuse every cell of our being with the light of hope.

Silent Blessings

If you're not sure what acts of kindness you want to perform, here's something you can do anytime, anywhere, even with complete strangers. I call it sending silent blessings. One day after September 11th, when things seemed so bleak, I was driving in my car praying we would all be okay. I spontaneously started looking at the people passing by and saying , "I hope you're safe, well, and happy." This is actually an adaptation of a Buddhist prayer that goes like this:

> *May all people be free from danger.*
> *May all people be well in body, mind, and heart*
> *May all people be at ease with whatever comes their way*
> *May all people be happy and free.*

Sending silent blessings lifted my spirits, so I started making a conscious effort to do it more often. Before long, whenever I was driving in the car or walking down the street, I would send silent blessings. One time I was waiting in line at a hospital to have some tests, getting impatient as the woman in front of me took a long time getting her paperwork in order. So I shifted gears and started sending her silent blessings. After all, we were in a hospital, and who knows what she was there for? She turned around, smiled at me and started talking—probably a coincidence but, in any event, a pleasant one. I'd like to believe that the blessings I sent her helped her through whatever tests she was there for and infused some positive feelings into what was probably a stressful day.

Try it yourself. When you're driving in the car or walking down the street, or in a store, send a silent blessing to the people you see. I guarantee, doing this will lift your spirits. Think of it this way: We share the earth with billions of people; why not send blessings to our unacknowledged co-compatriots? Who knows, the accumulation of all our blessing might in some small way add to the goodness in this world, and actually, it may not be such a small way at all.

END THOUGHTS

The power of connecting knows no bounds. When we forge connections of love and trust with our children, we give them the strength to face the world. Jonah Martin Edelman, the son of Marion Wright Edelman, founder of the Children's Defense Fund, wrote about the profound impact of his family's connection on his life: "When I am feeling paralyzed by a task that seems too difficult, I remember the love that lies at the core of my family and their legacy to me. The love gives strength, and I can move again." That is the indescribable power of connection.

Muhammed Ali once said, "Love is the net where hearts are caught like fish." May your loving connections be the net that catches your children's hearts and nurtures them for the rest of their lives. And may our connections to each other grow and strengthen in power and goodness, becoming the net where peace comes to rest for coming generations.

RESOURCES AND BIBLIOGRAPHY

Websites

MOMS Club
www.momsclub.org
Tells exactly how to form a support network of moms in your area; provides activities for moms and kids.

Parenting for Peace and Justice
www.ipj-ppj.org/ppjn-new.html
A national association of families of all types who seek peace, well-being, and justice at home and in the world.

The Institute for Peace and Justice
www.ipj-ppj.org
They help people find "learnable and doable" ways to incorporate justice and reconciliation into an active quest for peace.

Teaching Tolerance
www.tolerance.org
One of the best resource organizations in the world. Provides invaluable materials for homes, schools, and communities to promote acceptance.

United Network for Organ Sharing
www.unos.org
There are presently over 79,400 people waiting for some type of organ transplant; 50,955 people are waiting for a kidney. Here's where you can find out how you can help.

Books for Parents

Cox, Meg. *The Heart of a Family.* New York: Random House, 1998.
A beautiful book filled with wonderful family rituals for every occasion or purpose. Contains lots of stories from parents around the country. Highly recommended.

Edelman, Marion Wright. *The Measure of Our Success: A Letter to My Children and Yours.* New York: HarperTrade, 1993.
The head of the Children's Defense Fund describes her hopes for the improvement of American children's well-being. Touching and compelling.

Hallowell, Dr. Edward M. *Connect: 12 Vital Ties That Open Your Heart, Lengthen Your Life, and Deepen Your Soul.* New York: Pantheon Books, 1999.
Sensitive and beautiful book on elevating the human spirit through the power of connections.

Imber-Black, Evan, and Janine Roberts. *Rituals for Our Times: Celebrating, Healing, and Changing Our Lives and Our Relationships.* San Francisco: HarperCollins, 1992.
Shows how we can use the power of rituals to mark life's transitions, heal the past, and deepen relationships.

Vogt, Susan, ed. *Just Family Nights.* Elgin Ill.: Faithquest, 1994.
Sixty activities to teach kids about social justice, equity, and personal responsibility.

Kids Books and Joke Books

Anno, Mitsumasa, et al. *All in a Day*. New York: Philomel Books, 1986.
Ten internationally known artists depict a day in the lives of children in countries around the world. Our common humanity is revealed through words and pictures. (Grades 3–6.)

Bunting, Eve. *A Day's Work*. Boston: Houghton Mifflin, 1994.
A Mexican-American boy learns important lessons from his Spanish-speaking grandfather. (Grades 3–6.)

Carlstrom, Nancy White. *Light: Stories of a Small Kindness*. New York: Little, Brown, 1990.
Stories about children from different parts of the world who overcome obstacles. (Grades 3–6.)

Cole, Joanna, and Stephanie Calmenson. *The Laugh Book*. New York: Doubleday, 1987.

Keller, Charles, and Jeff Sinclair. *Best Knock-Knock Book Ever*. New York: Sterling, 2001.

Polacco, Patricia. *Chicken Sunday*. New York: Philomel, 1992.
The story of a group of children of different races who are friends and the wonderful woman who influences their lives. (Grades K–3.)

Sachar, Louis. *Dogs Don't Tell Jokes*. New York: Knopf, 1997.

Schmidt, Jeremy. *Two Lands, One Heart*. New York: Walker and Co., 1995.
The true story of TJ, a boy who journeyed from Colorado to Vietnam to see where his family was born. (Grades 2–5.)

Steig, William. *CDB!* New York: Simon & Schuster, 1973.
More jokes.

Wood, Douglas. *Old Turtle*. Duluth, Minn.: Pfeifer-Hamilton Publishers, 1991.
Book of the Year Award winner uses the voices of animals to look at our place in the world and the responsibility we have for taking care of it. (Grades K–2.)

Chapter 7

Nurturing Compassion

There are two ways of spreading light: to be the candle or the mirror that reflects it.

—Edith Wharton

When we are dead and people weep for us . . . let it be because we touched their lives with beauty and simplicity. Let it not be said that life was good to us, but rather that we were good to life.

—Jacob Philip Radic

We're here to love. Everything else is just stuff that happens along the way.

—Lori Simon

Compassion is another healing force. We saw it in our fire fighters and rescue workers after September 11th. We saw it in the outpouring of donations and assistance to families of the victims. We saw it in the overflow of people wanting to donate blood for the survivors. And for many, those acts of compassion felt nothing short of miraculous. In a world filled with violence, our ability to continue performing compassionate acts is desperately needed.

"To be truly compassionate, our first task is to open our own hearts and, with kindness for ourselves, confront our own discomfort, fear and suffering. True compassion is like the sun, always present in the sky, but sometimes hidden behind thick layers of dark clouds." This is what Dr. Adrian Bint teaches to doctors and nurses in his stress management courses. Compassion starts with how we treat ourselves, but it must not stop there. We must open our hearts, minds, and hands to all members of the human family. This sentiment shines through in a note I received from a mother in Japan shortly after September 11th: "No matter what race you are, now matter where you live, no matter what culture and religion you have, all the mothers are the same and worry about our children. Even the mothers of the suicide pilots. They may be crying in their deep places. As one of the mothers, I just cry for them." This is the essence of compassion.

THE URGENT NEED FOR COMPASSION NOW

Accepting others is one of the most important acts of compassion we can perform, and doing so may be one of the greatest challenges of our times. As much as we've seen a rise in compassion—at least temporarily—after September 11th, we've also seen so much hatred. Too many have looked with suspicion toward those of Middle Eastern descent, perceiving them as "the other." Blinded to our shared humanity, a silent disconnect has taken place.

This is how separations and divisions begin, be they racial, religious, ethnic, gender, age, political, socioeconomic, or sexual orientation. So many acts of violence are rooted in our inability to see beyond these divisions, and it's time for this to stop.

Arun Gandhi, grandson of the Mahatma, urges us to be much more cognizant of how we treat each other, calling prejudice, exclusion, and negative labels passive violence. Words like "Axis of Evil" are words of passive violence. They create deeper separations and feed the flames of hatred and suspicion.

Passive violence also rears its ugly head when we close our eyes to the needs of others. "Because we overuse the world's resources, there is less for those who need them," Gandhi said in a speech last November. "This is violence against humanity. We must display concern for others in our actions. We must be more conscious of what we do and how we behave."

Arun Gandhi urges us to see that there is too little compassion for those who are poor. The massive inequities that exist in our world are also forms of passive violence. These inequities often lead to physical violence and form the roots of war. Here are some examples Gandhi gives of inequities that exist today:

- In the United States, we spend $8 billion on cosmetics, the same amount it would take to educate all the illiterate people living in the world right now.
- Americans spend $1 billion a year on ice cream, enough to provide clean water and sanitation for every person living in Third-World countries.
- It takes an average of six minutes of work to earn a loaf of bread in the United States; it takes twenty hours to earn the same loaf of bread in Third-World countries.

What has happened to us that allows us to live with inequities like these—inequities that are so rampant in our world, and even in our own country? Has something inside us gone numb to the suffering of others? "I care about other people," one mother said to me. "It's just that when you're leading a comfortable life, you get wrapped up in your own stuff and forget about people who don't have as much." It's become too easy to forget. And each time we do, without even realizing it, we allow passive violence to exist.

"We can be violent toward others without being physical," Gandhi says. "Passive violence fuels the fire of physical violence. We are the fuel supply. *We must do things that are not just right for us, but are right for others.*" This is the true meaning of compassion.

Think about the figures you just read and now think of this item from the *New York Times:* "There was the Hollywood mom who hired dancers from the Cirque Du Soliel for her child's birthday party, spending $30,000, according to one guest." Another mother gave a $70,000 birthday party for her two-year-old child (*New York Times,* January 20, 2002). Yet as I write these words, 12 million American children are living in poverty, 4.2 million of them under the age of six. Think about it—*almost one in five American children under the age of six lives in poverty.* (National Center for Children in Poverty figures). How can we justify our own indulgence in the face of this? It reminds me of something Isadora Duncan once said, "So long as little children are allowed to suffer, there is not true love in this world."

Did you know that among all industrialized nations of the world, the United States ranks first in Gross Domestic Product and in the number of millionaires and billionaires, but eleventh in the proportion of children living in poverty, and twenty-second in infant mortality (Children's Defense Fund figures, 2001). How have we allowed this to happen?

In his book, *Chasing the Red, White & Blue,* David Cohen says, " . . . the gap between rich and poor is widening. 40 percent of American children live in poverty, and budget surpluses suggest that although the economic means exist to help the poor, *we simply choose not to . . .* America, moreover, has a child poverty rate that is . . . often two-to-three times higher than that of most other major Western industrialized nations."

The gap has been widening. Cohen says, "Inequality is dramatically on the rise in America. Between the late 1970s and the mid-1990s, the average income of the richest fifth of families increased by 30 percent, after adjusting for inflation, whereas the real incomes of the poorest fifth of families *fell* by 21 percent."

Marion Wright Edelman, head of the Children's Defense Fund, calls upon all of us to search our souls. "No other industrialized country in the world lets children be their poorest group as we do." Our compassion as a people has not reached far enough. Connie Mercer, director of Homefront, agrees. Listen to what she told me in a recent interview:

> People don't get it—there are families in need *all* the time. People have been so sympathetic to those who have been affected by September 11th, but they forget that there are families right in their own neighborhoods who are suffering. There's a total disconnect.
>
> A young mother came into my office today. Her husband died and she has three children. Even though she works full-time, she's about to lose her house because she can't afford to make the payments on her own. Why is there no outpouring for her? I meet people like this every day—85 percent of the homeless people I deal with have jobs. Can you imagine going to work every day, emptying bedpans or cleaning people's rooms in a hotel, then coming home to temporary shelter in a motel room because you can't afford to put a roof over your kids' heads? My people do the most difficult jobs there are and they show up for work every day, but they *still* can't afford a place to live. Yet nobody seems to care. I just don't get it.

According to the Children's Defense Fund, "The proportion of poor families with children that were poor despite being headed by somebody who worked full time throughout 2000 is the highest in the 26 years for which data exist." The way our social and economic structures are set up in America, working full time does not necessarily insure getting by. Author and social critic Barbara Ehrenreich found this out first hand. To research her latest book, *Nickeled and Dimed: On Not Getting by in America* (2001), she left behind her middle-class life and tried to survive on minimum wage jobs like waitressing, cleaning houses, serving as an aide in a nursing home, and working in Wal-Mart. Despite her high level of education, good health, childlessness, and race, she could barely cover her expenses and almost ended up in a shelter. Speaking out against a system that makes this common-place, she recently said, "Ours is a society that routinely generates destitution—and then, perversely, relieves its conscience by vilifying the destitute" (*New York Times Review of Books,* January 20, 2002).

Rather than averting our eyes from the poor, Gandhi urges us to think about the poorest person we know of and to ask ourselves this question every day: *What am I doing to help?* If every person who "has" pitches in to help, perhaps we will be able to start shifting the conditions that create so many "have nots." Oxfam International, a highly respected organization that has been actively working to eradicate hunger since 1970, says this: "Poverty and powerlessness are avoidable and can be eliminated by human action and political will." True compassion is not just feeling bad about poverty, hunger, and injustice, but rising above our indifference, and taking action. As theologian and author Matthew Fox says, "Compassion is not sentiment but is making justice and doing works of mercy." If one good thing comes out of September 11th, it should be that we all follow the lead of those generous people who performed compassionate acts, and start making this a part of our lives too.

EXERCISE: Do what Gandhi urges us to do—think of the poorest person you know of and ask yourself, "What am I doing to help?" If you are already helping, see if you can go a step further, perhaps by involving other people. If you're not helping yet, ask yourself how you will begin. When we make the commitment to reach out, somehow our time and energy expand. The websites at the end of this chapter are a good place to start.

THE POWER OF COMPASSION

We each reap tremendous benefits when we extend the hand of compassion to others. Listen to the words of psychologist and author Robert Brooks:

A child or adult's self-worth, dignity, hope, and resilience are nurtured when engaged in acts of caring. While being compassionate to others, we add value and meaning to our own life. . . . There are many, many values that we can teach our children and one of the most important is to be compassionate, caring people. This task will be facilitated when we model compassion in all of our relationships and when we involve our children in experiencing the joy of being contributing members of their society. We must strive to replace self-centeredness and selfishness with a genuine interest in and concern for others. In such a scenario, all will benefit.

There are so many ways we can express compassion toward others and model it for our children. The possibilities are endless. The point is to start now. Avoid the "Isn't it a shame?" syndrome, one that millions of people fall prey to every day. Here's what it looks like: You pick up the paper and read about people who are hungry, homeless, or without medical care, and you say to yourself, "Isn't it a shame?" Often this is followed by the thought, "I wish they'd do something about this problem." Then you turn the page and read about something else, or close the paper and get on with your day. The fallacy in this is that *we are "they."* We are the "they" who need to do something about these problems. Without our help, our action, and our will toward change, these problems will continue to exist. Our own complacency teaches our children to be complacent, too.

Something else that's easy to fall into is the "feel-good" syndrome. We might ocassionally pledge some money to a charity, or donate food to the hungry, or go on an AIDS walk, then pat ourselves on the back, feel good, and excuse ourselves from doing more. Performing intermittent gestures of compassion relieves us of guilt, but too often gives us the illusion that we have done enough. Enough is performing compassionate acts as an *ongoing* part of our lives.

You don't have to disavow material comforts or go live in Africa to make a difference. Think about weaving compassionate acts into your life on a steady basis and teaching your children to do the same. Imagine doing this with the same consistency as getting your hair cut. Imagine what the world would be like if everyone performed compassionate acts as an ongoing part of their lives. We actually might start eradicating some of the problems you just read about and begin creating peace from the ground up.

We each have this power within us. In this chapter and the next you'll meet people like you who've made a difference simply because they decided to translate their sense of compassion into concrete action. It is my hope that as you read about them, a deep and loving part of you will be sparked, and you'll get more involved than you ever have before. We create a better future for our children and strengthen the web of life, strand by strand, each time we lend a hand.

Compassion in Action

Every act of compassion can have an impact far beyond what we might ever imagine. Virginia, the niece of renowned political cartoonist Antonio Prohias, whose cartoon, Spy Vs. Spy, was read by millions (especially in *Mad Magazine*), shared a wonderful story of how her uncle's compassion touched a life in the most profound way.

Before coming to America from Castro's Cuba, Antonio Prohias barely escaped a firing squad. Arriving here with nothing but his life, he was haunted by the terrors he had left behind. His years of suffering had built in him a deep well of both sadness and compassion. "Any child who ever wrote my uncle received not only a personal letter, but also a signed copy of one of his books," Virginia recounts. "He would read between the lines of each letter and try to understand the heart of the person it came from."

"Over years of hearing from thousands of kids, one particular letter jumped out at him," his niece explains. "In this letter he saw a deep need." So Antonio Prohias decided to write a long personal letter back to the young man who wrote him, and along with it he included a stack of his books all personally inscribed.

Prohais never received a response. His niece described what happened next. "Years later my uncle passed away, and a letter finally arrived from the young man my uncle had sent all the books to. By now he was an adult. He poured out his heart in this letter and revealed that on the day my uncle's package arrived, he had been planning to take his own life. The care my uncle had shown in sending that letter and stack of books gave this young man the message that his life had worth. It was the package from my uncle that made him change his mind."

Antonio Prohias went to his grave never knowing that this simple act of compassion had saved a young man's life.

Sometimes we underestimate the impact of compassionate acts, but each one counts. A smile to a stranger, a helping hand, an ear when someone needs to be heard, kindness in the face of callousness, reaching out to a child who is lonely. One of the best ways we can honor those who died in the World Trade Center is to heighten our capacity for compassion every day of our lives, to translate the care we feel in our hearts into action, *and to teach this to our children.*

Our children benefit each time we do this. A study by Ziporah Magen, Ph.D., and Rachel Aharoni, Ph.D., found that "teenagers who were involved in helping others felt very positive about their lives and had high hopes for their own futures." We empower ourselves, our children, and others we might not even be aware of each time we perform acts of compassion.

> **EXERCISE:** Are there any obstacles in the way of your taking action to express compassion? Is there a place where you stop? Reflect on this and write about it in your journal. Is there a way you would like to express compassion but haven't? Write about this too.

NURTURING COMPASSION AND EMPATHY IN OUR CHILDREN

Myriam Miedzian, author of *Boys Will Be Boys: Breaking the Link Between Masculinity and Violence,* says, "Empathy is inversely related to violent behavior. The more we build empathy, the less violent people become."

This starts right in our own homes. The words of Maya, the mother of three, trying to explain the acts of the terrorists to her ten-year-old so beautifully demonstrate this. She said, "I know what they did was a terrible thing, but something inside them must have been so broken to have made them behave that way." And her child said, "I wonder what it was?" Then they talked. This is how we start building compassion and empathy.

Fran, the mother of three boys ages thirteen, ten, and eight, teaches compassion through example, awareness, and affirmation. "Affirmation is something children need to be taught," says Fran. "I always tell my children to affirm each other because their family's opinion of them is more important than anyone else's. When they say something kind, it means so much; when they say something mean, it hurts deeper. I remind them that a brother's opinion matters most. They are each other's mirrors." Fran continuously models this ethic for her children and encourages them to live it. In doing so she is helping them develop bonds of support and trust. "No matter what happens to you in the world," Fran says, "you should always be able to come home and feel safe."

How do we build empathy in our children so that our homes can be the place they feel safest, and the world becomes better because of who they are? Here are two crucial ways to make this happen:

1. Model compassion yourself. Treat your children with compassion and let them see you expressing care toward others.

Compassion comes in many forms. Psychologist and author Arthur Jersild says, "Compassion is the ultimate and most meaningful embodiment of emotional maturity. It is through compassion that a person achieves the highest peak and deepest reach in his or her search for self-fulfillment." As we express care for others, we ourselves become enriched.

In front of your children, make it a point to express care for people you may not even know. For example, you might say,

"That little girl over there just fell down. I hope she didn't hurt herself. Does she look hurt to you?" Or, "I don't wear this coat much anymore. I think I'll donate it to the homeless. The temperature is dropping and people who don't have a place to live might be cold. Is there something you'd like to donate?" Through simple expressions of care like these, children learn the habit of compassion.

2. Teach compassion. Some children innately have a sense of greater empathy than others. It's critical that we help those who haven't developed this virtue. As one mother says: "Whenever my children are unkind, I always ask them the question, 'Are you being positive and respectful?' I make them reflect upon the effects of their actions. Compassion starts by teaching our children, through our own actions, how to care.

"As a child you know how *you* feel but you're not in tune with how you affect the world."

Five Steps for Teaching Compassion

• *Help your child identify his own feelings.* Compassion begins with the way we treat ourselves. It's important to be able to name the emotions we feel and honor them. Once we can do this for ourselves, we're better able to do it for others. Help your child identify in himself emotions such as fear, anger, hurt, frustration, and embarrassment. Ask your child how he's feeling when his face shows emotion. Help him label the feeling.

When Juanita decided to help her eight-year-old son Carlos tune in to his feelings, she used movies and television shows they watched together as a vehicle. Here's a conversation they had together after watching a sad movie:

JUANITA: That movie made me feel really sad. How about you?
CARLOS: Yeah, I guess it was kinda sad.
JUANITA: When the dog died, it made me cry.
CARLOS: I felt tears coming behind my eyes when that happened. I hope nothing like that ever happens to our dog.

JUANITA: I would definitely cry if he died.

CARLOS: Me too. Lots.

JUANITA: You know, it's okay for boys to cry, don't you?

CARLOS: Daddy never cries.

JUANITA: I know he doesn't, but you can.

When we talk about emotions with our boys, we give them permission to feel. This is very important because studies show that the ability to empathize lessens in boys as they become socialized into a world where they are taught to be strong above all else. The only way our boys are able to empathize with others is when they can feel their own feelings first.

• *Ask your child to reflect on his or her actions and how they affect others.* Here's what one mother shared: "My younger son was crying. My middle son just stepped over him. I said, 'Eric, your brother's crying.' And Eric looked at me and said, 'But I'm not the one who hurt him.' It was then that I realized I needed to teach him to be more empathic. I said, 'Honey, if you walk right over him, he'll feel like you don't care about him. Plus if someone's hurt, they need your help even if you're not the one who hurt them.'" Some children more than others need to be guided to understand other people's feelings. It is not an innate capacity in everyone.

The American Psychological Association has a wonderful article on their website called "Teaching Gentleness in a Violent World." Here's an excerpt:

> It's important to let your children know how deeply you feel about their behavior toward others. If they see that you have a real emotional commitment to something, it's more likely that the issue will become important to them, too. This emotional reaction needs to be accompanied by information, some explanation of why you disapprove; for example, "Look, Joey is crying. He's crying because you took his toy away. That wasn't a very nice thing to do!" or "It hurts the cat when you do that; that's why he scratched you. It isn't kind, and I don't want you to do that anymore!'" Be frank, honest, and upfront with your kids about what kind

of behavior you do and don't like. Also, keep it short and to the point; the idea is to teach them, not the make them feel guilty!

Wayne, the father of two, often follows this advice with his daughters. "Whenever I see a me-first attitude in my kids, I tell them to think about how others might feel. I discourage them from saying and doing things that might hurt another person. The quicker you intervene, the more chance you have of curtailing that kind of behavior. If it's allowed to fester, it only gets worse. Children need to be aware of the feelings of others, and that doesn't always come naturally. They learn through our example and guidance."

> **EXERCISE:** Think about your children. Do they express compassion and empathy or do they have more of a me-first attitude? If so, plan to have a conversation with them like the ones above. When you see your children being uncaring, use it as a teachable moment. Remember, no guilt, just guidance.

• *Tell your child how you feel when he says or does something to upset you or another person.* "Amy, what you just said really hurt me. Adults have feelings too," is the kind of statement that helps children see the impact of their words. Or, "When you say that kind of thing I feel angry." Words have power. Let your child know the ramifications of what she chooses to speak.

The same applies to actions. "Jonathan, when you ignore what I ask you to do, I feel disrespected." *Our children need to be accountable for what they say and what they do.* By letting them see the impact of their actions, we guide them to understand our feelings and the feelings of others.

Patti, the mother of three, does this all the time. "I try to make my children continuously aware of how other people feel. This happened just the other day. My son has a boy in his class who doesn't do well academically, but he's a wonderful artist. The kids in the class were making fun of his test scores and my son was joining in. I reminded him that this boy's talents may exceed other people's even the ones who do better on tests. I told my son to put himself in the boy's shoes and imagine how it must have felt when the other kids were putting him down. I stressed how important it is to appreciate each person's unique gifts, and never feel you're better than they are. Everyone has something that's special."

Acknowledging when our children are kind and caring is also critical. In the article "What Makes Kids Care? Teaching Kindness in a Violent World," psychologist Julius Segal, Ph.D., points out that just as it's important to let them know how strongly you feel about their unkind acts, it's important to let them know how highly you regard their kind ones. For instance: "I saw you take care of the boy who fell on the playground. That was very kind of you, and it makes me feel very proud." Affirming the positive things our children do is a powerful reinforcer. Find every possible opportunity to do this.

• *Help your child identify the feelings of others.* You can start by doing this with characters on TV and in books. Then do the same with people you come in contact with. You might say, "The girl in this picture looks angry, doesn't she?" Or, "Why do you think Tommy is acting that way to his brother?" Or, "You said the teacher was crabby today. Do you think something might have been bothering her?" Questions like this get kids to start stepping out of the realm of their own experience and looking at the experiences and feelings of others. This is the beginning of empathy.

Watching a movie like *The Wizard of Oz,* for example, during the tornado scene you might say, "Look at Dorothy. How do you think she must be feeling right now?" Later you can talk about a time your child might have felt the same way, or times he's noticed the same feeling in other people. If your child tends to be less attuned to the feelings of others, he'll need more of your support and guidance. Empathy can be taught.

Listen to this example from Dan, the father of two:

I was in New York with my eight-year-old son Ben after the World Trade Center bombings. There were pictures posted all over the city of people who were dead and missing. At one point Ben leaned against a wall of pictures and thoughtlessly rested his foot on one of them. A woman nearby started having a conniption. I asked Ben if he realized why she was reacting like that. He knew the woman was angry but he didn't understand why. I tried to explain that she might have lost someone on September 11th and maybe the person's picture was on the wall he was leaning against. Ben hadn't grasped that when those buildings came down there were mothers, fathers, sons, and daughters inside. I didn't want to go into too much detail, but he needed to understand.

Dan's discussion with Ben opened a window of compassion for him. We can't always assume the things that are obvious to us are apparent to our children. Some children need us to guide them along a little more.

• *Involve your family in activities that express care for others.* "I try to instill in my children that life isn't just for your own fun—you have to give to others too," says Alan, the father of two. "In order to teach this, I involve them in activities where they can help others."

Another dad, Hank, the father of four, has the same idea. "My wife and I run the annual food drive every year for the local food pantry and homeless organization. It helps my children think about people who have less than we do. My children deliver bags for people to fill with food and clothing to every house in our town. Doing this has given them a sense of the needs of others."

All the experts agree—if you want to have caring children, you must model this yourself in the way you treat them, the way you treat others, and the ways you engage them to reach out and make a difference. Joan, the mother of nine-year-old Rebecca and six-year-old Hannah, has always had a deep concern about environmental issues. She has included her daughters in many activities that express compassion for the earth. Joan talked about two of her favorites:

My children and I worked on a wonderful project together. It was sparked one day when I read an article that told how acorns were needed to replenish the trees that are constantly being cut down. Overdevelopment of our land can cause flooding and depletion of reservoirs, so planting more trees keeps the ecosystem in balance. Acorns can be turned over to a local forestry service for cultivation. Then they get planted in park areas, at the sides of highways, and next to housing or commercial developments.

My daughters were only three and six when I started getting them involved. They loved collecting shells and pebbles, so why not have them collect acorns too? They enjoyed the project so much, we approached my daughter's teacher, and soon the whole class joined in. So did our extended family. Before long, tons of people were involved in the project and, as a result, thousands of trees have been planted. My girls are so proud that our work is helping prevent floods, preserve soil, and provide cleaner air.

This project led us to another—an Earth Day community cleanup. We pick up bags and gloves from our community center, put on our oldest clothes, and clean up places we love like the open space by our park. We encouraged our friends to start doing this too. Now there are so many people involved we have to look for extra spaces to clean up! My girls are very proud of making a contribution to their community. We even received a citation from the Governor.

As young as they are, Joan's girls have clearly picked up their mother's commitment to the environment. "What I like best about doing this," says six-year-old Hannah, "is that we're supporting the earth." Ten-year-old Rebecca says, "It felt good to do something to take care of the earth and show other people what they can do."

Joan says being involved in this kind of altruistic work gives her girls a special kind of pleasure. "Hannah and Rebecca are more enthusiastic about doing these types of activities than anything else they do, including ballet and gymnastics." They have a life-long example that expressing care for the earth can be joyful and satisfying.

ACCEPTING DIFFERENCES

An unknown writer once said, "Empathy is your pain in my heart." Sometimes the deepest pain a person can feel happens when they've been rejected, excluded, or treated with disrespect. There is an epidemic of cruelty in our schools, and our children know all too well the pain of being left out and made fun of. Remember the figure you read in Chapter 4—160,000 children a day miss school because of the way they are treated by their peers. The National Association of School Psychologists reports that 5 million elementary students a year are either bullies or victims of bullies. That's one child in seven.

Any child who is perceived as different or doesn't go along with the crowd can become a target. If this is happening to your child, speak to his teacher or principal. Parents need to intervene when their children are being hurt. Also, there are concrete things you can help your child do if he is being bullied. Teach your child these steps recommended by Michele Borba, Ed.D., in her comprehensive book *Building Moral Intelligence*.

Dealing With Bullies

• *Be assertive.* When kids cower in the face of a bully, it encourages him to go on. Teach this to your child through role play—have him stand tall, look you in the eye, and make a direct statement like, "Cut it out. That's not funny." Then have your child turn around and walk away with his head held high. Much as it hurts to be bullied, children who are need to assume a posture of dignity and strength. Practicing at home helps.

• *Ignore the bully.* Giving the bully attention can egg him on. Encourage your child to go to another part of the playground and talk to other kids instead of giving the bully the satisfaction of a reaction. Being with other kids is important. If the bully sees a child as a loner, that child can become more of an open target.

• *Use "I messages."* Here again, the victim takes a direct approach—looking the bully in the eye and assertively saying something like, "I don't like being called names. It's disrespectful." or "I totally disagree with what you're saying, and I want you to stop." The most important thing is the assertive stance and direct eye contact. Again, practice first. Have your child try doing this in the mirror.

Another very important thing for kids to know is that *they must learn to stand up for each other.* Too often bullies run a reign of terror by psychologically isolating their victims and turning other kids against them. And sadly, this goes on even as early as first grade. The mother of a six-year-old called me recently to ask what to do. She said, "My daughter has hardly anyone to play with anymore. A girl in her class has been spreading rumors about her, and the other kids are listening to what she tells them. No one wants to incur the wrath of the girl who's telling stories." We're talking about six-year-olds here!

It's critical that we teach our children to speak out on behalf of the underdog and to urge their friends to do the same. One of my favorite stories about the effectiveness of doing this came to me from a wonderful sixteen-year-old named Aaron, who goes to a large inner-city high school which is mostly black and Asian. After September 11th, Aaron grew concerned about the attitudes many of his classmates had toward the Muslim kids. So he put the word out to all his friends—"Don't let any Muslim kids be alone in the halls. Walk with them, talk with them, show your support and friendship." When other kids at school tried to use slurs against the Muslims, Aaron and his friends would try to get them to empathize, saying things like, "What if it was someone who was black or Chinese who attacked the World Trade Center? Would you still be talking that way?" Speaking in a respectful, nonaggressive manner got the other kids to stop and think.

Aaron's example is a good one for all of our kids. If we could get more of them to start standing up for each other—assertively and respectfully—we'd cut down tremendously on the incidence of bullying.

Kids see the need to do something about this trend too. A survey conducted by 4H found, "America's youth believe that build-ing respect and tolerance for others is the single greatest commu-nity need." What follows are three ways you can start doing this right in your own home.

FOSTERING ACCEPTANCE

1. Talk openly about prejudice. Help your children under-stand that we live in a world of differences, but underneath we are all alike. We all have the same basic needs for food, clothing, shelter, and love. And we all need the respect and acceptance of others. Stress that creating a more peaceful world starts with each of us, and that we must do what Gandhi says—be the change we wish to see in others.

Teach your children the meaning of "prejudice" and "discrim-ination." If they are old enough, talk about homophobia as well. Children need to learn that any kind of prejudice is unacceptable. They also need to learn how important it is to stand up for those who are targets the way Aaron did. Role play this with them so they become more comfortable doing it themselves, and so they have practice using the language of bravery standing up for oth-ers requires.

2. Expose your children to people who are different either through books, movies, TV shows, or events. Take your children to multicultural programs, ethnic restaurants, and cities that have a mix of different people. Also, visit nursing homes and places for people with disabilities. Helping your children develop a comfort level with differences is essential. Knowing about each other and being able to see our common humanity in spite of differences is a fundamental step in preventing biases.

3. Model acceptance. A disparaging word, a smirk, or a roll of the eyes can all convey prejudice. We need to be absolutely vig-ilant about conveying subtle unspoken messages of nonacceptance. It's critical to be aware of our own hidden biases—we all have them. To know what they are helps us free ourselves from their grip. Many people grew up in homes where acceptance wasn't taught and, as a result, have unconsciously absorbed their parents' biases. Awareness helps to change this.

Also, put a stop to racist or homophobic jokes, or any that poke fun at an ethnic group, gender, disability, or sexual orientation. When we tell jokes that diminish others, or even laugh at these jokes, we give tacit agreement to the insidious biases they convey. If someone tells a joke of this kind in your presence, give an "I message" like, "I'm uncomfortable around jokes like that." Or, "I really wish you wouldn't tell that kind of joke. I know you think it's funny, but it's actually a put-down to that race." By speaking up, we show our children that humor in any form that diminishes another person or group is not acceptable. We also show them that they can speak up too.

SUSPENDING JUDGMENTS

Our judgments of others often stand in the way of our ability to fully express compassion. Aileen shared this story about an important lesson she learned:

> There's an assisted-living facility for handicapped people near my house. This man used to sit outside in his wheelchair collecting donations. I would see him every day when I drove by, but his appearance was very odd and I would often look the other way. I eventually started making eye contact, even smiling. Before long I started honking and saying hi. He'd always give me a big smile and wave back. One day I decided to stop and talk to him. He turned out to be an extremely engaging man with a wonderful sense of humor. His name was Louie.
>
> After that, each time I passed by, I would stop and talk to him. Over the next five years I got to know Louie. His warmth and goodness touched my heart. Over time I started thinking about inviting him home for dinner, but I hesitated—he was

so different from me and my family. I let that stop me, a decision I will always regret.

Last week I read in the paper that there was a murder at the assisted-living facility. I was gripped with this sense of fear that it might be Louie. It turned out that it was. When his death was confirmed, I cried and cried, in part for his passing, and in part because I never opened my home to him—and now it was too late. I wished I could have told him what a difference he had made in my life. He was one of the friendliest people I ever met, always helping others, always smiling, even though he had so much to be sad about. Louie touched my life in such a special way and he never even knew it.

We all know the feeling of seeing someone who's different and looking away, as Aileen did. Because the handicapped were relegated to hidden corners of our society for so long, we have not had the opportunity to develop a comfort level with them. Schools that have handicap awareness programs do children a great service—both to those who have disabilities and to those who do not. We have so much to learn from each other. Often people who have mental or physical disabilities are blessed with an abundance of compassion. Having endured so much in their lives, their hearts open wider, and their capacity to care expands.

Listen to this story that psychologist Wayne Dyer often shares about an incident that took place at the Special Olympics.

A group of children were lined up at the starting line to begin a race. At the signal the children took off, except for one little boy who tripped and fell. As he lay on the ground crying, the other children turned around and one by one they ran to his side to see if he needed help. A little girl with Down's Syndrome planted a kiss on his cheek and said, "Do you feel better now?" At that the whole group helped the little boy to his feet, and together they joined hands and ran to the finish line.

Imagine a world full of children with hearts as big as these children's.

Denise Nover, an advocate for people who are handicapped and disenfranchised, has been including her eight-year-old daughter, Abby, in caring activities since she was little. Every year, Abby would come to Denise's office to wrap gifts for abused and neglected children and she'd always bring presents of her own. Having been around people with all manner of handicaps, Abby has developed a heightened awareness and concern for those less fortunate than she. "It's not only what you say, it's what you do," says Denise. "Abby knows I have been working all my life to help provide services for people in need. This is a value she has inherited."

Mattie Stepanek is one of those wonderful children who, because of his handicaps, has a heart as wide as the world. His life exemplifies the golden quality that comes to people with extreme challenges. Mattie suffers from a rare form of muscular dystrophy, and has been at death's door many times throughout his young life. Yet Mattie is the most compassionate person imaginable. He knows he may not live to adulthood, like his three siblings who also suffered from the same disease, so Mattie has dedicated his life to bringing peace to others. He says, "We are a mosaic of gifts. When we look upon our differences as bad, we're breaking the mosaic." Living each day of his life with a desire to make the world a better place has enabled Mattie to transcend the debilitating effects of his illness and focus on a larger purpose.

REACHING OUT

Tom Smith has tracked Americans' attitudes toward their neighbors as part of the General Social Survey he directs at the University of Chicago's National Opinion Research Center. "I think the shift in charity was that if you lived in a neighborhood or small town thirty or forty years ago and you knew someone down the street and the husband was thrown out of work or disabled, you might help him out in some way," Smith said. "It was personal volunteer work more than giving money."

"I think now those things are done less on a person-to-person level, but more through organized charity efforts. . . . That means people have fewer obligations in their immediate surroundings, but also fewer opportunities to find satisfaction in lending a hand. There is that very strong emotional gain that you get from seeing the good you've done," Smith says. This is the kind of emotional gain I've been talking about—the kind that comes from giving to others.

Gail experienced this firsthand when she reached out to help an aging friend. Listen to her story:

> When my mother was alive, she would always tell me sto-ries about her best friend, Helen. My mother died very sud-denly, and I realized that Helen was my only connection to her. She was old, alone, house-bound, and barely managing, so I decided to help out. I started dropping in to see her on a regular basis and arranged for a visiting nurse. Then I started coming by once a week to help Helen pay her bills. Whenever she was sick, I would check in.
>
> Helen needed me, but I didn't realize how much I needed her. Over time I realized I was being most compassionate to myself by helping her. Helen brought so much joy into my life with her love and warmth, more than I could have ever imag-ined. When I'd come over after a long day of work, she would always comfort me. 'Dahling, come lay down. You look tired. What can I give you to eat?' She would say these things, just like my mother used to. Helen loved my son, too. 'Tatela, look, I have chocolate for you. Come sit with me,' she would say. Theo no longer had his natural grandmother but now he had Helen. By reaching out to help, I gained so much. When we're compassionate, we create bridges to the heart.

Now let us all think about how we can build bridges of the heart through our own acts of compassion.

END THOUGHTS

Lori Simon, who has worked with children with disabilities for over twenty years, says, "When I see other people's kids, I see them as my responsibility too. We are all responsible for all children everywhere. We're here to love. Everything else is just stuff that happens along the way."

Lori was blessed to have been taught this by one of the greatest living sages of our time, Elie Wiesel. As a student of his at Boston University, Lori discovered this key to living that she has held on to ever since. "From Elie Weisel I learned that whatever one person experiences, we all experience. If one of us is in pain, we are all in pain. But if you give love, that spreads, too. Whatever we feel and express affects everyone else." Lori speaks passionately about how Elie Wiesel's teachings inform everything she does. Here's something else she learned from him: "We all have pieces of each other inside of us. We separate ourselves and don't want to look at other people's pain because somewhere inside we recognize it as our own. We need to look into each other's eyes and see ourselves." This is what compassion is all about.

Yet how many of us look into the eyes of another and see ourselves? How many times do we walk by someone who is suffering or handicapped and look the other way? God created enough food to feed every person on earth, enough water to relieve our thirst, and enough ability within each of us to take care of one another, with no one left out. Why is it not working? Morality compels each of us to open our eyes to the inequities that exist in our world, and to do something about them. Our goodness as human beings will shine brightest when we truly take care of each other. Let us record a million more good deeds spurred by heightened compassion and the recognition that we must *never* let one of our own want for the essentials of life. May the lessons of September 11th teach us that if we truly want to create hope, healing, and peace on earth, this is where we need to start.

RESOURCES AND BIBLIOGRAPHY

Websites

The Children's Defense Fund
www.childrensdefense.org
Visit their website and find out how you can help America's children, particularly those in need. Provides comprehensive statistics on poverty, gun violence, and more.

Children Now
www.childrennow.org
Promotes solutions to the most pressing problems facing children today, including violence and poverty.

National Center for Children in Poverty
cpmcnet.columbia.edu
Provides statistics on child poverty and ways we can eradicated it.

Oxfam America
www.oxfamamerica.org
Dedicated to "creating lasting solutions to hunger, poverty, and social injustice through long-term partnerships with poor communities around the world." Find out how you can help.

Books for Parents

Arnow, Jan. *Teaching Peace*. New York: Perigree, 1995.
Teaches parents and teachers how to raise children to live in harmony, free of violence or prejudice.

Ben Jelloun, Tahar. *Racism Explained to My Daughter*. New York: New Press, 1999.
In this book, which won the United Nations Global Tolerance Award, the author shares insights about racism with his ten-year-old daughter.

Borba, Michele. *Building Moral Intelligence: The Seven Essential Virtues That Teach Kids to Do the Right Thing*. San Francisco: Jossey-Bass, 2001.
Exceptional book filled with incredibly useful activities. Buy this one for sure.

Brooks, Robert, and Sam Goldstein. *Raising Resilient Children*. New York: McGraw-Hill, 2001.
Ten essential guideposts for parents for nurturing resilience, positive self-esteem, and emotional health in their kids.

Cohen, David. *Chasing the Red, White & Blue*. New York: Picador, 2001.
This book explores the growing gap between rich and poor in America. It also looks at how race and religion have become divisive social factors, and how, for an increasing number of Americans, the dream of upward mobility has become futile.

Dalton, Harlon. *Racial Healing: Confronting the Fear Between Blacks and Whites*. New York: Anchor Books, 1995.
Insights on racial divisions written by a Yale Law School professor; a pleasure to read.

Ehrenreich, Barbara. *Nickeled and Dimed: On Not Getting by in America*. New York: Henry Holt, 2001.
The author gave up her middle-class life, tried to subsist on minimum wage jobs, and almost ended up homeless. This is her story.

Elias, Maurice, et al. *Raising Emotionally Intelligent Teenagers*. New York: Three Rivers Press, 2002.
Warm, sensitive book on how to raise compassionate, committed teens who are willing to help others.

Ellis, Susan, et al. *Children as Volunteers*. Philadelphia: Energize, 1991.
Tells how children under the age of fourteen can be included in volunteer programs.

Jacobs, Bruce. *Race Manners: Navigating the Minefield Between Black and White Americans*. New York: Arcade Publishing, 1999.
Deals with the countless ways we confront racism that occurs between blacks and whites on public transportation, on the street, at work.

Miedzian, Myriam. *Boys Will Be Boys: Breaking the Link Between Masculinity and Violence*. New York: Doubleday, 1992.
Looks at the roots of violent behavior in males and ways we can break this pattern.

Miles. Betty. *Save the Earth*. New York: Knopf, 1991.
Environmental activities you can do with your children.

Pollack, William. *Real Boys*. New York: Holt, 1998.
Helping boys with self-confidence, self-control, depression, and violence.

Stern-LaRosa, Caryl, and Ellen Bettmann. *Hate Hurts: How Children Learn and Unlearn Prejudice*. New York: Scholastic, 200.
An essential guidebook by the Antidefamation League on confronting and conquering biases and accepting differences. Tips, role plays, and anwers to tough questions.

Teaching Tolerance. *Starting Small*. Montgomery, Ala.: The Southern Poverty Law Center, 1997.
Tells teachers and parents how to teach tolerance to young children.

Wiesel, Elie, and Richard Hefner. *Converstions With Elie Wiesel*. New York: Schocken, 2001.
Collection of interviews with the great Nobel Prize winner. Includes such diverse topics as moral responsibility, the anatomy of hate, compassion, and mercy.

Books for Children

Adoff, Arnold. *Black Is Brown Is Tan*. Montclair, N.J.: Great Owl Books, 1991.
This sensitive book is the story of an interracial family. (Grades K–2.)

Blume, Judy. *Iggie's House*. New York: Bradbury Press, 1970.
A young girl learns about prejudice and tolerance when a black family moves into her all-white neighborhood. (Grades 4–6.)

Birdseye, Debbie Holsclaw, and Tom Birdseye. *Under Our Skin*. New York: Holiday House, 1997.
Six children of different racial backgrounds talk about the issue of race and their own experiences with prejudice. (Grades 3–6.)

Bruchac, Joseph. *Eagle Song*. New York: Puffin, 1999.
Fourth-grader Danny Bigtree moves from a Mohawk reservation to Brooklyn and must find ways to deal with stereotypes about his Native American heritage. (Grades 3–6.)

Cohen, B. *Molly's Pilgrim*. New York: Lothrop, Lee & Shepard, 1978.
Beautiful, moving story of a Jewish immigrant child and her desire for acceptance amid anti-Semitism. Molly triumphs. (Grades 1–4.)

Dodds, Bill. *My Sister Annie*. Honesdale, Penn.: Boyds Mill Press, 1997.
Charlie has a sister with Down's syndrome. He must deal with teasing and various emotions. (Grades 2–4.)

Estes, Eleanor. *The Hundred Dresses*. San Diego: Harcourt Brace, 1972.
Shy Wanda comes from Poland. The children who tease her eventually come to understand the effects of what they have done. (Grades 3–6.)

Hahn, Mary Downing. *December Stillness*. New York: Harpers, 1991.
A thirteen-year-old girl befriends a homeless Vietnam veteran and learns a lot about the meaning of compassion. (Grades 4–6).

Hamanaka, Sheila. *All the Colors of the Earth*. Fairfield, N.J.: Morrow Junior Books, 1994.
Through beautiful oil paintings and lyrical words, children see that people of different colors are as beautiful and unique as the elements of nature. (Grades K–2.)

Houston, Jeanne W., and James D. Houston. *Farewell to Manzanar*. New York: Bantam. 1983.
A young girl's memoir of growing up in a Japanese internment camp during World War II. (Grades 4–6.)

Kidd, Diana. *Onion Tears*. New York: William Morrow, 1993.
A young girl from Vietnam grieves over the loss of her family, deals with teasing, and must make new friends in America. (Grades 2–4.)

Osborn, Kevin. *Tolerance*. New York: Rosen Publishing Group, 1990.
This book of nonfiction helps children understand the meaning of tolerance and shows them how to be tolerant of people in a world filled with too much intolerance. (Grades 3–6.)

Seuss, Dr. *The Sneetches and Other Stories*. New York: Random House, 1961.
The issues of tolerance and discrimination are addressed though humorous illustrations. (Grades K–4.)

Uchida, Yoshiko. *A Jar of Dreams*. New York: Simon & Schuster, 1985.

Eleven-year-old Rinko wants to be like everyone else, but is ridiculed because she is Japanese. She eventually learns the value of her own strength and uniqueness. (Grades 3–6.)

Vigna, Judith. *Black Like Kyra, White Like Me.* Morton Grove, Ill.: Albert Whitman. 1996. A story of friendship between two young girls and the prejudice of the adults in their lives. (Grades K–4.)

Yashima, Taro. *Crow Boy.* New York: Viking Press, 1976.
The issue of accepting differences is addressed as a little boy goes to school for six years in a village in Japan. (Grades K–3.)

PART III

THE RACE TO PEACE

Chapter 8

Making a Difference

Service is the rent we pay for being. It is the very purpose of life, and not something you do in your spare time.

—Marian Wright Edelman

When people come together to do the right thing, anything is possible.

—Nino Vendome

There is a marvelous story of a man who once stood before God, his heart breaking from the pain and injustice in the world. "Dear God," he cried out. "Look at all the suffering, the anguish and distress in your world. Why don't you send help?"
  God responded, "I did send help. I sent you."

—David Wolpe, *Teaching Your Children About God*

Taking altruistic action empowers us in the face of fear and uncertainty. It helps us step beyond our narrowness and touch lives in ways we may never have thought possible. Each time we perform acts of compassion, we light a candle that illuminates the people we reach out to, and casts a glow on our own souls.

In this chapter you will meet people who have stretched beyond their own boundaries to make a difference in the lives of others. These are stories of people like you and me who decided to step out and support other individuals, their communities, and in some cases, the world at large. May their lives inspire you and your children. My fondest wish, my deepest vision is that these stories will reach into your hearts and empower you to make a difference too. And through the accumulated acts of people like you and the children you're raising, the callousness and violence in our world will start to change.

CREATING HOPE BY HELPING OTHERS

We heal ourselves when we help others. And through our reaching out to those around us, we help the world heal. One of the most powerful stories of healing I know came to me from a woman named Maria who transcended overwhelming personal crisis by reaching out. Here is her story:

> All I ever wanted was to be a mother. At age twenty-nine, I became pregnant for the first time. I was overwhelmed with joy, but my dream was not meant to be. Severe complications set in toward the end of my pregnancy, and when I finally gave birth, the baby I had prayed for all my life didn't survive. The cause of his death was almost as devastating as the death itself: I had ovarian cancer and only a radical hysterectomy would save my life. My dream of being a mother was shattered. And when it seemed things couldn't get worse, I learned that the cancer had spread and I had only one year to live.
>
> I raged at God and went into a period of deep despair. How could he let this happen to me?
>
> After recuperating from my surgery, I decided to go back to my job in a social services agency for handicapped chil-

dren. One day a woman came in with the most severely deformed child I had ever seen. I watched this mother handling her child, and what I saw moved me profoundly—it was absolute unconditional love. She was so gentle, so accepting that I felt a sense of transcendence in the mere act of watching her. Although I never saw this mother again, she touched something deep inside me and changed my life. Through her expression of unconditional love I saw what I most needed to give to myself in the face of all this loss, and what I still needed to give to a child.

I promised myself that if I lived, somehow, I would find a way to give the same kind of unconditional love to a child of my own.

In spite of the doctors' prognosis, I started to heal. No one could understand it. Each day I got better. Before long, my husband and I decided we would go to India and adopt a child nobody else wanted. We found a run-down orphanage filled with children who had been literally abandoned on the streets. One child caught my eye. He was swathed in netting and covered with sores, but something in his face pulled me toward him, and I knew this was the child I was meant to love.

That was seventeen years ago. Anil is now a teenager and we are both in perfect health. Having him has given me a second chance at life. Raising him has been my way of saying thank you.

Maria's story is such a beautiful example of what Wayne Muller writes about in his book *Legacy of the Heart*. "Even as we serve others we are working on ourselves; every act, every word, every gesture of genuine compassion naturally nourishes our own hearts as well. It is not a question of who is healed first. When we attend to ourselves with compassion and mercy, more healing is made available for others. And when we serve others with an open and generous heart, great healing comes to us."

Who can you reach out to? What might motivate you to transcend the boundaries of your life and allow compassion to become a driving force? Sometimes this motivation comes in unexpected ways, as happened with Maria. Her grief and loss opened her heart, and in walked the woman who, unknowingly, changed her life indelibly. Maria's moment of revelation was totally spontaneous. This is how it often happens. The key is opening our hearts—to others, to caring, and to making a difference. For some, the events of September 11th did this. And for all of us, the spirit of giving we saw then needs to continue and become a way of life.

> **EXERCISE:** With your notebook at your side, close your eyes and breathe deeply. Ask your higher self these questions: How can I best make a difference in the time I have here on earth? Is there a way I need to reach out that I have not been aware of before? What is the legacy I might leave?

Sometimes fear stands in the way of doing what we envision. We don't feel able enough, smart enough, strong enough, unique enough. Please know this—you *are* enough.

Sometimes we stop short of doing what we dream because we're afraid we'll fail. But everyone who has ever accomplished anything of value has risked failure; it's inevitable and impossible to avoid. A wise person once told me, "If you're not failing enough, you're not taking enough risks." There's nothing wrong with failing, but it's a horrible loss to never have taken a risk.

Sometimes we just have to breathe deep and move forward in spite of our fears, because to let them hold us back would be too much a sacrifice of our own potential. And our children must see us doing this, for each time we take action to manifest our visions, we give our children permission to do the same. Eleanor Roosevelt once said, "You gain strength, courage, and confidence by every experience in which you really stop to look fear in the face. . . . You must do the thing you think you cannot do."

We each have a unique path, and every time we move forward in the face of fear and doubt, we begin to find it. As we find ways to make a difference, a sense of peace starts to unfold.

What touches your heart? Is it children in poverty, homelessness, hunger, gun violence, war? Whatever calls out to you most is where you can start thinking about making your unique difference. The world so desperately needs your participation.

> **EXERCISE:** What issues most call to you? Start thinking about this and write down whatever comes to mind. Ask yourself what you might do to start making a difference in an area you are concerned about?
>
> Have your children do the same thing. You're never too young to start. As you read this chapter, you'll see this firsthand.

When you step out to make a greater difference, you set the wheels in motion for your children. By your example they see the value of giving and often follow suit. In fact, your example is the most critical factor in fostering altruism and resilience in the face of fear. Your children's sense of hope expands each time they reach out to others, and so does yours.

Please share the following stories with your children as a confirmation of the goodness in this world and the power regular individuals can exert when they choose to take action for the good of others. For many of us, our ability to make a difference is like a hidden gold mine waiting to be discovered. Once that gold is mined, the world changes.

FAMILIES MAKING A DIFFERENCE

There is a Swedish proverb that says, "The best place to find a helping hand is at the end of your own arm." Everyone of us has the ability to help, but we don't always extend a hand to do it. Yet, when we see others reaching out, we can be inspired to do the same.

This is what's been happening to young people across the country. A nationwide survey commissioned last October by 4-H reported that 90 percent of America's youth, touched by the heroic acts of rescue workers on and after September 11th, said they would now be more likely to help in their community. But just as critical is your example as a parents: 83 percent of the kids interviewed said they would be more interested in volunteering and getting involved in their community if they saw their parents doing it.

This has been the case in thirteen-year-old Anna Albert's life. Anna's mom, Sue, has been a community activist for many years. Continuously involved in her mother's projects, Anna has become an activist herself. After the events of September 11th, Anna realized that kids her age needed a way to feel better without turning to drugs or alcohol. She came up with the idea of the Teen Vision Café, a place where kids could go to meet, talk, and have fun. "The goal is to bring teens together," Anna said, "to 'un-bore' them and help kids of different races and colors connect. It'll be good for our whole community." Kids like Anna who put themselves out for the good of others reap important benefits—increased self-esteem and a greater sense of mastery in life. "Being involved makes me feel important," says Anna. "You're a part of something."

Fifteen-year-old Megan's mother has also set an example of community involvement. Megan now follows her mother's path by volunteering, and it gives her a sense of empowerment. "You feel like you're a part of changing the world, like you're indirectly helping everyone."

Single mom Judy Lepore has been teaching her children to contribute to others from the time they were little. She's found many ways to include her children in acts of giving, and her children are learning that even small acts of generosity can make a big difference. "Whenever we go to the city, I give my children a pocketful of change to give to homeless people." Judy's thirteen-year-old son Frankie says, "I feel so good when I help. You see how much the people need it. One man was in an old wheelchair. Another guy had bags he was walking around with that looked like everything he owned was inside. They were so grateful when I handed them the money." Judy's nine-year-old daughter Tess says, "It makes me feel proud that I can do something."

Some people recoil from giving to people on the street. I follow the philosophy offered by psychologist Wayne Dyer that opening our hearts and expressing care to those who need it is one of the most important things we can do. It's not the coins we put in someone's hand that matter so much as our acknowledgment of someone's pain and humanity. It's like we're saying, "You are not invisible." That's the gift. What the person does with the money really doesn't matter. Knowing there are people who care does.

Nobel prize winner Elie Wiesel feels the same way. In the wonderful book *Conversations With Elie Wiesel*, he talks about responding to a man with an outstretched hand: " . . . on the one hand reason tells me that if I give him a dollar, he will go and buy alcohol. But then I say to myself, So what? Who am I to decide what he will do with the money that I give him? I cannot see an outstretched hand and not put something there. It's impossible."

Judy Lepore believes that her overall sense of satisfaction in life is elevated when she gives to others. "When I come from a spirit of generosity, it makes me feel like I have more. Goodness always comes back to you in many ways." Judy thinks it's critical to set this kind of example. "I think people have a responsibility to help others. In this country where there's so much wealth, we have been negligent. It's absurd that so many people don't have their basic needs met." She realizes, too, what a difference she makes each time she sets a positive example. "As a mother and a teacher I see how much influence I have. I can teach compassion instead of criticism, generosity instead of greed, giving back instead of just taking."

Community volunteer and mother of two, Barbara Lerman-Golumb agrees. She frequently involves her children in her work. "We must be role models for our kids, now more than ever," says Barbara. "Our kids need to be involved in social justice work. I take my kids to the soup kitchen when I volunteer and they love it. They've become very caring individuals who've learned how to make a difference. It's become a part of their lives."

Each time we help, the world changes a little bit for the better. Psychologist Robert Brooks says, "The healing power of displays of charity should never be underestimated. Seemingly small gestures of kindness become lifelong indelible memories."

Joy has been teaching her children to make a difference since they were very little. Even though her girls are only ten and seven, they've been helping others for years. For many, this past holiday season was a sad time. Separated from their families and alone in the world, the events we had just lived through magnified their loneliness. For Joy, the project she and her girls have been doing each year took on a special meaning.

We have a tradition of taking our kids to a nursing home every year the day after Christmas. Every year we bring gifts and sing songs to the people there. We contact the home before we go to find out which seniors didn't have any visitors or gifts on Christmas day. This year we brought them pillows that we decorated by hand with colored fabric glue. On each one we wrote the words "Wishing you nights of peace and days of hope." Our friends joined us and brought gifts too.

The seniors we visited were so grateful. There was one woman we were told never had any visitors. "She's not very nice," a staff member commented. When we approached the woman, she had a scowl on her face, but when my girls handed her the pillow and wished her a happy holiday, she broke into a smile and gave them each a hug. There was an old man who was bed-ridden. When my girls gave him his gifts, he started to cry.

My daughter's friend came with us for the first time, and she'd never seen older people like this before, so I explained to her how much our being there meant to them. Slowly she became more comfortable. By the time we left, she said she wanted to come back again. She saw for herself what it difference it made to be there and extend some warmth.

This activity has taught our children so much about the art of giving. When you set the example and give with joy in your heart, the residual compassion rubs off on them.

Joy's seven-year-old daughter, Taylor, clearly reflects this: "It made me feel so good to give presents to people who didn't have any. They were so happy and excited. One man couldn't talk but I knew he was trying to say thank you. I want to always keep doing this."

Ordinary people like us are capable of making a huge difference in other people's lives. Everyone you read about in this chapter is a "regular" person who, for whatever reason, decided to step beyond his or her usual boundaries and offer help to others. They are no different from you or me. We each have the potential to change lives.

PROMPTED BY A NEED

Sometimes we are compelled to act when an issue pulls at us so hard that to ignore it would be ignoring something deep in ourselves. I clearly remember an instance when this happened to me. Connie Mercer, the director of Homefront, an organization that helps find shelter and services for homeless people, spoke at a religious service I was attending. She told us there were over a hundred children without beds right in our area. "They're sleeping on floors," is what she said. When I heard her words, I thought, "How can I go home tonight and sleep in my nice warm bed knowing that children only a few miles from me are sleeping on a cold, hard floor?" My sense of injustice and outrage spurred me to approach Connie right away and ask how I could help. "You could find us some mattresses," she replied. "How many?" I asked "Fifty for starters," she answered. "Used would be fine. We can sanitize them."

"They're yours," I answered, having no idea how in the world I was going to find fifty mattresses that were in decent condition. It didn't matter. I knew I had made this promise, and somehow I would keep it.

So I started the next day, calling mattress showrooms during my lunch break to find out what they did with people's old mattresses when new ones were delivered. It turned out that many old mattresses were simply discarded even if they were in good shape. The problem was, none of the distributors wanted to bother storing mattresses for a homeless organization or making an extra stop to drop them off. So I kept calling. And my pleas kept getting a little more heartfelt and a little more desperate. Finally, after about fifteen or twenty phone calls a kind voice on the other end said, "We can help." It was a man who also felt that children sleeping on cold floors was too intolerable to close his eyes to. He arranged for all the used mattresses from his store to be dropped off at Homefront—hundreds of them over a year's time. As Connie Mercer said, "What you did was relatively easy, but it made a huge difference in so many people's lives." Doing it helped me sleep better at night.

TOUCHING LIVES AFTER HIS ENDED

Bradley James Fetchet was twenty-four when he was killed in the attacks on the World Trade Center. Seeing his sweet face smiling out from a picture on the memorial page of the *New York Times,* I felt compelled to cut out his story and save it. Bradley was not only a hero in his death, he was a hero in life, simply by sharing his compassionate heart. The *Times* article told about the thousands of letters and calls that came in after Bradley died recounting stories of his extreme generosity, yet stressing that he was a person who never wanted to be in the spotlight. He gave to others simply for the intrinsic value of giving.

Buying elaborate gifts for his family and surprising people in countless ways was one of his favorite things to do. Bradley Fetchet cared about people he knew and even those he didn't, never asking for anything in return. The article ended with a quote he kept in his journal: "You can tell the character of a man by what he does for the man who can offer him nothing." People like Bradley, with such beautiful spirits, have the capacity to change the world even when they are no longer here. May his life inspire us to follow in his magnificent footsteps.

HEALING BY HELPING

Amy Callahan was a victim of September 11th in a different way— her fiancé, Scott Hazelcorn, was killed in the World Trade Center. In an article in the *New York Times* (November 12, 2001), Kelly

Crow described how Amy, a thirty-year-old special education teacher, refusing to give in to despair, decided to use her life to honor Scott's. He'd always had a dream of starting a camp for children, and in the wake of his death Amy decided to make Scott's dream a reality. She started the Scott Hazelcorn Children's Foundation and earmarked all the proceeds to a camp for children affected by the September 11th tragedy. Within two months of making this commitment, Amy garnered the help of friends, family, and strangers, and raised over $65,000.

The camp Amy plans to open will be called "Camp Haze," after Scott's nickname. When asked how she does it all—fundraising, networking, planning and organizing a camp, while holding a full-time teaching job, Amy replied, "This is my reason to get up in the morning." You can find out more information about Camp Haze by going to www.camphaze.org.

LOSS AS A CATALYST FOR GIVING

Loss spurred Ken Rutherford to action as well. While in Somalia in 1993, the car Ken was driving exploded as it passed over a landmine. At the age of thirty-two, Ken lost both of his legs. When Oprah Winfrey featured Ken on her show last October, he told how this experience profoundly heightened his sense of compassion. Rather than seeing himself as a victim, Ken saw himself as someone who had been offered a second chance at life and felt compelled to give back. He started learning more about the effects of landmines and discovered that there were millions of people worldwide who had lost life and limb in landmine explosions. With a colleague he created the Landmine Survivor's Network.

"We're the lucky ones," says Ken. "We survived." Here are some of staggering statistics Ken brings to light in his speaking engagements and on his network's website www.landminesurvivors.org: "Landmines claim nearly three victims an hour. That's one new victim every 22 minutes—24,000 new victims a year. 1200 are maimed every month. Today, over 80 million landmines remain buried waiting to go off. There are 16 mine-producing countries—including the United States. Together they have created a world of more than 80 mine-infested countries."

Ken now travels all over the world helping other people who have been injured, and works to ban the production of more landmines. After meeting Princess Diana, whose campaign against landmines brought this issue into the public eye, Ken remarked, "One person really can make a difference in this world."

Ken himself is a shining example of this. He is indeed a person who has let the passion in his heart propell him ahead full-throttle to make a difference in the lives of others.

TURNING GRIEF INTO ACTION

Tragedy led Heather Metzger to make a difference too. The Giraffe Heroes Project featured Heather on their website, www.giraffe.org, and described how her father's death led her to become an activist at the age of seventeen. Heather's father had been driving under the influence of drugs and alcohol when he was killed. On that day Heather decided she would dedicate her life to preventing other people from suffering the kind of loss she had. She joined Mothers Against Drunk Driving, began studying the effects of alcohol, and created a presentation for elementary schools called "Drug-Free Me." Heather also talked to owners of stores where teenage boys rented tuxedos for the prom and convinced them to put statistics on drunk driving in every pocket. She even used her own funds to print and distribute a booklet on substance abuse prevention.

Even in the face of ostracism by her peers, Heather continued her work. Being touted as a "goody-goody" didn't stop her from pushing forward with the goals she had committed herself to.

After graduation from the University of Maryland, Heather started lobbying for stronger drunk driving laws. She was asked to serve as the Maryland State Chairperson to the 2000 National Youth Summit. High school students are her primary focus because she knows the value of early prevention. Her personal story and pictures of her father's crash make teens stop and think. For Heather, loss and sorrow have been a catalyst for saving lives.

FROM OUTRAGE TO ACTION

Eighteen-year-old Craig Kielburger works to save lives too. A native of Toronto, Craig started speaking out for children's rights since the age of twelve. That's when he read about a young boy from Pakistan who was forced into slave labor and was murdered for speaking out. "Kids Can Free the Children," the world's largest network of children helping other children, grew out of Craig's concern. Now in thirty-five countries Craig's organization has over 100,000 active members all over the world.

Craig has traveled all over the world and has witnessed shocking abuses of children: an eight-year-old girl forced to recycle bloody syringes without gloves, children working in a factory with extremely hazardous materials to make fireworks, children sold for sex on city streets. Craig continuously asks the question, "If child labor is not acceptable for white, middle-class North American kids, then why is it acceptable for a girl in Thailand or a boy in Brazil?"

His organization has already accomplished so much. They have been instrumental in creating alternative sources of revenue for poor families so children can be free from hazardous work. They've also helped build over 300 schools, two live-in rehabilitation centers for children, and two health centers in Nicaragua. Free the Children has distributed over $2,000,000 worth of medical supplies and 60,000 school kits for children. They have also raised money to build schools in 23 countries so 15,000 children can go to school. On top of this, Free the Children has helped convince members of the international business community to adopt codes of conduct regarding child labor.

Kids Can Free the Children is now working with the United Nations to create a "Children-Children" network. Their mission is to create partnerships among children around the globe to help kids affected by war. Later in this chapter you will find out how you can help this incredible organization. You can reach them at www.freethechildren.org.

When I think about Craig Kielburger starting Kids Can Free the Children at age twelve, I wonder how any of us can still believe that one person can't make a difference.

Putting Himself on the Line

Caleb is another young man who is making a tremendous difference in the lives of others. What's unusual about Caleb is that he's a gay rights activist who happens to be straight. Do Something.org featured his inspiring story and described what led him to take on this role. As a freshman in high school Caleb became friendly with some kids who were members of the Gay-Straight Alliance. "A new window opened for me, a window into another world where not everyone's parents love them for who they are, and where people could not expect to be accepted wherever they went."

As Caleb became increasingly concerned about the problems his friends faced, he decided to translate his concern into action by joining their organization. Taking this kind of stand caused negative reactions in some classmates, but undaunted, Caleb remained firm in his commitment. "People always ask why I care about a movement that does not include me. I care because the gay rights movement *should* include me. Although I am straight, I know people affected by hate and prejudice. These people are my friends and I believe that everyone who has seen the face of hatred should be involved in preventing it."

Caleb lives his beliefs every day. He sits with his gay friends in the cafeteria and works to teach respect to those who don't understand its true meaning. He knows that any great movement for social change cannot be carried on only by those for whom change is needed. "There are white people fighting for black people's rights in the civil rights movement. There are men fighting for women's rights in the feminist movement. I would be greatly ashamed if there were no straight people fighting for gay rights in our movement." Now, as president of the Gay-Straight Alliance, Caleb continues to be a role model for respect, equity, and justice. With all the stories of bullying and cruelty in schools, Caleb stands out as a young man of true courage.

IT DOESN'T MATTER HOW YOUNG YOU ARE

Some kids think you have to wait till you're grown up to make a difference. Not John Holland-McCowan. The Kids Cheering Kids website (www.kidscheeringkids.org) tells the story of how John gave birth to a whole organization when he was only four. It was then that John heard for the first time about children his age who were so poor they had no toys. Learning this upset him so much he began to cry and immediately decided to start saving his allowance to buy toys for these kids. John even asked his friends to join in. Before long a meeting was held with John, his mother, John's friends, and their parents, and a toy drive was launched. But in John's mind, that wasn't enough.

Concerned that deprived children might not have friends to play with, John asked his mother to bring him to the place where they'd been donating toys. They started visiting a shelter for abused children where he made friends with another little boy. Seeing his friend's face light up each time he visited sparked in John another idea: the vision of kids connecting to kids in need to offer support, friendship, and warmth. And Kids Cheering Kids was born.

The idea started spreading like wildfire, and chapters started forming in neighboring areas of California. According to an article in the *Los Gatos Weekly-Times* (January 20, 1999), John and about thirteen other kids ranging in age from five to twenty-three now make up the core of KCK along with eight adult directors. A pediatric daycare center is one of the main recipients of KCK's services. Children in this center have a variety of specialized medical needs like respiratory disorders and cerebral palsy. KCK volunteers pair up with patients to help them do exercises that build motor skills and foster rehabilitation. A child volunteer also reads illustrated books to their partners. And once a month they help out with "Date Night," when the center stays open late and welcomes in brothers and sisters.

One young KCK volunteer commented, "It just feels good to know you've helped somebody." It's hard to imagine that this wonderful project was started by a four-year-old child! Do your children have any ways they'd like to reach out and make a difference? If so, do what John's mom did—help them get started. You never know what kind of miracles your child is capable of creating.

IT DOESN'T MATTER HOW OLD YOU ARE

The urge to make a difference can transcend age, race, and gender. When eighty-year-old Claude Cox heard about the growing numbers of poor and hungry people in his area, he thought about the thirty-five acres of land he and his wife owned. No longer used for growing hay, Claude approached his church to see how his land might be of help. In an article in *UU World Magazine* (November–December 2001) Kimberly French describes how Claude's offer led to the creation of the Cornucopia Project, where large qualities of organic corn are grown to feed the hungry.

Excited by this idea, other church members joined in, and before long, people of all ages were tilling soil, picking corn, and irrigating Claude's field. During the first year Cornucopia volunteers grew 20,000 ears of corn for local food pantries and crisis distribution centers. Many of the people who benefited were children and working parents who couldn't make ends meet. Area food pantry shelves had been getting more and more sparse, so this infusion of fresh corn met a very important need.

Church pastor Stephen Shick commented, "People are hungry to find out how in this complex world you can make a difference and contribute from our abundance." Everybody wins in projects like this one.

STILL MAKING A DIFFERENCE
AT 100 YEARS OLD

Of all the people I've interviewed, Mathilda Spak had to be one of the most extraordinary. At 100 years old, Mathilda is out there volunteering every day from morning till night. This feisty lady has more energy than people half her age, even though she is nearly blind, has severe arthritis, and suffers from blackouts. Yet Mathilda completely relishes life. She said to me in a recent interview, "I'm having a ball!"

Every day Mathilda either takes a bus or gets a ride to one of her many pet projects. Pay attention to the following words of wisdom from this rare gem of a woman. People like her don't come along very often:

> I made a promise to my mother that I would work on myasenthia gravis—the fatal debilitating illness she died of—till I found out what caused it and how to cure it. I've been asking questions ever since. Twenty-five years ago, I started a research project and we're getting closer to finding out the causes. We've been able to cut the death rate from 85 percent to 5 percent.
>
> I also work at the Children's Hospital in Long Beach, California. When babies who have been abused are brought to the clinic, their soiled clothes are thrown out and they end up being released wrapped in a towel. Can you imagine! When I saw that, I lost my temper. I told the people at the hospital, "These children need decent clothes!" So they put me in charge. I convinced a yarn company to donate skeins of yarn. Now I have members of different churches knitting beautiful blankets and sweaters for the babies. I also get do-nations of new clothing. Now every single baby is properly clothed, with a pretty new blanket.
>
> I also fund-raise for the City of Hope. Each year we have a Grand Prix fund-raiser for twenty different charitable organizations. Hundreds apply to be included but the rule is that each organization can only participate every three years. A few years ago I made a deal with them to keep myasthenia

gravis on their schedule every year. How did I convince them? I told them that I'm in my nineties and I can't afford to wait around three years between cycles.

There are six days a week and I try to fit it all in. What I can't do at the office I take home. You have to stay busy, otherwise you get stagnant and you start to feel sorry for yourself. I also serve as a guide for the Long Beach Symphony, helping out when the children visit from schools.

I got started on this path because my mother taught me from the time I was a child that you must always give back to the community in service. We had a little store in a poor neighborhood and my mother was always helping people. I learned it from her.

There's a lot of goodness in people waiting to come out. One day I was on my way to work. I got off the bus and blacked out. Our office is in a very poor area of the city. Two down-and-out men came over and helped me. They could have stolen my purse and run away, but they didn't. I looked at them and said, "Are you hungry?" And they said yes. So I asked them come with me to the diner across the street and have breakfast. But the men said, "They won't let us in." And I said, "Oh yes they will!! Watch!" We went inside together and I wouldn't take any guff from the waitress about serving them. We had a nice breakfast, then I gave the waitress a $20 bill and told her that she had to feed these men till the money ran out, and I would be back to check. The men ate all week long.

I live every minute of my life as if it is the last, and I enjoy every second. I have two rules: At my funeral, anyone who sheds a tear will be haunted because I have lived a great life. The other rule—continue my charity work.

My advice to this generation is—Give of yourself. There's no one who cannot give something. You can take care of a child, volunteer, help your neighbor. No excuses. My mother taught me to never say can't, and that's how I live. I have to walk with a cane. Big deal. So I buy myself fancy canes.

Only by giving do you get back. My mother also taught me to only use the dollar for what good you can do with it, and to never turn away a hungry person.

I get people to do all kinds of things. I go to the nursing

home and have the older women knit for the babies. If some-one says they can't help out, I ask for one Wednesday. But people started saying, "Don't let Mathilda ask you for one Wednesday or you'll be doing one Wednesday for the rest of your life!" I have one man who has been doing one Wednes-day for forty years.

Tomorrow is Valentine's Day and I'm going to the hospi-tal. I'm delivering a teddy bear to every person there.

And she's 100. Are you speechless yet?

NINO'S

Another person with a huge heart and a deep capacity for caring is Nino Vedome. When I walked into Nino's Restaurant on Canal Street in New York last winter, I felt like I'd come home. The mir-acle of compassion turned this restaurant—only blocks from the World Trade Center—into a place of solace and healing for the thousands of rescue workers who were fed here twenty-four hours a day, seven days a week for six months. Fire fighters, po-lice officers, Coast Guardsmen, Salvation Army workers, and vol-unteers who worked at Ground Zero came to Nino's to be fed in body, mind, and spirit.

As of January 2002, Nino raised enough in donations to give away over $6 million' worth of food. Over 20,000 volunteers came through his doors as of that date, approximately 115 a day. *Time* magazine wrote about Nino's spectacular contribution, say-ing, "Overnight it went from serving 150 meals a day to 7000" (January 7, 2002).

When I talked to Nino, what came through most was his fierce belief in the need for all of us to show concern for each other through our actions. He expressed deep gratitude to all of the or-ganizations, corporations, and individuals who contributed time and money and he's hoping that what happened in his restaurant will encourage more people to reach out and help as an ongoing part of their lives. Listen to his words:

We've forgotten about each other and we've become a "fast-food society." Our actions on Canal Street contradicted this. There needs to be a new social order, and I hope one of the core parts of it will be knowing we are *all* responsible for tomorrow by what we do today. *We are all responsible.* Whether that means jury duty or helping your neighbor with their child. No human being should be alone, because we have each other. But we have been so busy and so motivated by our materialistic needs that we've become immune to each other.

We, as a people, need to be more involved. What happened here at Nino's should exemplify what can be done with no resources. This all came about through the work of so many people. People came from across the country and all over the world to help. For all of us it's been a work of love and concern, a level of commitment and drive. When people come together to do the right thing, anything is possible.

Having two children of his own, Nino looks to the future and feels strongly that parents can't do it alone. "My community is also responsible for what happens to my children, all of our children." He also believes that social problems like homelessness and hunger need to be addressed in a very focused, aware, and humane manner.

"In the end," says Nino, "if everyone looks to help one another, it'll affect us all. Being concerned about others gives me satisfaction, and the greatest return is knowing others are okay. We need to get back to some basic core values: community and taking care of one another." Nino is a living example of this.

HEROES IN THE TRUEST SENSE

The meaning of "hero" has shifted since September 11th. Before, our skewed perceptions had us see movie stars, athletes, daredevils, and millionaires as heroes. Now, thanks to the courageous efforts of the firefighters, police officers, and rescue workers at Ground Zero, we've begun to understand the true nature of heroism. I had the opportunity to talk to some of these real-life heroes as they went on break during the recovery effort. Their words say it all:

"When they asked for volunteers to work at the World Trade Center, we had people drive here from Queens just to see if there was a way to serve. We would do this work for free," says Lieutenant Bonsignore, of Engine Company 6. "My men would walk through fire to rescue people. Sometimes I actually have to pull them back. They're like fearless lions." Lieutenant Bonsignore speaks with a blend of humility and strength that characterizes true heroes. "I really don't want to be a hero. We're just trying to do our jobs. That's all that matters. The police and fire department work like a family. You eat together, sleep together, and you die together." In a society thrown off course by the quest for wealth and fame, we need to follow the lead of people like Lieutenant Bonsignore. A dedicated father, he talks about the values he strives to pass on to his kids: "I want my children to care about others over everything else. Baseball players make $20 million a year. Life is not about money. It's what you can do for others. It's how you can serve. Helping humanity is what it's all about."

Fire fighter Karl VanKasten of Engine Company 326 agrees. His eyes fill with tears as he talks about the many friends he lost. "About a hundred fire fighters who weren't on duty ran into the World Trade Center to rescue people, and they were trapped . . ." He looks away and gathers his composure. "It's such a feeling of helping people, you can't even explain it. It's like nothing in the world. It doesn't matter how old they are, what color they are, or anything else—it's a human life." It's absolutely clear that Lieutenant Van Kasten would give his own life in an instant to save someone else's. "My friends who were lost rescuing others, I know that's how they wanted to die—for a reason and a cause. They're still watching over all of us, taking care of us from another place."

People like Lieutenant Bonsignore and Fire fighter VanKasten help us understand what real heroism is about. Their passion for the work they do, their drive to make a difference, their willing-

ness to give their lives to save others has touched us all indelibly.
May we all be inspired to rise to their call.

WAYS YOU CAN MAKE A DIFFERENCE

So now you've read about some wonderful people who are literally changing the world, merely out of a desire to help. They may
not have any more talent and skill than you or I, but they each
have one thing that defines them—the will to make a difference
and a commitment to taking action. How about you? Are you
making a difference in some special way? If not here's how you
can get started. This is also an excellent activity to do with children age nine and up.

Finding Your Path

Consultant-educator Pat Windom counsels people from all
walks of life. She offers this highly effective four-step process to
help you discover what your "making a difference" role might
be:

*1. Ask yourself: "What are my personal strengths and tal-
ents?"* If you're not sure, ask other people. Friends, family, and
colleagues often see things in us that we don't see in ourselves.
Everyone has unique strengths and talents, *everyone*. Sometimes
we're just not aware of what they are. Our strengths and talents
can remain hidden like diamonds beneath the surface. When we
unearth them, our lives change. If you question your capacity to
make a difference, think about these words by author Shad
Helmstetter, *"You are as unlimited as the endless universe."*

Start by writing down any strengths and talents you have,
even if they seem minor. For example, one person I interviewed
said she was good at organizing things. "So what?" she said.
"How could that possibly make a difference?" Actually, this skill
does make a big difference. So many organizations could use
someone working behind the scenes to help them get organized,

even if it is just once a week. When I ran a not-for-profit organization, I totally depended on a wonderful woman who organized our materials, correspondences, and schedules. Her talent made a huge difference.

A man I know said carpentry was his special talent, but he couldn't imagine how it could be of use in a "contributing" kind of way. Well, Habitat for Humanity would love to have his help. Also, many communities also have local "handyman projects" where people who are good at fixing things or building things help the elderly, disabled, and impoverished. My father is seventy-seven years old and he offers handyman help to people in his community. Don't discount any of your talents; somebody out there needs them.

2. Create a "Me Profile." This is a great way to help you further discover your unique way of contributing. Pat Windom recommends writing down the following:

- Your strengths
- Your talents
- Things you like to do
- Things you can do quickly
- Things that give you joy
- Things you feel passionate about

The things that surface as you write are your unique talents. Listen to what comes out as you do this activity. It will give you some powerful insights.

3. Ask yourself this very important question: "How can I use my strengths and talents to benefit my community, or world?" This question is critical. Close your eyes, breathe deeply, and let the wisest, highest part of you guide you to the answer. Be patient if you don't get it right away. Just keep asking. Before long, you'll know the answer.

It might come as a sudden insight or a distinct physical sensation—a thump of the heart, a surge of energy, a quickening of the pulse. This is what happened to me when I discovered that my path was peacemaking. When the realization hit me, my entire body and brain felt energized. I even felt a little surprised, like, is this really what I was meant to do? Yet something inside me knew it was.

As I allowed myself to receive the inspiration this newly found direction brought me, I had to trust that the specific nature of the work I needed to do would become apparent. I had to be willing to live in the question, because moving toward one's purpose in life is not a linear path. Answers can come in many forms—a book, a person, something you see on TV, a dream, a memory, an insight, or an answered prayer. It's essential to have faith that the wisest part of yourself is guiding you, along with whatever higher power you believe in. Also, trusting that *we each have a unique purpose.* Our job in the time we have here on earth is to find it and follow it.

Staying open is also fundamental in finding our unique path of contribution. The minute we close the door of our mind, we stop the process. So suspend disbelief and trust that you *do* have a very special purpose, and by staying open, you will discover what it is. Share this message with your children. The earlier they start learning it, the better.

4. Now ask yourself what specific ways you can use your talents for the common good. Look at the organizations and websites at the end of this chapter, and see what calls to you. Imagine your passions, priorities, and strengths being put to work for the betterment of the world we live in. Pat Windom suggests that you also reflect on this question: "How can I use my strengths for the greatest benefit and highest level of integrity of the world we live in?"

Write down your ideas, and any action steps that occur to you. Clearly defining the ideas you come up with is critical. Be as concrete as possible in determining where you will start—with a phone call, a letter, marking a date on your calendar. Also, tell a friend what you are doing, and invite him or her to join in.

Having a partner when we start a new venture can spell the difference between achieving what we set out to do, and letting our visions fall into the dusty wastebin of discarded ideas. Don't let this happen to you. Call a friend now.

I remember doing this when I got the idea for my second book. Writing a book at that time seemed to be a very "unreasonable" thing to do—I was teaching full-time, leading workshops, taking graduate courses, and still had a child living at home. But somehow this book called to me, and I knew I needed to write it. How I'd fit it into my life was another story, one that worked itself out later.

But first I had to get started. So I called a colleague from graduate school who also had dreams of writing a book. We made an agreement to call each other every Wednesday night no matter what. We also agreed that we'd make promises during our phone calls, like "I promise to get a chapter outline done by next week." I hung her number over my phone and with it the words, "Call Gail every other Wednesday night." (We took turns calling each other.) This continued for two years, and that's how my second book got written. Thank you, Gail. Without your support and encouragement, and the knowledge that you would hold me accountable, that book never would have gotten written.

Think of a friend you can call. Now pick up the phone and call her. Tell her what you want to do, even if it's the tiniest embryo of an idea. Take another look at the resource section at the end of this chapter, and if there's something that speaks to you, get moving while the motivation is strong. Visit a website, make a phone call, mark your calendar, and get started.

One of the key reasons people don't move forward on new ideas is procrastination. "I'll get started when my schedule lightens up." Or, "I'll get around to it when my kids are all in school." But when you wait, the spark of inspiration that could have changed your life gets lost in the muck and mire of everyday living. We make our lives more golden by giving. In this moment—right now—you can take the first step to a path so powerful that when you come to the end of your life, you'll say, "I leave this life satisfied—I have lived my highest purpose, and my time here on earth has made a difference." It is never too late to start, and the moment to do it is *now.*

RAISING KIDS WHO CARE ENOUGH TO MAKE A DIFFERENCE

I had the pleasure of interviewing Craig Kielburger's mom, Theresa. When I asked her what she had done to raise such an extraordinary son, this is what she said:

> We raised Craig with an attitude of concern about one's neighbor. When he came home and talked about kids in the schoolyard being mean to other kids, we would encourage him to help the person who was being hurt. It is so important to teach our children take the risk of being kind to the child being picked on. He learned to stand up for the underdog.
>
> From the time Craig was little, we taught him that people are basically the same inside and have the same needs. We stressed how important it was to treat each other with respect. The way we behave as adults affects our kids a lot too. It's how we act that influences them most.
>
> Reading plays a big part too. We read a lot to our kids when they were little, lots of stories about people who were kind, patient, honest, and understanding. These stories left a deep impression.
>
> We always nurtured our children's unique talents and interests. Craig's older brother had a passion for the environment. He started a petition drive to support the environment when he was younger, and Craig would follow him around and help. His brother was a very big influence in his life.
>
> I think a lot of kids feel a sense of passion inside. Kids want to help and we need to encourage them to do so. They also need to join with kids their own age. Kids can be the best role models for each other.
>
> Next year Craig will be traveling across the United States to talk to kids in schools as part of his new project. Free the

Children is organizing a Culture of Peace program that stresses peacemaking and tolerance. A team of young people will be joining him and they will be picking team leaders in each schools. Tell your children about this project. You can find out more about this on the Free the Children website.

SPECIFIC WAYS YOU CAN HELP RIGHT AWAY

If you don't have the time to research all the organizations listed at the end of this chapter and you want some very specific ways you and your children can make a difference right now, here they are.

Helping Children Around the World

If you and your children would like to help impoverished children from different parts of the globe, here are some wonderful suggestions with immediate applicability from Craig Kielburger's organization, Kids Can Free the Children (www.freethechildren.org).

Provide School and Health Kits

School and Health Kits were designed to fill a need. Millions of children around the world do not go to school because they cannot afford school supplies.

A School Kit Contains:
2–3 spiral notebooks, approx. 75 pages each, 8½ in x 11 in (21.5 cm x 28 cm)
4–6 unsharpened pencils with erasers
1 small pencil sharpener
1 metric ruler
1 regular-sized eraser
1 box of 12–16 crayons or pencil crayons
12 sheets of colored paper
1 pair of scissors

1 ball (similar in size to a tennis ball)
Book bag (either cloth or plastic)

A Health Kit Contains:
1 hand towel
1 washcloth
1 toothbrush
1 family-sized tube of toothpaste
1 bar of soap
A small box of Band-aids
1 comb or brush
1 pair of nail scissors

New items only!

FTC receives requests from organizations all over the world for School and Health Kits. They have been sent to Nicaragua, Ecuador, Brazil, India, South Africa, Peru, Sudan, Israel, the Philippines, and Kosovo. Supplies or donations toward the purchase of supplies can be sent to:

Kids Can Free the Children
50 High Oak Trail
Richmond Hill, Ontario Canada L4E 3L9

Building Schools Campaign
One of FTC's projects is to fund the construction of schools for children who would otherwise never receive an education and forever be caught in the cycle of poverty and exploitation. Young people are the primary supporters of the School Building Project but it also has the support of many adults and service organizations.

How much does it cost to build a school?
Costs vary anywhere from $2,500 to $15,000, depending on the location and the type of school constructed. If you can't afford to build a whole school, you can buy new desks for a classroom,

pay for a teacher's salary for a year, bring in water for a bathroom, or help students pay for their school supplies. These costs vary from $50–$800.

If you would like to contact Kids Can Free the Children for ideas on fundraising, or on establishing a FTC Chapter, please contact Tanya Reda at: youth@freethechildren.com. (This information has been reprinted with permission from Kids Can Free the Children.)

Bringing Comfort to Other Kids

The "Comfort Quilt" Project is another wonderful way for your child's school, scouting troop, or religious education program to help others. Visit their website www.iearn.org/projects/ comfortquilts.html and learn how your kids can design and create quilts to share with children in need of comfort.

The project was created in response to the caring needs of children receiving hospital or clinic care. Many of these children were harmed by the devastating effects of natural disasters, national crisis, or displacement from their homes. Participating schools or groups can make one or more quilts using fabric squares they've decorated.

Schools and organizations have found many ways to comfort others through this wonderful project. Many groups made quilts for the victims of September 11th. A first-grade class made a quilt for their emergency medical team's ambulance so children on the way to the hospital could receive a little extra comfort. When Hurricane George hit Puerto Rico several years ago, another class wanted to help children whose homes and schools had been damaged. They sent e-mail messages and comfort quilts to show how much they cared. Two primary classes joined together and made a comfort quilt for a Ronald McDonald House for critically ill children. In their words, "When we care for each other, it makes the world a better place. It makes everyone feel happier and stronger inside."

END THOUGHTS

The world is made of tiny grains of sand as well as huge mountains. Each plays a vital role in the elegant ecosystem that comprises nature. So it is with peace. Be our role large or small, each is vital.

My mentor, Norman Cousins, whom you read about in the Introduction, was a passionate believer in the enormous power each individual has, and he urged us all to play a part in creating peace. As I mentioned earlier in the book, his beliefs spurred me to step beyond my self-doubts and get involved. The power surge that propelled me beyond the closed door of inaction, into the wide-open vista of making a difference, was in large part from the following words from Cousins's book *Human Options:*

"The starting point for a better world is the belief that is it possible."

"We are more than the shadow of our substance, more than a self-contained and self-sealing entity. We come to life in others. . . ."

"Nothing about human life is more precious than that we can define our own purpose and shape our own destiny."

"There are vast surges of conscience, natural purpose and goodness inside us demanding air and release. And we have our own potentialities, the regions of which are far broader than we ever guessed at. . . ."

Where do you want to put your potential? Giving a meal to a neighbor who can't get to the store, tutoring a child in reading, or mailing a monthly check to UNICEF? If you can't afford to give money, give time. There are charitable organizations that need help addressing envelopes, answering phones, giving rides. Offer to dish out food in a local soup kitchen, or knit blankets for children in hospitals, or booties and small hats for preemies. There's such power in helping others, and showing your children you care gets them to help too.

Like the silent heartbeat of a sleeping tiger, this power is always present, even when we are not aware of it. Now is the time to set it free. Get out and make a difference!

RESOURCES AND BIBLIOGRAPHY

Websites

Do Something
http://www.dosomething.org
  Fabulous website with a mission "to inspire young people to believe that change is possible." They train, fund, and mobilize kids K–12 to be leaders. For activities specifically for younger kids, go to: http://coach.dosomething.org/coach/sitepages/index.cfm?formid= 120.

Kids Cheering Kids
www.kidscheeringkids.org
  Children and young adults, five and up, reaching out to enrich the lives of children less fortunate.

Kids Can Make a Difference
http://www.kids.maine.org/prog.htm
  Kids in middle school and high school ending hunger and poverty; click on "What Kids Can Do." Addresses root causes of hunger and poverty; shows kids their role in helping.

Kids Can Free the Children
www.freethechildren.org
  Founded by twelve-year-old Craig Kielburger. Shows kids how they can help children in need around the world.

TeenHoopla Activism Page
http://ala8.ala.org/teenhoopla/activism.html
  For teens who really want to make a difference. Shows what they can do and has superb links to organizations.

America's Second Harvest
http://www.secondharvest.org/index.html
  Collects and distributes food to hungry people. See how your whole family can get involved.

Bread for the World
www.bread.org

"Seeking Justice, Ending Hunger" is the motto of this organization that doesn't provide bread, but pushes governments to help the poor with more humane policies.

National Coalition for the Homeless
http://www.nationalhomeless.org
Focuses on housing, health care, civil rights, and justice. With your help, we can eradicate homelessness.

Habitat for Humanity
http://www.habitat.org
Visit this site and see how your family can help rehabilitate houses for low-income families. Create a miracle.

VolunteerMatch
http://www.volunteermatch.org
Want to volunteer but don't know how? This website has tons of information on volunteer work and provides an online database where you'll find opportunities by zip code, category, and date.

ServeNet
http://www.servenet.org
Another site that will help you find a place to volunteer. There's a database of service roles. Click on RESOURCES to find information for kids under eighteen who want to volunteer.

Network for Good
www.networkforgood
Helps you volunteer, speak out, donate, and make a difference in the environment, education, health, human services, peace, and other international issues.

My Hero
www.myhero.com
This inspiring site introduces you to people of all ages who've made a difference in the world, their communities, and the lives of others.

Project Linus
www.projectlinus.org

Provides homemade blankets and afghans to children all over the world who are ill, traumatized, or in need.

The Giraffe Project
www.giraffe.org
Features stories of people who have "stuck their necks out" for the common good.

Camp Haze
http://www.camphaze.org
Helps children who lost a parent or loved on September 11th. Provides a network of peers and a specially trained staff—certified teachers, therapists, and experienced counselors. Provides support to parents also.

Comfort Quilts
www.iearn.org/projects/comfortquilts.html
Find out how your child's school, scouting troup, or organization can create quilts to give to children in need of comfort.

UNICEF
www.unicef.org.
Find out how to help children around the world. Many opportunities on this website.

BOOKS FOR PARENTS

Cooney, Robert, and Michalowski, Helen. *The Power of the People: Active Nonviolence in the United States.* Gabriola Island, B.C., Canada: New Society Publishers, 1987.
Documents the struggle by peace leaders against war, and their impact on history. (Grades 7–12.)

Cousins, Norman. *Human Options.* New York: Norton, 1981.
Thoughts from one of the world's great thinkers on war, peace, and personal responsibility. My bible.

Farnham, Suzanne G., and Joseph Gill. *Listening Hearts: Discerning Call in Community.* Philadelphia: Morehouse, 1991.

Asks us to listen to our hearts so that we may discover what our calling is and how we can remain faithful and accountable to our purpose.

Helmstedder, Shad. *What to Say When You Talk to Yourself.* New York: Pocketbooks, 1982.
The definitive book on using affirmations to self-actualize and find your purpose.

Kushner, Harold S. *Living a Life That Matters.* New York: Knopf, 2001.
Insightful book shows how we each have the capacity to make a positive difference in the world and in other people's lives.

Meltzer, Milton. *Ain't Gonna Study War No More.* New York: Harper & Row, 1985.
"Theories, thoughts, and actions of generations of heroes who bravely rejected all violence, or participation in wars they considered unjust." (Grades 7–12.)

Muller, Wayne. *Legacy of the Heart: The Spiritual Advantages of a Painful Childhood.* New York: Simon & Schuster, 1992.
Lessons learned and won the hard way. Teaches people to find "a place of grace" in the pain they've experienced.

Parks, Rosa. *Rosa Parks: My Story.* New York: Penguin Putnam, 1999.
Compelling story of the mother of the civil rights movement told in her own words. (Grades 6 and up.)

Peavy, Linda, and Ursula Smith. *Dreams Into Deeds: Nine Women Who Dared.* New York: Charles Scribner's Sons, 1985.
Nine courageous women who made a difference from 1880–1930, including Jane Addams, Marian Anderson, and Babe Didrikson Zaharias. (Grades 7–12.)

Wallace, Aubrey. *Green Means: Living Gently on the Planet.* San Francisco: Bay Books, 1994.
Highlights people who have worked hard to help the environment against big odds. "Ordinary people with extraordinary commitment can make sweeping change for the long-term benefit of the earth and its residents."

Wiesel, Elie, and Richard D. Hefner. *Conversations With Elie Wiesel*. New York: Schocken, 2001.
Wisdom and insight on compassion, tolerance, personal responsibility, and more, from one of the greatest men of our times.

Wolpe, David. *Teaching Your Childen About God*. New York: Henry Holt, 1993.
Sensitive guide for parents about the nature of God and spirituality.

BOOK FOR KIDS

Coles, Robert. *The Story of Ruby Bridges*. New York: Scholastic, 1995.
The true story of the little girl who was the first black student in her segregated school. (Grades K–3.)

Lewis, Barbara A. *The Kid's Guide to Service Projects*. Minneapolis: Free Spirit Publishing, 1995.
Helps older children develop service actvities and carry them out. (Grades 5–7.)

Lewis, Barbara A., *The Kid's Guide to Social Action*. Minneapolis: Free Spirit, 1991.
Activities you can guide your children to do to help their communities.

Lewis, Barbara A. *What Do You Stand For?* Minneapolis: Free Spirit Press, 1997.
Real children challenge the reader to build traits such as empathy, citizenship, leadership, and respect. Focuses on volunteering. (Grades 3–6.)

McKissack, Patricia. *Martin Luther King, Jr., a Man to Remember*. Chicago: Children's Press, 1984.
King's story of leading the fight against racism and his efforts to bring tolerance, dignity, and understanding to this fight. (Grades 4–6.)

Chapter 9

Creating Peace in Our World, One Family at a Time

If we have no peace, it is because we have forgotten that we belong to each other.

—Mother Teresa

The opposite of love is not hatred but indifference.

—Elie Weisel

I'm re-thinking violence for us—it doesn't do any good.

—Ghazi Ahmed Hamad, Hamas spokesperson

Martin Luther King once said, "The ultimate weakness of violence is that it is a descending spiral, begetting the very thing it seeks to destroy. . . . Returning violence for violence multiplies violence, adding deeper darkness to a night already devoid of stars. Darkness cannot drive out darkness; only light can do that. Hate cannot drive out hate; only love can do that." Yes, we've been angry about what our country has gone through. Those who lost loved ones will live with the pain of their passing for the rest of their lives. Yet we must move beyond hatred and the need for vengeance. And we must move beyond the fear that pushes us toward reactivity and closes down our ability to seek creative solutions.

There was a time I would recoil somewhat when I'd hear people talk about the concept of love as the strongest force of all. Even though Gandhi and King preached these words, they didn't quite pierce through the veil of my own cynicism. How could love be stronger than a bomb that can kill millions, or a landmine that can blow up a car, or a gun that could take the life of a child? Love seemed too amorphous, too idealized to have such power. But then I had children.

I look at my children and my love for them infuses me with a power beyond words. My love for them would have me me lay down my life—gladly, in an instant, to save theirs. I remember seeing a mother interviewed on television after her son had been shot in the head and a bullet lodged in his brain. She said to the doctors, "Take mine." It was so obvious to her—of course she would give her life for her child. That is the intractable power of love.

Love moves us to greater courage. It energizes and calls us to be something larger.

Those who love live in the light of their expanding souls. A room full of darkness can be illuminated by a single flame—no amount of darkness can drown out its light. As Martin Luther King said, "Darkness cannot drive out darkness; only light can do that." Love has that kind of energy.

You are holding this book in your hands clearly out of love for your children. The power of love is motivating you to transcend your boundaries and find a path to peace. Let the light that emanates from your heart guide you. Use the legacy of your life to help create more peace in this world for the sake of *all* of our children.

More than a decade ago, the playwright Tony Kushner wrote the following prophetic words: "There are moments in history when the fabric of everyday life unravels, and there is this unstable dynamism that allows for incredible social change in short periods of time. People and the world they're living in can be utterly transformed, either for the good or the bad, or some mixture of the two."

This is such a time, and the way things go will be up to us. We are faced with a choice—to fall back into the familiar patterns of the old normal or to create a new normal—one of compassion, inclusion, equity, and concern for *all* human beings. Retreating into the old normal mode of self-containment and apathy is, sadly, the easiest thing to do—and the choice certain to guarantee that the status quo becomes the future we leave to our children. Yet we are faced with an unparalleled opportunity that challenges us to rise to a higher way of being. The choice is up to each of us. We are on the cusp of a new era, and which way it will goes lies in our hands.

MOVING BEYOND WAR

Norman Cousins once said, "War is an invention of the human mind. The human mind can invent peace." The question is, "How?"

How can we use our resources, our time, our energy, our common visions, and moreover, our *will* to invent peace during an era when billions of dollars a year are spent worldwide on war?

By peace, I don't mean pacifism or turning the other cheek. What I'm talking about is a dynamic, proactive process whereby we address the conditions that lead to war early enough to prevent future wars from happening. War goes against one of the most fundamental tenets of the Judeo-Christian ethic and other world religions: "Thou shalt not kill." The most important question facing humanity today is, *How do we transform the conditions and beliefs that have us choose to kill?*

It is *critical* that we find the answer. We must assert the same diligence in preventing war as we have in preparing for it, seeking viable alternatives to violence so that the use of force becomes our last option, not our first. This is not to suggest that we should leave ourselves unprotected. Even Gandhi didn't recommend

doing that. But there is a midpoint we are not using, a place between overarming ourselves—as we are now—and pacifism. It is
a place of balance where we keep ourselves protected and, at the
same time, pursue the ways of peace.

Unfortunately, when we speak of nonviolence, we imagine
people throwing down their arms and turning the other cheek.
This is a fallacy. Nonviolence is a dynamic process that employs
effective proactive alternatives. It is daring and courageous, not
weak and capitulating. This is illustrated brilliantly in a book
called *A Force More Powerful: A Century of Nonviolent Conflict,* by Peter Ackerman and Jack DuVall. The authors describe
numerous situations throughout history where nonviolent options were successfully employed to combat conflict and oppression. "To succeed, a nonviolent movement cannot simply take a
principled stand for 'nonviolence.' It has to devise a strategy for
action. In turn, this strategy must broadly communicate goals,
mobilize people, and select sanctions to punish opponents. To
shift the momentum of conflict in their favor, nonviolent resisters
must diversify the scope and variety of these sanctions, defend
their popular base against repression, and exploit their opponents' weaknesses and concessions."

This is exactly what the people of Denmark did during World
War II. When the Germans marched in and attempted to arrest
7,000 Jews, the Danish people were successful in foiling them.
How did they manage to accomplish this seemingly impossible
task without the use of violence? Through unified, direct actions
that weakened the Germans' power base: by orchestrating mass
strikes and protests, by refusing to honor curfews, by students refusing to speak German in language classes, by creating a system
for saving the lives of their Jewish citizens, even by having Danish
songfests throughout the nation to show strength and unity.
Through the combination of all of these, the Danes reasserted
their power in the face of oppression. The strength of their collective acts of resistance weakened the stranglehold the Nazi's were
attempting to apply, and by the time October 1, 1943, rolled
around—the date the Nazis ordered the arrest of 7,000 Jews—a

system had been put in place for saving them. Again, from *A Force More Powerful*: "All kinds of Danish organizations sheltered Jewish families—in private homes, in hospitals—and shuttled them to the coast, where fishing boats carried them across a narrow channel to Sweden." As a result, close to 6,600 of 7,000 people whose lives had been marked for death were saved.

Why is it more important now than ever to follow this lead and prevent further violence? Read on.

THE "NOW" IMPERATIVE

At the start of this book, I told you how I was propelled into action twenty-one years ago, when my boys were five and eight, by the harsh realization that the weapons of mass detraction could short-circuit their futures. This issue gripped me so hard I could no longer ignore it. And now for the sake of all of our children, it is absolutely critical that we address it together. *We* have the power to change things now. You, with this book in your hands, have this power. Every parent on earth has this power, and now is the time we must use it. Here's why:

> The world spends some $750 billion annually on military forces and weapons, while for a fraction of this amount everyone on the planet could have clean water, adequate food, health care, education, shelter, and clothing. . . . We have developed and deployed tens of thousands of nuclear weapons capable of destroying humanity and most of life. Many people think that this problem has ended, but it has not. Ending the nuclear weapons threat to humanity and other forms of life is the greatest challenge of our time. It wouldn't be so difficult if the governments of the nuclear weapons states accepted their share of responsibility and took leadership of the effort. Since these governments have failed to do so, it is left to the people of the world to take responsibility and fight for a world free of nuclear weapons. It is a fight for a humane and human future.

These are the words of Dr. David Krieger, who has lectured all over the world on the threat of nuclear weapons and has written more than eight books on the subject. Founder of the Nuclear Age Peace Foundation, he's been waging peace since 1982. Spurred by growing urgency, he's put aside his work as a judge, and now focuses all his energy on bringing his message to others.

The destructive capacity of America's nuclear warheads is 100,000 times greater than the single Hiroshima bomb, and the number is growing. The all-encompassing danger of these weapons has brought other prominent people to the forefront as well. Admiral Noel Gayler, former commander-in-chief of the U.S.S. *Pacific,* says, "Does nuclear disarmament imperil our security? No. It enhances it." The reason—because the presence of nuclear weapons is destabilizing and leads to the production of more.

After spending twenty-seven years of his military life working on nuclear weapons policy, Admiral Lee Butler arrived at what he calls "a deeply held conviction—that a world free of the threat of nuclear weapons is necessarily a world *devoid* of nuclear weapons." Why? Because "nuclear weapons are inherently dangerous, hugely expensive, and militarily inefficient. . . ." Our nuclear arsenals keep growing, and even desparately poor countries like India, Pakistan, and North Korea are spending millions on nuclear weapons. The more we raise the bar, the more others arm.

For this reason, many Nobel laureates and prominent people have also begun speaking out. Queen Noor of Jordan has said, "The sheer folly of trying to defend a nation by destroying all life on the planet must be apparent to anyone capable of rational thought. Nuclear capability must be reduced to zero, globally, permanently. There is no other option."

Dr. Krieger tells us this: *"If nuclear weapons are to be abolished, the people must lead the way."* In a recent phone interview he outlined what each of us can do:

• Educate yourself about the issue, and join with others working on it, like the Nuclear Age Peace Foundation, Physicians for

Social Responsibility, or the Lawyers Committee on Nuclear Policy. Visit their websites (listed in the Resources section at the end of this chapter) and find out how you can help.

• Contact our leaders and call for an end to the production of these weapons. Let them know this is an issue you want them to take action on.

• Rent a copy of the movie *Amazing Grace and Chuck* and watch it with your children. This movie shows that when people make a commitment, the impossible can become a reality. After you watch the movie, discuss what it's about. Decide what actions you want to take as a family.

• Organize a meeting at your place of worship or your child's school. Get a group together and bring this issue to the PTA and other organizations that care about the future of our children. By the way, this is what I did when my boys were little. As a result, our school board voted to send home nuclear "freeze" information with every child in the school.

• Read your children the story of *Sadako and the Thousand Paper Cranes*—the true story of a little girl who died of radiation poisoning after the bombing of Hiroshima. Together make paper cranes to send to our leaders and ask them to rethink their position on nuclear weapons.

Tremendous power is unleashed when people like you and me join together to overcome seemingly impossible challenges. Again the words of David Krieger:

> Know that *we* have the power to change things. Change doesn't happen without people like you becoming involved. The Berlin Wall fell, the Soviet Union disintegrated, apartheid ended in South Africa. These things happened because enough people had the courage, compassion, and commitment to make them happen. People like you.
> I believe this problem will be solved when we have a Million Child March or a Million Parents March on Washington on behalf of children everywhere. I believe it is possible that some of you who are reading this book right now will use your creativity, energy, and ability to make it happen.

And when you do, I want to meet you. I'll be there marching at your side.

CREATING A VISION OF PEACE

Think for a moment about what the world would be like if all people were truly united in the common goal of eliminating war from this planet. Imagine people all over having made the decision to share resources, put down their arms, and resolve differences nonviolently. Imagine just for a moment that, in spite of our differences, we found a way to live in peace. I know this is a tall order, but just for a moment indulge in this vision, and imagine that, in spite of it all, we have achieved a world at peace.

Imagine that fifty years from now this actually comes to pass. A major shift started in the year 2002, led by people who refused to accept that their children were destined to grow up in a violent world. And imagine that those people, you among them, taught their children the ways of peace, and together they started taking steps to rectify the conditions that lead to war. Imagine that the voices of those people were so strong, the governments had to listen. And one by one they started using the same resources that have gone to war, to create peace.

Now imagine that this massive shift started right in our own homes. Parents and children knowing that peace starts with each individual, refusing to accept the status quo. Parents and children realizing that you are either part of the problem or part of the solution. Parents and children taking action against cruelty, racism, hunger, and homelessness. Imagine us being guided by all those people who lost their lives on September 11th. Imagine them saying, *We gave our lives so you could learn this lesson.*

And now imagine that because enough of us heard their voices, the conditions that lead to war have been slowly eradicated. Food, homes, clean water, and medicine are now available to *all* people; illiteracy is a thing of the past, and the weapons of mass destruction have been abolished. What has emerged is a tangible sense of world community, a reverence for life, a reverence for each other—a world at peace—all starting in the year 2002, because of the steps *you* took today. In Chapter 10, "A Call to Action: Starting the Race to Peace," you will find out how—together—we can actually begin to make this happen.

Now for the most important exercise you will ever do:

Completely suspend disbelief and imagine that the vision you just read could actually become a reality. For now, suspend any voices of doubt or cynicism. They have never served you. And let the voice of your highest vision speak. Now ask the wisest part of yourself this question: What was my role in creating a more peaceful world? Go back to the vision and see what you did.

Pull out all the stops and let your mind flow freer than it ever has. Keep suspending disbelief, and allow whatever visions emerge to fully take shape. Now write down what you envisioned as specifically as you can. Don't discount anything. As the writer Richard Bach says, "You are never given a dream without also being given the power to make it come true."

What gets revealed in this process may indeed be your mission in life.

Guiding Your Children Toward a Vision of Peace

Ask your children to do the exercise you just did. Have them envision a world at peace fifty years from now, and ask them to imagine what role they had in making it happen. Encourage them to be as specific as possible, and to suspend all vestiges of disbelief. Remind them about Craig Kielburger, who started Kids Can Free the Children when he was twelve years old, and John Holland-McCowan, who started Kids Cheering Kids at only four. Let them know they possess the same wonderful abilities these children have.

Now have your children write down whatever vision comes to mind, and if they're too young to do this for themselves, write it down for them. Remind your children: "The starting point for a better world is the belief that it is possible," and that they have the ability to create a better world.

Here's the most important part: Help your children come up with specific steps they can take to make their vision real. Have them write down at least one step they will take within the next week. Hang it up and put it on your calendar. This will be a life-changing step for both you and your children. Perhaps you can combine both of your visions.

Talk with your child at least once a week to plan the next step, and the next, and the next. Don't just stop at the initial vision. Keep going.

You can also have your children create drawings, paintings, or murals of their visions of peace. Hang them up in your home as a reminder. Make making your visions real a top priority.

PEACEMAKERS AMONG US

Throughout this book I have stressed the power individuals have to change the world. Individuals like you and me. Individuals like the children you are raising right now. Regular people like the ones you are about to meet. And knowing this gives me hope. Here are just a few of the many people who have decided to honor their visions of peace and make them real. May they each inspire you to make your visions a reality, too, because, like them, you have this power inside of yourself.

Melodye Feldman: Breaking Down Walls of Hatred

In 1993, Melodye Feldman had the dream of bringing young Israeli and Palestinian women together to find ways to live and work with one another. She imagined creating an inclusive, integrated community where opposing groups could retain their own unique qualities while learning to accept each other. Her vision led to "Seeking Common Ground," a summer camp that has been bringing children of opposing sides together for nine years.

Melodye sees it as a safe place where kids can tell their stories to their "enemy" and be heard. "I wanted them live, eat, and interact together, and to find their own voice and self-esteem." Melodye's idea was that by listening, and coming to know each other, the concept of "enemy" would begin to dissolve. She was right.

Here's how it happens. In a twenty-one-day program, Israeli and Palestinian girls ages fourteen through eighteen come together to live and work. The camp program focuses on skill building, socialization, integration, and leadership training. "This is a building block," says Melodye. "The idea is that when they go home the girls will use these skills in their own communities." Ground rules are set right away—no violence of any kind, no name calling, no put-downs. The girls have to learn how to communicate honestly but respectfully. It's hard at first, but before long they start to understand their shared humanity. In nine years there has been only one incident of fighting, and that was between two girls on the same side. Through negotiation they were able to work things out.

"We provide a safe environment where the girls can take risks and stretch. I use a rubber band to symbolize stretching out of one's comfort zone." The girls also participate in a ropes course. "We call it challenge by choice. Imagine an Israeli girl holding a wire that supports a Palestinian girl going across a ravine. The Palestinian girl must ask, 'Are you willing to support me?' And the Israeli girl needs to answer, 'I'm here to support you.' This alone is a stretch for so many of the girls."

The staff, which is comprised of the same ethnic mix as the campers, also does the ropes course. Once a young Israeli girl said to a Palestinian staffer, "I'm here to support you," and the staffer asked, "But are you willing to support me when we get home?" The Israeli girl thought about it for a minute and then said yes. Melodye counts this as one of the most profound moments she can remember—the essence of what Seeking Common Ground is about. Through experiences like this, walls break down, stereotypes fall away, and trust builds. Melodye says, "The camp's motto is 'In order to ensure your safety, you must ensure the safety of others,' the same thing we need to be doing in the world."

According to Melodye, the kids have a heightened sensitivity when they get home. They continue to stay in touch with each other via e-mail, and they voice a range of emotions. They'll say things to each other like, "I can't believe what your side is doing!" But then they'll end the e-mail with a request for their friend's phone number. In the midst of war they have concrete experiences to counterbalance what they are living with.

"We must be proactive rather than reactive," Melodye says. "This is the key to peace: Living peace in every aspect of our lives—in the way we parent, how we treat people we meet, and by valuing each other. People in conflict who come together intentionally, and who create relationships through social interaction, and practice new communication skills, approach their conflicts from a place of connection rather than detachment."

"It's one person at a time, one relationship at a time. Small steps build on each other. Living this way gives me the encouragement to go on," Melodye says. "I have a Palestinian and an Israeli girl living with me who are training to work in my program. They give me hope every single day."

Melodye's philosophy is this: "We have three choices: To walk backwards, to stand still, or to walk forward. In my life, the commitment I've made is to walk forward. If I were to die tomorrow, my life will have been complete."

Lin Evola: Promoting Peace Through Art

For ten years, Lin has been traveling to the far reaches of the world urging people to give up their weapons. When warring gang members from the streets of East and South Central Los Angeles heard Lin's message, they turned in guns for her to melt down and transform into the beautiful "Peace Angel" sculpture that was placed in front of the Crossroads School of Arts and Sciences in Los Angeles. At the dedication, black and Latino gang members joined with the sheriff of Los Angeles, to take a stand for peace.

Lin is now working on similar projects in thirteen sites around the globe, including Johannesburg, Jerusalem, and Ciapas, Mexico. One of her Peace Angels stood until recently, near Ground Zero at the entrance of Nino's Restaurant, which you read about earlier. This magnificent sculpture honored those who were lost and inspired those who saw it toward a vision of peace. One of the firefighters at Ground Zero commented, "Each time I look at the sculpture, I get a peacefulness. I think about all the friends I lost and I know they're all together, guardian angels still watching over all the people."

In an intangible sense, this Peace Angel tells us that there's something higher, something larger than hatred and violence, that lives within us all.

This is the message Lin Evola brings everywhere she goes. Prompted by the 1992 race riots in her former hometown of Los Angeles, Lin felt an urgency to draw people's attention to the issue of peace. She began collecting every mode of weapons she could get her hands on, from guns to cluster bombs, from landmines to missile casings. "Peace is a continual process, a way of life and a strenuous journey," Lin says. "If our work results in people reconsidering their way of thinking and acting—from a mindset of violence to one of peace, we will have had a profound effect on the world."

Imagine a Peace Angel on the Mount of Olives, in Jerusalem, a sacred site of spiritual significance to Muslims, Jews, and Christians. Lin is now working on making this vision a reality. "This is a small symbolic gesture, and a leap of faith, that we *can* possibly move toward a more peaceful world. Allowing their weapons to be used in a sculpture representing all of them symbolizes their desire for the same thing: that their children be safe and that they live in peace. Giving up some weapons, knowing they will be mixed with the weapons of their enemies, is a step toward honor and dignity."

Lin believes that if more and more people can be inspired toward a vision of peace, we will see the world begin to change. "Terrorism happens when people are fractured. We can't justify these acts, but we must understand that every person who commits an act of terrorism is a lost soul in a valley of darkness. We must each look at the world we live in and find ways to bring wholeness to children everywhere so we can prevent these acts from ever happening again."

Having been a peace activist most of her life, Lin sees the urgency for greater numbers of us to get involved. "People must realize that we have this opportunity now, to own our lives and live from our most powerful place." But she also cautions us against spreading ourselves too thin. "We have so much anxiety about trying to solve everything now. Each generation creates new problems and new solutions, and each will solve some of the 'unsolvable' problems of the generation before it. We must remember this—it's a process that's gone on since the beginning of time."

Urging each of us to do our part, Lin says, "If you don't like the way the system is working, do something about it. Instead of going down the old road, create a new one. We must never give up the power we have within ourselves."

Lin Evola's Peace Angels are an eloquent symbol of hope and transformation. They call us each to look inside ourselves and see what our role is in bringing peace to the world we live in.

You can learn more about the Peace Angels project by visiting this website: www.evola.enewspro.com.

Lynn Elling: Creating Peace at Eighty-one

Lynn Elling has been waging peace for most of his adult life. It began during World War II, when as a young naval officer, he witnessed the carnage of the Battle of Tarawa, which killed 6,000 people. The result was a profound realization that war is unthinkable. The question that began haunting him was, "How can we abolish war like we did slavery?" Lynn Elling has been on a quest to do so ever since.

In 1980, Elling convinced Yugoslavia's President Tito to sign a Declaration of World Citizenship. Since then he has met with such luminaries as Jimmy Carter, Indira Gandhi, Hubert Humphrey, and Norman Cousins to talk about ways to bring peace to this violent world.

In 1988, the original founder of the Peace Sites Program, Lou Kousans, asked Elling to take over. Now he had a new mission—to persuade schools, churches, and organizations to proclaim themselves as peace sites, places where understanding, acceptance, and nonviolent resolutions of conflicts are taught. Because of Elling's tireless work there are now 750 Peace Sites internationally, and the number is growing.

"Our peace site program is becoming a major player in creating a more peaceful healthy world," Elling told me in a phone interview. He talked about the enthusiasm kids have for participating in the program. For example, 900 high school students came to school on their day off—Martin Luther King Day, 2002—to witness their school being dedicated as a peace site.

Churches synagogues, and mosques also rank among the growing number of peace sites. But schools, primarily elementary, make up the greatest number of active peace sites. The most famous is the Carter Center in Atlanta.

In 1995 Elling's program took a new and exciting turn. They started working with the Nobel Peace Prize Forum, a group from Norway that links Nobel laureates to schools. Elling described how the program works:

> The Nobel Prize Forum wanted the Nobel laureates to meet young children because they see them as the hope for the future. Together we created the Nobel Peace Prize Festival, which involves about 1,000 elementary and middle-school children from thirty to forty schools. Our first festival was held in 1996 in my home state of Minnesota. Before the children get to meet the Nobel laureates, each school is charged with "adopting" one of them. The children have to learn about their laureate and they plan a celebration on his or her behalf. On the day of the festival, all the laureates come and each school does a stage performance in their honor. We plan to have Kofi Anan at the festival in 2003 to help celebrate the one hundredth anniversary of the Nobel Prize. This idea has

been introduced to the children of Norway and now they have a Nobel laureate festival there too.

Along with this we've started the "Planet in Every Classroom" project. The idea is for every classroom across America to have a picture of the earth in space. We ask each teacher to teach that we are part of one big human family. By looking at this photograph, we are reminded that the earth is our home and we are one family regardless of race, religion, or country. An international and human value perspective can be woven into every subject.

We provide lesson plans too. This is the best possible way to start promoting nonviolence. People must identify that we are all part of the human family. We've got to find a way to live together in peace and we have to start with children. It's simple but powerful.

If you would like to learn more about the Peace Sites program, the Nobel Laureates program, or the Planet in Every Classroom, go to www.peacesite.org.

Peacemaker Kids

Nickole Evans

Sixteen-year-old Nickole Evans has been working actively as a peacemaker for years. She is featured on the My Hero website for her courageous and far-reaching actions. Ironically, Nickole had every reason to become cynical—in 1998, she was beaten up by a gang of Bosnian kids. Yet she chose peace over vengeance, reconciling with the kids who had hurt her. Ultimately, she came to understand that these children had been traumatized by war, so she started working to help them peacefully coexist with others.

Nickole has developed a website, www.y2kyouth.org, where young people from all over can share their feelings about war and violence. It was created in conjunction with the World Junior Peace Summit, and allows kids to express their views about race, religion, overpopulation, and other issues of concern.

Nickole has been a peacemaker since she was little, playing with kids from Nigeria, the Ukraine, Mexico, Bosnia, and Kosovo, and helping her peers resolve conflicts, which she still does as a peer mediator. She also started a branch of Students Against Violence Everywhere (SAVE) in her area.

According to the My Hero website, Nicole has been honored at the United Nations, winning the Peace & Tolerance Award in the category of Technology. She was also invited to attend a junior summit at MIT, where she met with other teens from around the globe to explore how technology could be use to improve the quality of life for people everywhere. Nickole says, "The more of us that are helping others, the better our world will be."

Mattie Stepanik

You met twelve-year-old Mattie in Chapter 5, where we talked about the altruism he exhibits even in the face of his debilitating illness. Mattie's rare form of muscular dystrophy doesn't stop him from continuously reaching out to others with his message of peace. He has written thousands of poems, many of which talk about the need to care for one another, and his book *Heart Songs* has risen to the top of the best-seller list. He says, "I think that's so important, especially now, when everybody is feeling a sense of fear and having been terrorized, to look at what you have in your life and have a sense of gratitude and see the miracles in your life."

Although he's been sick as long as he can remember, Mattie has dedicated himself to helping others. As a representative of Children's Hospice International, Mattie speaks on behalf of sick children everywhere and is trying to find ways our government can make it easier for them to get the services they need. Director of Children's Hospice International, Jim Hawkins, says, "Even though he has been facing a terminal illness for the last six years, Mattie has never seen his condition as an obstacle between him and his goals. Little Mattie has somehow acquired more wisdom in his short life than most of us do after decades of living."

"My biggest role model for this is Jimmy Carter, who has been a wonderful peanut farmer, politician, and peacemaker," says

Mattie. "I call him the 'perfect hero.' I would like to work as a mediator, and share my poetry, essays, and philosophy with others so that they may be inspired to work with other people, too."

Through Mattie's public appearances and poems about peace, he is touching the hearts of millions of people. Oprah Winfrey was so taken with him that during one of Mattie's hospitalizations, she asked viewers throughout the country to pray for him every day for a month. That's the effect Mattie Stepanik has on people. He lives and breathes peace and conveys it to everyone he meets. Let's all share in prayers that Mattie will live a long life. We need him in this world more than he can ever know.

Ibrahim Alex Bangura

Sixteen-year-old Alex Bangura's hero is Nelson Mandela and he is clearly following in his footsteps. In an article by Wendy Jewell on the My Hero website, I learned about the work this extraordinary young man from Sierra Leone has been doing for the past ten years. His contribution spans many areas.

Alex has been spreading peace through a group called Peace Links Musical Youths. With other members of the group, he writes and performs music that brings a message of peace, tolerance, and reconciliation to people throughout their war-torn country. Alex is so good at what he does that in 1993 his peers selected him to attend a United Nations Peaceways conference, where he received training in leadership, conflict resolution, and human rights.

What he learned there really paid off—Alex helped save lives by distributing oral rehydration packets for UNICEF during cholera outbreaks. He also works on environmental clean-up and helps build shelters for people who have been displaced from their homes. On top of all this, Alex still finds time to lead workshops on tolerance.

Although Alex's family is very poor, he manages to work tirelessly for people who are less fortunate. Currently he is working to rehabilitate thousands of children in Sierra Leone who were taken from their homes and forced to serve as soldiers. One of the ways he brings a message of peace to these children is through the music he composes with Peace Links.

If you would like to learn more about Alex or order one of his tapes, go to www.myhero.com.

It is essential that we share these stories with our children to give them a sense that people—including kids—really *can* make a difference. Why is this so critical? Because without it, many children fall into a descending spiral of hopelessness, apathy, and cynicism. I have seen this happen too many times when I've worked with young people. "Why should I bother about caring others? No one cares about me," said a poor seventeen-year-old African-American male. Then, from seventeen-year-old white female at a private school: "I don't believe we can have peace. It's impossible. So why bother?" Comments like these are not atypical. Yet on the other hand, there are many kids like the ones you just read about above, who are hopeful and empowered. "Yes, people *can* make a difference," a nine-year-old peer mediator told me. "I know 'cause I'm doing it."

Kids like this *know* they can change the world because they see the results of their actions right in their own schools and communities. Energized and inspired, they see the future as a place of possibility.

Isamar Martinez is one of these children. A fifth-grader living in a public housing project where violence is prevalent, Isamar arrived in the country from the Dominican Republic and didn't speak a word of English until two years ago. Even though her clothes aren't the newest, she always walks with her head held high and a sense of purpose.

As one of sixty students in her school trained in mediation skills, Isamar wears with pride the badge that designates her as a "peacemaker." Short in stature but courageous in character, she is known by peers and adults alike as one of the most outstanding peacemakers her school of 450 children.

Her guidance counselor says that when Isamar observes children on the brink of a fight, she'll walk over and convince them to stop. She urges them to sit down and talk, and small as she is, Isamar exudes a quiet dignity that has them follow her lead.

If you have any doubt about the ability of kids to make peace, listen to Isamar's words:

> Kids really *can* learn how to help the world be more peaceful. If they learn how to make peace themselves, someday they will be able to help countries of the world stop fighting like they are now.
>
> I help kids make peace all the time. I tell them how to work things out and they follow me. One of the things I do is get them to understand how the other person feels. Kids really can work things out when they have some help.
>
> I think teachers and principals need to start training peacemakers and teaching their kids to believe in peace. And if they do, I think it *will* be possible to have a more peaceful world. We're doing a project in our school with the United Nations. Maybe we can help them help the people of the world become more peaceful. If you have peace in your heart, you can help people who fight learn how to stop.

Isamar's experience of empowerment is not atypical. In an article for *Teaching Tolerance* magazine ("Someone Else's Problem," spring 2001), high school teacher Benjamin Dow wrote about how getting involved and making a difference literally transformed his students. He said, "I've found that, without the belief that change is possible, student outrage is just as likely as ignorance to lead to apathy." For this reason, Benjamin decided to involve his juniors in a project that would "not only challenge their perception of the world but also challenge their perceived inability to make a difference in it."

With his three teammates he created the Hunger at Home Project, one that would help his students understand that hunger and poverty are not only national and international problems, but problems that affect people right in their own school and community. More importantly, Benjamin and his colleagues wanted to "push our students to take action, designing and implementing programs that would meet real community needs and, in some small ways, change the world."

The teachers started by challenging their students' perceptions that their suburban middle-class town had no hungry people in it. When the director of their local food bank came to speak, Benjamin's students could hardly believe what she told them— that over 2,400 people right in their own town were using emergency food services every month, and over half of them were white. What shocked them even more was that 40 percent of these people were children, two-thirds coming from families with working parents.

Learning this was a big step. One young man said that he realized for the first time, "The poor are not just lazy, but most are responsible people who need a little boost."

Now Benjamin's students were ready to take action. With the help of their teachers, they got involved in a wide range of community service projects. They volunteered at the local food bank, they translated community outreach materials into Spanish and Hindi to let people know where they could get food services, and they even created legislation that went before the state senate.

Before long Benjamin's students started carrying their newfound commitment into other areas of their lives. Several got their church youth groups to join them in feeding and clothing the poor. Inspired by what the juniors at their school were doing, the freshmen decided to launch a letter-writing campaign to get free day planners—required for all students—for kids who couldn't afford them. The spirit of altruism spread to the sophomores too. Spearheaded by several kids who'd been previously failing in class, a project was devised to rectify an ethnic inequity that existed in the school's attendance policy.

Benjamin says the results were stunning: "We watched our students move from apathy to activism. It became clear that, given the tools to take action in their lives, community, and world, students will meet the challenge wholeheartedly." The experience of making a difference literally changed their lives.

Taking action empowers, and peace will come when enough of us move from powerlessness to activism. It is critical that we help our children see that *every one of us,* regardless of age gender, or socio-economic group, has the ability to change the world, and that we need to start doing this *now.*

MODELS FOR PEACE

We know all too well about plans, preparations, and expenditures for war, but what structures do we have in place for peace? What follows are some models for peace that already exist, and one—a United States Department of Peace—that is being proposed in Congress. With your help we can make it a reality. Read on to find out more.

The U.S. Department of Peace

On July 11, 2001, Congressman Dennis J. Kucinich (Dem.-Ohio) introduced a bill to establish a Department of Peace. This bill, H.R.2459, calls for a "Cabinet-level department in the executive branch of the Federal Government . . . dedicated to peacemaking and the study of conditions that are conducive to both domestic and international peace." Among the innovations, this bill would provide are:

- Development of new structures in nonviolent dispute resolution both nationally and internationally.
- "Policies that promote national and international conflict prevention, nonviolent intervention, mediation, peaceful resolution of conflict."
- Development of programs that address "the root sources of conflict in troubled areas."
- A Secretary of Peace to serve as a delegate to the National Security Council and work with each branch of the federal government.

We have a Department of Defense (war). To balance the equation, shouldn't we also have a Department of Peace? Pursuing peace does not mean leaving ourselves defenseless or abandoning our arms. In today's climate that would be foolhardy. What it does mean is concurrently pursuing alternate ways of preventing conflict and non-violently addressing those conflicts that already exist.

When Arun Gandhi was asked about what we should have done in response to September 11th, he said, in essence, that by the time September 11th rolled around, it was too late. We had ignored the opportunity to do the work that might have prevented it in the first place. If we had used the United Nations more, instead of shirking the payment of our dues, if we had strengthened our worldwide coalitions, if we had gone into Afghanistan and set up democratic schools for the people there who ended up in Taliban-sponsored schools, if we had learned the language of the people of impoverished Middle Eastern countries and given them some other form of hope, perhaps we might have averted what happened. Fanatics can't function in a vacuum. They need a following to gain power. If we had done some of these things an advance, maybe so many people would not have become blind followers of a man so filled with hate.

A Department of Peace could help us prevent this kind of tragedy from happening again. Ask your legislators to support this important bill. If enough of them hear from us, we can make it a reality.

To learn more, go to Congressman Kucinich's website: www.house.gov/kucinich/action/peace.htm.

The Carter Center

The Carter Center is a wonderful example of proactivity in the quest for peace. It was founded almost twenty years ago "to reduce conflict and to alleviate suffering in the world." Based on the philosophy and vision of President Jimmy Carter, the Center sees prevention as the key. Take a look at their statement:

> We discovered early that to be successful in our mission we had to address the root causes of suffering. That is why our health programs focus on eradicating and controlling diseases

and reducing hunger by increasing food production, and our peace efforts help to achieve democratic government, resolve and prevent conflicts, safeguard human rights, and achieve long-term development. We work in regions of the world with diverse ethnic and religious beliefs, offering our services to all who are in need. We believe that these methods, which provide a voice for the voiceless and hope to the hopeless, are critical to eliminating the desperate conditions that terrorists attempt to exploit.

The Center is working with countries around the globe to help foster free elections, open media, human rights, reconciliation among opposing groups, and more. Most recently they've worked in Guyana, Liberia, East Timor, Zambia, and a village outside Shanghai to help set up and monitor free elections. In the Dominican Republic, another country where the Carter Center monitored free election, its president signed a moratorium on the purchase of sophisticated weapons. Twenty-eight other heads of state joined him in doing this.

The list is long of all the concrete steps the Carter Center is taking to create peace and freedom around the world. If you'd like to find out how you can help, visit their website: www.carter center.org.

The United States Institute for Peace

The United States Institute of Peace (www.usip.org) is not to be confused with the proposed U.S. Department of Peace. The institute is "an independent, nonpartisan federal institution created and funded by Congress to strengthen the nation's capacity to promote the peaceful resolution of international conflict." It sponsors a wide variety of programs, including conferences, workshops, educational services, grants, fellowships, and publications. Among their objectives are the following:

- To involve the best and the brightest from academia, research organizations, and government to assess how to deal with international conflict situations politically.

- To provide conflict management/resolution training to international affairs professionals. This includes mediation and negotiation skills.
- To strengthen curricula and instruction, "from high school through graduate education, about the changing character of international conflict and non-violent approaches to managing international disputes."

Another objective is the prevention of regional conflicts. Each year the U.S. Institute of Peace trains approximately 2,000 foreign affairs, national security, public security, and humanitarian relief practitioners. "Participants include diplomats, government officials, police, and military personnel from the United States and dozens of foreign countries. In addition, most Institute training programs include representatives of international and nongovernmental organizations. . . . "

The Institute has created an international educational program to train greater numbers of people in negotiation/conflict resolution skills. So far, faculty workshops have been held in the Balkans and Southeast Europe, and in Cairo. Workshops are also being planned for Southeast Asia and the Middle East. According to the Institute, the ultimate goal is to help people manage regional conflicts and develop a shared vision for the future so they will work together, rather than destroy each other. If you would like to find out how you can become directly involved in their educational programs, you can e-mail the United States for Peace at education@usip.org.

The Hague Appeal for Peace

In 1999, the Hague Appeal for Peace held a conference that drew over 10,000 people from all over the world. This was one of the largest conferences of its kind, and it was here that a worldwide agenda for peace was established. According to the Hague Appeal, peace is "not only the absence of conflict between and within states, but also as the presence of economic and social justice." There are four major strands to their agenda: addressing root causes of war, human rights, transformation of violent conflict, and disarmament.

Peace education is a big part of their initiative. The educational component of the Hague Appeal for Peace focuses on building "public awareness and political support for the introduction of peace education into all spheres of education, including nonformal education, in all schools throughout the world . . . and promoting the education of all teachers to teach for peace."

On December 10, 2001, the Hague Appeal was joined in their commitment to the abolition of nuclear arms by the Nobel Centennial Appeal, in Oslo, Norway. Here is an excerpt from the statement that was signed by twenty-three Nobel laureates including Elie Wiesel, Desmond Tutu, and Lech Walesa:

> We, the undersigned Nobel Peace Laureates . . . hope that our message of peace and justice will reach the hearts and minds of those in and out of government who have the power to make a better world. We look forward to a world in which we the peoples, working in cooperation with governments, with full respect for international law, will enable the UN to fulfill its mission to save this and succeeding generations from the scourge of war. . . . We commit ourselves to work for the elimination of all weapons of mass destruction and the reduction and control of small arms and other conventional weapons.
>
> We call on the human family to address the root causes of violence and build a culture of peace and hope. We know that another world is possible, a world of justice and peace. Together we can make it a reality.

The Hague Appeal for Peace invites your participation and urges greater numbers of people to get involved. Find out what you and your children can do by going to www.haguepeace.org.

END THOUGHTS

There is a proverb from Greenland that goes like this: "When you have gone so far that you can't manage one more step, then you've gone just half the distance you are capable of." Life gets so busy that sometimes we feel we can't go one more step. And too often the tumult of everyday activity deafens us to the sounds of others' suffering. Yet when we engage in altruistic acts, our senses heighten and we become energized. We are then imbued with the passion that makes moving forward easy. Sometimes ignoring the voice of our highest purpose takes the most energy. When we give ourselves permission to define our purpose and live our highest vision, everything changes. It's like allowing light into a darkened room.

In his wonderful book *Living a Life That Matters,* Rabbi Harold Kushner talks about the need we all have to make a difference, and to leave the world a better place from having lived in it. He says, " . . . it is not the prospect of death that frightens most people. People can accept the inescapable fact of mortality. What frightens them more is the dread of insignificance, the notion that we will be born and live and one day die, and none of it will matter."

We have the opportunity now, to seize the moment, *this moment in time* when our contribution is needed so desperately. As I write these words, a statistic keeps haunting me: 27,000 people a day worldwide die of hunger-related diseases—27,000 people a day! And what's worse is that it is *preventable.* By our noninvolvement, we allow this number to repeat day after day. Those who have must reach out a hand to those who have not, and until such time, we will never have peace. But if one person at a time extends a hand in a gesture of care, and someone else sees this and follows, and then the next, and then the next, we will begin creating the path to peace.

Gandhi once said, "War will only be stopped when the conscience of mankind has become sufficiently elevated to recognize the undisputed supremacy of the law of love in all walks of life. Some say this will never come to pass. I shall retain the faith till the end of my earthly existence that it *shall* come to pass."

Think of Gandhi's words: "... when the conscience of mankind has become sufficiently elevated." This is what we are called to now, the elevation of our consciousness individually and collectively. Our children's futures depend on it. The peace and stability of our world depend on it. The conscience of us all rising to the call—when this happens, we will see the roots of war transform, because *we* will transform them. Rabbi Kushner says, "The small choices and decisions we make a hundred times a day add up to determining the kind of world we live in."

What kind of world do you want? Begin creating it now.

RESOURCES AND BIBLIOGRAPHY

Websites

The Hague Appeal for Peace
www.haguepeace.org
Goal—to create a culture of peace, and prevent and transform violent conflict. Sponsors conferences, peace education programs, and offer materials on teaching peace. You can order their free e-newsletter by e-mailing this address: hap@ialana.org.

The Carter Center
www.cartercenter.org
Working to set up democratic governments, eradicate hunger, and other roots of war and violence. Mission: "To reduce conflict and to alleviate suffering in the world."

The Nuclear Age Peace Foundation
www.wagingpeace.org
Offers up-to-date research, educational programs, and policymaking guidance. Working toward the "creation of a peaceful and secure future based upon nonviolence, justice, and human dignity."

The United States Institute of Peace
www.usip.org
Mission: "to strengthen the nation's capabilities to promote the peaceful resolution of international conflicts."

International Peace Academy
www.ipacademy.org
Promotes "the prevention and settlement of armed conflicts between and within states through policy research and development."

Physicians for Social Responsibility
www.psr.org
Winner of the 1985 Nobel Prize. Twenty thousand doctors worldwide, committed to the elimination of nuclear weapons. Students
can set up a PSR chapter; student newsletter available.

The Lawyers Committee on Nuclear Policy
www.lcnp.org
Provides legal information to policymakers, diplomats, activists,
and the media on disarmament and international law; works with
the UN and the World Court, and provides up-to-date information
to people like you and me.

Urgent Call
www.urgentcall.org
Working for international nuclear arms control. Tells us specific
things we can do to help now.

International Peace Bureau
www.ipb.org
Nobel Prize–winning organization working to support UN peace
and disarmament initiatives. Focus on peace education, conflict resolution, and human rights.

The Elie Wiesel Foundation for Humanity
http://www.eliewieselfoundation.org
Works for human rights; combats "indifference, intolerance and
injustice." Holds international conferences and seminars bringing
together scholars, artists, scientists, politicians, and young people
from all over the world.

The Project on Preventing War
www.pon.harvard.edu

Working to change the way people, organizations, and nations resolve their disputes—from "win-lose" outcomes to "all-gain" solutions.

Global Action to Prevent War
www.globalactionpw.org
International organization working on "a comprehensive program for moving to a world in which deadly conflict is rare, brief, and small in scale." Chapters in approximately fifty countries.

PeaceWomen
PeaceWomen.org
For women who care about peace seeking to "nurture communication among a diversity of women's organizations and the UN."

Seeking Common Ground
buildingpeace.com
Mission: to create understanding. Hosts summer camp programs for Israeli and Palestinian girls as well as girls from the United States from varying ethnic and racial groups.

Children's International Summer Villages
http://www.cisv.org
Promotes peace education and cross-cultural friendship in sixty-seven different countries.

Center for the Advancement of Nonviolence
www.nonviolenceworks.com
Focuses on education, social action, and the development nonviolent institutional models; offers curricula and teaching tools. You can order their poster and curriculum guide—*64 Ways to Practice Nonviolence*—in English and Spanish.

Tikkun
www.Tikkun.org
A growing community of people from different religious backgrounds working to create a world based on economic justice, peace, human rights, and compassion.

People for Peace
http://hometown.aol.com/pforpeace/index.htm
   Includes stories and activities for kids on creating more peace in their communities, schools, and world.

UNICEF's Voices of Youth program
http://www.unicef.org/voy/meeting/meethome.html
   Helps children learn about what affects other kids in today's world; includes information on children and war, children rights, and other important issues.

Y2KYouth
Y2KYouth.org
   Motto: "It only takes one child to educate a village."A clearing-house of information on peace, violence, and service for teens.

Youth M-Power
www.youthm-power.org
   For kids who want to make peace. "M" stands for mediation. Links kids nationwide, provides resources and activities.

Books for Parents

Ackerman, Peter, and Jack DuVall. *A Force More Powerful: A Century of Nonviolent Conflict.* New York: St. Martin's Press, 2000. Inspiring. Shows how nonviolent action was successfully used to topple dictators, stop invaders, and gain human rights in many countries over the past century. Thoroughly researched. A must-read. You can order the PBS video of "A Force More Powerful" by calling 800-221 7945, ext. 270.

Bush, B., and J. Folger. *The Promise of Mediation: Responding to Conflict Through Empowerment and Recognition.* San Francisco: Jossey Bass, 1994.
Mediation skills for a variety of purposes.

Eisler, Riane. *The Chalice and the Blade: Our History, Our Future.* San Francisco: HarperCollins, 1997.
This revolutionary book examines the roots of war in our society. Ashley Montagu calls it "the most important book since Darwin's *Origin of Species.*

From the Ashes: A Spiritual Response to the Attack on America collected by the editors of Beliefnet. Emmaus, Penn.: Rodale, 2001.
A collection of essays from some of the top spiritual writers in the world today. Includes the words of the Dali Lama, Archbishop Desmond Tutu, Thcih naht Hanh, and more.

Krieger, David, and Carah Ong. *Maginot Line in the Sky: International Perspectives on Ballistic Missile Defense.* Santa Barbara, Calif.: Nuclear Age Peace Federation, 2001.
Explores the dangers of our ballistic missile defense system and its possible impact on the world.

McCarthy, Coleman. *Strength Through Peace.* Washington, D.C.: Center for Teaching Peace.
Compilation of writings by leading peacemakers and analysts on peace and nonviolence.

Moore, Christopher. *The Mediation Process: Practical Strategies for Resolving Conflict.* Second Edition. San Francisco: Jossey Bass, 1996.
Tools for mediating conflicts.

Ury, William. *Getting to Peace.* New York: Viking, 1999.
Visionary book by renowned expert on creating peace on every level of human interaction.

Ury, William. *The Third Side: Why We Fight and How We Can Stop.* New York: Penguin, 2000.
Paperback version of *Getting to Peace.*

Weber, T., and E. Boulding. *Gandhi's Peace Army: The Shanti Sena and Unarmed Peacekeeping.* Syracuse, N.Y.: Syracuse University Press, 1996.
The principles of nonviolence in practice.

Books for Children

Byars, Betsy. *The Cybil War.* New York: Viking, 1981.
A conflict between two long-term friends arises from misinformation. (Grades 3–6.)

Coerr, Eleanor. *Sadako and the Thousand Paper Cranes.* New York: Penguin-Putnam Books for Young Readers, 1999.

After the bombing of Hiroshima, Sadako is hospitalized with radiation disease. She races against time to make one thousand paper cranes as a call for peace. (Grades 2–7.)

Crane, Stephen. *The Red Badge of Courage.* New York: Vintage, 1990.
In this classic, a young Civil War soldier learns about the horrors of war firsthand, and finds a way to exercise his conscience. (Grades 9–12.)

Keene, Ann T. *Peacemakers: Winners of the Nobel Peace Prize.* Oxford, England: Oxford University Press, 1998.
Tells how the Nobel Peace Prize was established and all the individuals and organizations that have received it since 1901. (Grades 6 and up.)

Lowry, Lois. *Number the Stars.* New York: Houghton-Mifflin, 1989.
The must-read story of a Jewish family's survival during the Holocaust as they are protected by their Danish neighbors. (Grades 5–9.)

Lucas, Eileen. *Peace on the Playground.* New York: Franklin Watts, 1991.
Shows kids why it's important to work out conflicts and how to do so. (Grades K–6.)

Millman, Dan. *The Secret of the Peaceful Warrior.* Tiburon, Calif.: H.T. Kramer Inc., 1991.
Wonderful story of a young boy's courage and humanity in the face of a bully. (Grades 1–6.)

Paulus, Trina. *Hope for the Flowers.* New York: Paulist Press, 1972.
A fable of peace, hope, and the power of one.

Polacco, Patricia. *Pink and Say.* New York: Philomel, 1994.
Incredibly moving story of two young boys, one black and one white, who fought in the Civil War. Shows the outcome of intolerance and the power of love. (Grades 2–6.)

Scholes, Katherine. *Peace Begins With You.* Boston: Little, Brown, 1990.
A simply written book on peace, conflict, and how to work out conflicts. (Grades K–2.)

Seuss, Dr. *The Butter Battle Book.* New York: Random House, 1984.
Dr. Seuss shows how perceived differences can escalate to fighting and ultimately to war. (Grades K–4.)

Tate, Eleanora E. *Thank You, Dr. Martin Luther King, Jr.!* New York: Bantam Doubleday Dell, 1999.
Mary Eloise is African-American. Her attitude about her heritage improves when two wonderful storytellers come to her school. (Grades 3–6.)

Thomas, S. M. *Somewhere Today: A Book of Peace.* Morton Grove, Ill.: Albert Whitman & Co., 1998.
Text and photos show children from all parts of the world. Designed to inspire kids to take responsibility for making the world a better place. (Grades K–4.)

Chapter 10

A Call to Action: Starting the Race to Peace

We now have the most promising opportunity in 10,000 years to create a co-culture of coexistence. . . .

—William Ury, Director of Harvard University's Project on Preventing War

There comes a time when silence is betrayal.

—Martin Luther King

Ordinary people with extraordinary commitment can make sweeping change for the long-term benefit of the earth and its residents.

—Aubrey Wallace, author of *Green Means: Living Gently on the Planet*

Those of us whose hands touch this book walk a special path—we are parents. The future lives in our houses. It lives in the faces we look at each morning and put to bed each night. And how the future turns out will be the direct result of what we do today. We owe it to our children to do *whatever* is in our power to create peace. And we cannot wait. The amount of violence in our world increases every day, and each minute we turn away from this problem, it gets worse.

The key to changing this is in our hands. Morally and ethically, we are compelled to use that key. We cannot leave it up to governments—they are too involved with their own self-propagation. We cannot leave it up to politicians—they are too busy catering to the big-business interests who keep them in office. We cannot leave it up to other people—creating peace is up to each of us.

Listen to these powerful words by poet and writer Wendell Berry: "How many deaths of other people's children by bombing or starvation are we willing to accept in order that we may be free, affluent and supposedly at peace? To that question I answer, none. Please, no children, don't kill any children for my benefit." I agree—the thought of any more children dying for my comfort is unthinkable, yet it happens every single day. Every 3.6 seconds, someone dies from hunger and other preventable causes, and the majority are children. *Just in the time it took you to read this sentence, someone died unnecessarily.* This is unfathomable, and absolutely unacceptable.

How can we turn over to our own children a world where other children die in wars, and thousands upon thousands die of starvation every single day? Many people think there's no way to change this, but that's simply not true. We have the resources; we have the solutions. What's missing is the will.

Time and time again as I have been researching this book, what has become painfully clear is that the solutions to ending war, poverty, and hunger exist in this moment. The problem, inconceivable as it may seem, is that we are not using the solutions available to us.

Listen to this statement from the United Nations FAO (Food and Agriculture Organization) Report delivered in Rome, 2001.

One of the great achievements of the past century has been the production of enough food not only for the needs of a global population which has doubled, from some three billion in 1960 to over six billion in 2000 but also to ensure a better standard of nutrition. . . . Looking back on the century, however, future historians are likely to point to the anomaly that hunger should have coexisted on a vast scale with more than adequate aggregate global food supplies. The simultaneous persistence of widespread extreme food deprivation and plentiful food supplies in a world with excellent means of communications and transport, can only suggest that there are fundamental flaws in the way in which nations are functioning and the relationships between how they are governed and managed. . . . Yet the world continues to live with it.

Why is this happening? According to a UN report issued in 2001—it's because *the political will does not exist*, precisely the same reason we are not using tools that already exist to create peace.

Poverty and war are inextricably linked. At a gathering of world leaders in March of 2002, President of the U.N. General Assembly, Han Seung Soo, quoting poet Octavio Paz, said, "The richest nations could no longer afford to be 'islands of abundance in an ocean of universal misery.' The consequence, he said would be the poorest nations becoming 'the breeding ground for violence' " (*New York Times,* March 22, 2002).

We see the direct ramifications of this in the countless conflicts and uprisings that go on around the world every day.

Committed individuals working toward a common goal *do* have the power to reshape the world. This has happened over and over again throughout history. The abolition of slavery, women's suffrage, the dismantling of Apartheid, the fall of the Berlin Wall, the civil rights movement—all of these massive changes came from people, not governments, and now is the time for the biggest change ever: moving beyond war toward a culture of peace, starting with regular people like us.

For this reason we must embark on a new race—one far more important than the race to space, and having far more impact than anything our species has ever before accomplished—the Race to Peace.

And why does this have to be a race? Because time is running out. According to the United Nations, thirty-six wars are being waged in our world as I write these words. The weapons of mass destruction are just a hair trigger away from being used. In our schools and neighborhoods children are killing each other—remember this statistic from the Children's Defense Fund, "Every day in America 9 children and youth under 20 die from firearms," the highest number in the industrialized world. And as you read these words, new wars are being planned, and the production of nuclear weapons is increasing.

But *we* have the ability to turn this tide. Read on to find out how.

FEEDING THE VISION

There is a story that goes like this: A Native American grandfather was talking to his grandson. He said, "I feel as if I have two wolves fighting in my heart. One wolf is the vengeful, angry, violent one. The other wolf is the loving, compassionate one." The grandson asked him, "Which wolf will win the fight in your heart?" And the grandfather answered, "The one I feed."

In the past hundred years we have been feeding the wolf of war. The wolf of peace has gone hungry, and now is our time to feed it. The place to begin is with our *will*.

Consider the possibility that with the combined power of parents all over the world we could accomplish this. . . . That people will one day look back and say,

> In the year 2002, families everywhere, no longer willing to accept the violence their children were growing up with, decided they'd had enough.
>
> One by one, mothers, fathers, grandparents, and children of all ages and colors made a huge decision—they started working to create peace. The idea started to catch. Friends told friends, cousins told cousins, e-mails started flying from one coast to the other, across oceans, and beyond all conceivable boundaries. Suddenly people all over the world caught

the bug. And the Race to Peace began. United in a common theme, individuals and organizations started chipping away the roots of war—poverty, homelessness, hunger and the inequitable distribution of resources. They joined voices and called for an end to nuclear weapons and the availability of street weapons.

Before long their efforts took on the momentum of a tidal wave. Voices of nay-sayers were drowned out by its strength, and politicians started listening—after all, they wanted to get reelected. In time, new laws were passed and treaties signed. A change in people's consciousness began to take shape—they started seeing war as unthinkable and barbaric as cannibalism. And they realized it was indeed within their collective power to stop wars from continuing.

Ultimately they created the most massive social change in human history—the beginning of peace. We began empowering our United Nations to intervene more in global conflicts, a halt was put to the development of nuclear weapons, and every person who served in governments around the world was taught the skills of negotiation and mediation. Over time democratic schools were set up throughout the world, and the skills of peacemaking were taught to children everywhere, thereby grooming a generation trained in the tools and methods of peace. Crimes of international significance were dealt with in the World Court, and nations started sharing resources. A collaborative world order began to take shape, and we were a part of its initial inception.

WHAT IS THE RACE TO PEACE?

It's a common theme, the purpose of which is to unite organizations and people all over the world committed to making the vision of peace a reality. It's also a way of connecting to each other through the Internet. The Race to Peace website will enable you to find each other, communicate, collaborate, and support each other.

There's power in numbers, and what we need more than ever is a sense of cohesion. Many wonderful groups are already doing important work in creating peace nationally, locally, or globally. Others are addressing the roots of violence, such as hunger, homelessness, and intolerance. But everyone is working separately. The Race to Peace can potentially be the glue that pulls us all together—the spark that spreads from person to person, family to family, group to group, nation to nation. The ultimate result? A social epidemic where greater and greater numbers of people "catch" the idea that peace can be created, and take action to make it happen.

This type of phenomenon is elegantly described in Malcom Gladwell's book, *The Tipping Point*, where he shows how trends can actually spread like viruses. The most powerful force is word of mouth. Just by communicating, networking, and reaching out, you have the potential to make the Race to Peace a trend that spreads like a healthy virus.

In the following pages you will find out exactly how you can get involved.

THE CHALLENGE

To begin now. As Margaret Mead said: "Never doubt that a small group of thoughtful committed citizens can change the world. Indeed, it is the only thing that ever has." *We are the people of whom she speaks.* Right now, tap into that spark of power that's beginning to ignite, and get ready to begin.

THE PREMISE

The Race to Peace stands on one simple premise: *that peace will be reached through small concrete steps taken by committed people.* If every parent makes a commitment to taking actions toward peace once a day, once a week, or even once a month, the race to peace can be won. What kind of action steps am I talking about? They fall into five areas:

Ending Hunger and Homelessness
Ending the Production of Nuclear Weapons
Eliminating Gun Violence
Building Tolerance and Equity
Taking Local or Global Action for Peace

Which one calls to you? In the following pages, you'll discover how you can get involved in the area you choose, whom to contact, and specific action steps you can take.

THE FIRST STEP: CREATING THE MIND-SET

The next question is, "How do I mobilize myself?" If you haven't done the "Finding Your Path" process in Chapter 8, do it now. The image that comes to mind is Superman in his Clark Kent outfit. So many of us are like Clark Kent, waiting to rip off that dull gray suit and reveal the hero that lives inside. We all have an enormous capacity to make a difference, but too often we ignore our "hero" voice. May this book be a bolt of lightning that strikes you deep, and has you rip off that suit and start living the power you possess.

What does the hero inside you want to achieve? Write it down. Also write down these affirmations to read every morning and every night:

I am the key to peace.
I take action every day to create peace in my life.
I take action every day to create peace in the lives of others.

As your inner hero becomes more and more empowered, new affirmations will start to evolve. Write them down and hang them up too. Keeping yourself surrounded with visual reminders is a critical part of manifesting your most important purpose. The same goes for your children. Tell them about their internal hero too.

Commit to living these affirmations every day. If you get side-tracked and start veering off the path, acknowledge it and get back on. Like anything worth doing, winning the Race to Peace will take patience, commitment, and energy. Your involvement will give you energy—ask anyone who's out there making a difference.

Age doesn't matter. If you can lick a stamp or hold a phone, you're needed in the race. Think of Mattie Stepanik, only 12 and fighting for his survival against a fatal illness, but out there changing the world with his passionate words. Think of Mathilda Spak, who's changing the world at 100 years old. As in a marathon—you can be at the front, or be at the back—what counts is that we create a massive body of determined people moving step by step toward a common goal. The Race to Peace needs all of us, and it needs us *now*.

RACE TO PEACE ACTION GROUPS

Action groups are the heart of the Race to Peace. Here's how to form one. Invite some friends and neighbors to your home. Share this book with them and explain why it's so important that they join you in the Race to Peace. Have them read this book, and in the meantime, choose one of the five strands above to commit yourselves to.

Now, with your group, start exploring the organizations listed in the following pages and see which one you will build your action project around. Visit the websites and talk to the people who staff these organizations. Find out which organization is the one for you. Decide on a concrete project with measurable steps and a goal you believe in. Later in this chapter you will find specific project ideas.

Keep your group small—no more than ten people. If it gets larger, split off into smaller groups. The idea is for groups to keep expanding.

Important: Every person in your group should do the "Finding Your Path" process in Chapter 8. It's critical that people contribute from their talents and unique strengths.

When you run your meetings, you can rotate the role of facilitator, or if the group is comfortable, have the same person facilitate each meeting. So the process of your meetings reflects peace, follow these ground rules:

- Listen with an open mind.
- Work through dissenting viewpoints respectfully.
- Suspend judgment, and work with a spirit of compromise.
- Be peaceful—remember above all else to be accepting and kind.
- Share warmth, care, and support.
- Make it fun.

Have refreshments and meet in a comfortable room. Even though you're doing important work, your meetings should be enjoyable. Start each one with an opening exercise—a prayer, affirmation, a reading from this book or another. Light a candle to signify the flame that your work will ignite this world. Rotate leading the opening so everyone gets a turn.

The body of your meeting should be devoted to action steps—choosing them, giving yourselves deadlines, and reporting on what you have accomplished. If you are in touch with any other Race to Peace action groups, set aside part of your meeting to share what they're doing. Make sure someone takes notes at every meeting. Create a Race to Peace Notebook, in which you keep a purpose statement, action steps, and notes from past meetings.

End with a review of the action steps people will take and "by when's." Like, "I will contact the principal of our local school by April 1st to offer coordinating a Peace Fair." Also, at the end of each meeting, have each person affirm a partner. This is a time to offer sincere compliments about positive qualities you've observed, courageous actions, or innovative ideas. Always leave your meetings on a note of affirmation. This gives people energy and a sense of being appreciated—essential for keeping your enthusiasm over the long-term.

Also, tell everyone you know what you're doing. Remember

what I said earlier? Word of mouth can be the most powerful way of spreading a new idea. Call your friends, send e-mails—make the Race to Peace a household phrase.

ORGANIZATIONS TO CHOOSE FROM

One guideline—the organization you work with needs to be one that addresses the roots of violence, or directly creates peace. If you prefer to work with an organization that's not on this list, go ahead. There are many others to choose from at the end of Chapters 7, 8, and 9. The following organizations are just a starting point. Whatever organization you choose, be sure to register at www.racetopeace.com so other people can find you. We need to keep supporting and inspiring each other.

Ending Hunger, Homelessness, and Poverty

Oxfam America www.oxfamamerica.org
The Hunger Project www.thp.org
Kids Can Free the Children www.freethechildren.org
America's Second Harvest www.secondharvest.org/index.html
National Coalition for the Homeless www.nationalhomeless.org
Habitat for Humanity www.habitat.org
The Children's Defense Fund www.childrensdefense.org

Eliminating Gun Violence

Million Mom March www.millionmommarch.org
The Brady Campaign to Prevent Gun violence
www.bradycam paign.org

Ending the Production of Nuclear Weapons

Nuclear Age Peace Foundation www.wagingpeace.org
Urgent Call www.urgentcall.org

Building Tolerance and Equity

Teaching Tolerance www.Tolerance.org

Do Something www.dosomething.org. Go to
http://coach.dosomething.org/coach/sitepages/index.cfm?formid=
120 for activities for elementary-aged children.

Local or Global Action for Peace

The Hague Appeal for Peace www.haguepeace.org
UNICEF's Voices of Youth Program www.unicef.org/voy/meeting/
meethome.html
ACR Association for Conflict Resolution www.acresolution.org
Youth M-Power www.youthm-power.org (for young people)
Peace Sites www.peacesite.org

PROJECTS YOUR ACTION GROUP CAN ENGAGE IN

Once your group has chosen an organization, set some goals.
Below are actions you might want to consider for whatever organization you choose:

Get your child's school involved. Peace is an issue that affects
every child. Share some of the statistics in this book with your
child's teacher and principal. Offer to create a service or peace
project the school can participate in. More and more educators
are seeing the value of getting kids involved in helping others, so
your child's school might appreciate the help you're offering.

Also, tell your child's teacher and principal about peacemaking programs and curricula listed in the resource sections of this
book, and if they're not already teaching peace, strongly encourage them to do so.

Talk to the librarian at your child's school too. Ask her to
order some of the books recommended at the end of each chapter.

*Get you child's religious education program or scouting group
involved.* Every major religion has compassion at its core, and
what better way of expressing care for others than by reaching
out to help. So many projects recommended in this book would
be a perfect adjunct to a Sunday school or scouting program.

Get your PTA/PTO or home/school association involved. All of the issues we have talked about in this book affect the world's children. Parent groups are about kids, not just about schools. What more wonderful way to expand the reach of your parent group than by involving them in some of the projects in this book.

Build public awareness. Many people don't take action simply because they are not aware of how pressing some of these problems are. Or they simply don't know what to do to help. Create an evening when you can share information, provide a speaker, and allow for questions and answers. This is also a wonderful opportunity to expand your group or help others begin one of their own. Have a sign-up sheet available and request everyone's e-mail address. This way, even if they don't sign up to join a Race to Peace Group, you can stay in touch and let them know about activities your group sponsors. Building awareness is a fundamental step in the Race to Peace.

Get your church, temple, or mosque involved. What better way to spread good will than to have your place of worship reach out to the larger world in an effort toward peace. Join with another congregation to work on a project together. In fact, join with a congregation of a different religious persuasion. In the Special Resource Section at the end of this book you'll meet an imam of a mosque who has joined with all the religious leaders in his community to sponsor interfaith services every Thanksgiving. He also talks about pulpit exchanges where kids speak at different places of worship to help people build a greater understanding of each other's faiths. Try doing something like this in your place of worship.

Fund-raise. Every organization you have read about needs two kinds of support—people power and donations. Hold a carwash, bake sale, raffle, art show, talent night, or carnival to raise money for the organization you choose to help. Make your fund-raising efforts ongoing. See how creative you can be in coming up with new ideas.

Fill a pressing need. Build a school or hospital in Africa. Kids Can Free the Children has already built hospitals and three hundred schools in twenty-three Third-World countries, and this is an organization almost entirely staffed and run by kids! Contact them and find out how you can do this too. Everything you'll need to know to get started is listed Chapter 8. Can you imagine your efforts saving lives? It's actually possible to do this. Start now.

Engage in direct service. When I interviewed Connie Mercer, Director of Homefront, she talked about many things people like us can do to help people who are struggling to get on their feet. She said, "A father I know who lost his job and home due to illness is finally getting back on his feet. His family now has a place to live, he has a job, and he was recently able to get a car but he can't drive it because he can't afford to pay for car insurance. I wish there was an angel out there who could write a check." Think of the thousands of dollars we spend going out to dinner and to the movies. Imagine sometimes forgoing these activities and writing the check that would change somebody's life. You'd be performing a real miracle.

Find out who needs a miracle and what you can do to help. If you're not sure how you can help poor people in your area, go to the National Coalition for the Homeless website.

Make a child's dream come true. One guidance counselor I interviewed told me about a child in her school who is an outstanding student, but barely has enough clothes to wear. This counselor brings in clothing for her on a regular basis. Think about the huge wardrobes so many of our children have. If we could spend just a fraction of that money on new clothing for a child in need, we'd be performing another real-life miracle. Call the local chapter of Catholic Charities or Jewish Family Services. Or call your child's school and see if there are any children in need you can anonymously donate to. Also, ask your local homeless organization or food bank. Almost every county has one. You'll be shocked when you see how many children right in your own area are in need of the basics.

Tutor. It's a gift to be able to help a child who, with a little extra support, could make it in life. A helping hand in a time of need makes all the difference in the world. Contact your local homeless organization or school and see if you can help a child who's struggling. Your involvement could be a turning point in his life.

Start a letter-writing campaign. Massive social change comes first from the voices of the people. The abolition of slavery, women's right to vote, ending discrimination—all of these were the direct result of people like you who refused to accept the status quo.

Organize a letter-writing campaign about the issues that most concern you.

Call and e-mail. Legislators really *do* listen to the voices of their constituents—they want to be reelected. Use your voice and have your children use theirs. These websites will tell you how to reach your senators and congressional representatives:

http://www.house.gov
http://www.senate.gov/senators/senator_by_state.cfm

Write your local newspapers, too, and have your kids do the same. Newspapers appreciate getting letters from concerned kids, and they often print them.

Help coordinate the Race to Peace. I know there are wonderful administrators out there reading this book right now. There are also people who have the resources and talents to make the Race to Peace international in scope. To you I say this: If you feel the spark, start now. Create an event. Invite entertainers to promote the Race to Peace as a unifying global theme. Let's give them the opportunity to use their talents for the betterment of humanity. Bono of U2 is already doing this. *Time* magazine (March 2002) reported that he has become a powerful force in ending hunger and poverty in Africa—he felt the call and decided to answer it. Now he's saving lives.

One of you reading this book right now is saying, "Maybe it's me." If you're thinking these words, then it *is* you. Step up to the plate. Use your gifts to make the Race to Peace a household word. Use your networking abilities to make the Race to Peace as familiar as Starbucks or Nike. Use your power to make the Race to Peace something we can actually win while there's still time.

Imagine Race to Peace bumper stickers, billboards, posters, and commercials. Imagine a Race to Peace theme song—one that could potentially become as familiar as "We Are the World." Imagine Race to Peace marches, conferences, symposia, and a documentary highlighting this growing grassroots movement. Imagine a Million Parent March. Imagine making all this happen. You can.

RACE TO PEACE ACTION GROUPS FOR KIDS

Encourage your kids to form action groups in their school, scouting troop, religious education program, or neighborhood. Help your child create a group just like John Holland McCowan's mother did when he thought up Kids Cheering Kids. Support your kids turning their visions into actions. Sit down together and see how you can help them begin. Write up a plan, then get started. Children *are* capable of launching national movements. Whatever your child's role mught be, encourage it.

EMPOWERMENT PARTNERSHIPS

Ask someone from your group to be your empowerment partner, or ask someone outside it—a friend, relative, neighbor, or someone you find on the Race to Peace website (www.racetopeace. com). Have your child do the same. Your empowerment partner is a mutual support person and cheerleader, someone with whom you share goals, discuss plans, and maintain accountability through biweekly phone calls. Empowerment partners are like those Special Olympics kids you read about earlier who helped lift a fallen friend off the ground, and ran together to the finish line. To make the Race to Peace work we'll all need to cheer each other on and pick each other up when the job feels too big.

Empowerment partnerships will help you do that. Pick a specific night every other week for your phone call to each other. Honor the night religiously. If something pressing comes up and you absolutely can't talk on your designated night, pick another night to do it. Don't skip. This pattern of biweekly phone calls is critical in building and sustaining momentum. During each phone call, tell each other about action steps you've committed to in your action group and jot them down. For example, "I said I'd call the Coalition for the Homeless and see if our group can set up a tutoring network for children." Or "I've already called the Nuclear Age Peace Foundation and they're sending a speaker to our area. By Friday I promised I would get a list of places we can hold the event."

When you check back in with each other, if one of you hasn't been able to fulfill a promise, then recommit to doing it before your next phone call. And always, always affirm each other for what you have done. Affirmation and support are the juice that keeps us going.

Make the Race to Peace a part of your family. Check in with your kids every week and share what you're each doing. You may have chosen to work on different aspects of the same project, or different projects altogether. In either event, keep each other informed, and be sure to affirm, encourage, and take joy in each other's accomplishments.

RACE TO PEACE OUTREACH

Whether through fundraising, letter-writing campaigns, community events, or e-mail newsletters, let other people know about the Race to Peace and invite them to join in. Contact your local newspapers and radio stations and tell them what you're doing. Ask them to do an article on the Race to Peace. Anytime you host a community or speaker's event, invite them to send a photographer.

Keep your efforts in the public eye—commitment is contagious. Share the knowledge you've accumulated since you've been reading this book. Many people aren't aware, for example, that every 3.6 seconds someone in the world dies of starvation or preventable diseases, and that poverty and inequity are at the heart of war. Educating people about the facts is a very important step. Consider creating fact sheets, posters, and booklets—use what you've read in this book. The Race to Peace requires resourcefulness and creativity—but most importantly, make it fun. Allow your involvement in the Race to Peace to be the spark of energy that lights your life and gives you a sense of purpose beyond anything you've ever known.

WORLDWIDE NETWORKS

On www.racetopeace.com you can link with people across the globe who are also involved. Stay connected. Share stories, ideas, goals, accomplishments. We need each other—a mom, dad, or child in China, Spain, Israel, or Egypt is only an e-mail away. Connecting and communicating will bring us closer to winning the Race to Peace.

STAY IN TOUCH

Keep in touch with me and let me know what you are doing. I will share your stories on the Race to Peace website and in my e-newsletter *Peaceful Parenting*. With enough of us out there working, who knows what we can create?

CONCLUSION

For the sake of all of our children we are faced with this new mission—one we must be unwilling to postpone—creating peace. Why must we do this now? Because we have everything in our favor but time. As I said earlier, the knowledge of how to make peace is there, so are the resources—the only thing missing is the will of the people. With your participation we can change that.

May we harness our collective energy, and let the love we feel for our children be our power source. Together we can win the Race to Peace.

On the Minds of Parents: Answers to Our Most Pressing Questions

This has been a year of difficult questions for parents—our own and our children's, including the existential questions that arise when we are faced with a crisis. How do we maintain hope? How do we transcend personal trauma? Is it possible for regular people to make a difference? Is peace possible? These are some of the many questions that parents have been asking over the past year.

To answer all of them would take many chapters, maybe even an entire book. What I've attempted to do in this section is highlight questions that parents seem most concerned about and provide answers from some top experts. Every answer you are about to read was based on lengthy personal interviews with each person. Each in-depth answer below is in the voice of the person interviewed. May their wisdom and insight provide you with additional information to further elucidate topics that have been discussed in this book.

This section has been divided into five parts:

Healing Our Emotions
Moving Beyond Grief and Trauma
    This section also contains a special resource: Steps to Helping Children Through Grief

Raising Peaceful Kids
Creating Hope
Creating Peace

HEALING OUR EMOTIONS

How do we process what we've lived through in the past year?

DR. TERESA BENZWIE: What we need now more than ever is con-nection among all people. Whether we're Christian, Muslim, or Jewish, we all want the same things for our children. It is in our connections that we will find more peace.

Grief is complex and difficult to experience, yet it can hold the potential for helping us grow spiritually and emotionally. By ex-periencing our feelings of fear, rage, or sadness, we can transition to another realm, a safe place where we can receive, accept, and connect to our deeper selves. Possibly grief can be a source to help us move closer to our humanity and help us find out more about who we are as individuals and who we are in relation to others.

Since September 11th, many of us have come face-to-face with grief and loss—not only loss of those we love, but also the loss of innocence, control, and safety. We feel much more vulnerable and open and realize how little control we have over our world and our powerlessness to protect the people we love. However, these losses can also be an important part of our growth.

All our life experiences remain a part of us to some degree of consciousness and we recognize how each new loss triggers our past losses. Our personal histories of losses are an integral part of our current daily living and with each new loss we have an op-portunity to heal. It's essential to allow the full grieving process, no matter how long it takes to move through all its stages of de-nial, bargaining, anger, and finally acceptance.

We need to reach out and help each other through the difficult times so many of us are experiencing. Connection is vital. Possibly together, we can move to a better place as individuals and as a nation. Our society has become separate and alienated, and what we desperately desire and really need is community. Anytime we feel a part of a community or something greater than ourselves, we feel safer and more comfortable. This sharing can restore hope and that wonderful sense that things may again be "right" which we experience when we look at our children sleeping.

Hopefully, the tragedy of September 11th can be the catalyst which brings us all closer together. I really believe that goodness can come out of chaos. However, we need to readjust our priorities. We must look into our hearts and ask ourselves what is important? Then we must forge ahead, pouring our energies into the answer we hear and simply "do it."

DR. TERESA BENZWIE is a nationally recognized therapist and author of *A Moving Experience* and other books.

How can parents help their children cope with anxiety, anger, and other difficult feelings that have come up over the past year?

DR. HEIDI KADUSON: Parents need to realize that children might not talk about their reactions to the events of the past year, but they are there. Understand that whatever issues your child had going on before may be magnified in the face of what's been happening in the world. A child who's shy may be more shy, an oppositional child may be more oppositional. If your child is acting out, his or her anger is a shield for something else—fear or anxiety perhaps. Be as understanding as possible and help your child express whatever emotions are there.

It's very important to recognize your own reactions to what's been happening in the world or your underlying feelings will be conveyed to your children. Parents who reassure their children that they are safe, but are themselves feeling anxious and fearful will convey confusing messages. It's absolutely essential to deal with your own emotions so you can authentically help your child to do the same. False reassurances don't work. Children are very aware of the things we whisper when we think they're not listening, or phone conversations they pick up on when they're within earshot. Realize that they are listening and taking it all in.

Many parents believe the traumatic events we've lived through in the past year don't bother their children because their children haven't been asking questions. But when I work with these same children, their fears come out through play.

Play and artwork are the best tools for helping kids express feelings. Many children tend not to talk about things they're most afraid of because they believe that by putting the fear into words it might actually happen. The best thing parents can do is encourage them to play and draw about whatever's on their minds. Encourage, allow, and be present for your child's expressions of fear, anger, or anxiety. Parents can actually narrate what they see in their child's dramatic play or artwork. Plato once said that you learn more through play than through a lifetime of conversation.

It's very important to be honest while still assuring the child that you are there to protect them. If your child asks if something bad might happen again, answer him honestly and say, "I don't know, but I'll be here for you no matter what."

DR. HEIDI KADUSON is an internationally recognized play therapist specializing in posttraumatic reactions. She is the author of many books including *Short Term Play Therapy,* which she coauthored with Charles E. Schaeffer.

What can we do to take care of our emotional well-being in these times of stress and uncertainty?

BETTY LEVIN: There are a number of specific things you can do. The first is having what I call a centering practice. Start each day with even a few moments of meditation, yoga, t'ai chi, prayer, or journal writing. One of my clients recently told me how doing this helped her take control of her "hyper habit." It was just a small change but it made a big difference in the quality of her life. Taking time to do a short meditation helps her transcend the frenzy of the moment and gets her in touch with her true priorities. The psychologist Joan Borysenko calls this kind of centering practice a "minivacation." Minivacations help us become more mindful and savor the moments of our lives rather than rushing through them.

Next, is live by your core values. Another client of mine left her longtime job because staying in it was compromising what she valued most. Her internal wisdom told her there had to be something more fulfilling she could do. She was right. After exploring her talents and most deeply held values, she discovered a better alternative. Now she has not only job satisfaction but the realization that she possesses the ability to exercise options and the courage to take risks.

Healthy relationships are essential. Family, friends, community, and organizations knit a human web that reinforces our sense of connectedness. They cut down on isolation and fear. Too often we become alienated from others through misunderstandings, poor communication, grudges, or even indifference. It's so important, especially now, to bridge our misunderstandings and nurture our relationships.

Perhaps the most important aspect of emotional well-being is the spiritual dimension—an awareness of the sacredness of all human beings. In our society it's so easy to become self-involved. The spiritual dimension helps us discover our capacity for compassion, gratitude, love, forgiveness, and faith in the humanity of others. Now more than ever, this is critical. Listen to this quote from Bo Lozoff, cofounder of the Prison Ashram Project. He said, "Every great spiritual, philosophical, and religious tradition has emphasized compassion, reconciliation, forgiveness, and responsibility. These are not suggestions, they are the laws of the universe, like gravity. If we follow them, we will thrive; if not, we will suffer."

The last critical piece is forgiveness. I saw how important this was in my own life when my ex-husband was dying of Lou Gehrig's disease. We'd been married for twenty-seven years and divorced for five. Even though he'd been hostile and punishing, I felt a strong need to find a way to forgive him before he died. One of my greatest obstacles was his treatment of our daughters. But as he lay dying, I felt I had to acknowledge the good years and forgive him for what he had done.

It was so hard, and I struggled to separate his goodness from his bad behavior. But I was finally able to get to the point of writing him a letter expressing forgiveness for what he had done. By the time he received it, he was unable to speak, so I never got a response. I'd like to think the letter helped release him from any more suffering. By writing it, I was released in a different kind of way—I was able to let go. Forgiveness benefits the forgiver. This is why it's so important for our emotional well-being that we let go of past grievances, and find a place inside where we are able to forgive, especially now.

> BETTY LEVIN, M.A., is a psychotherapist, speaker, and consultant in human relations. She has been in private practice for twenty-eight years and has been published in a number of professional journals.

MOVING BEYOND GRIEF AND TRAUMA

How do I cope with severe loss and help my children to do the same?

RON LEWIS: In the Bible, the story of Jacob provides an interesting lesson. After wrestling with an angel Jacob's leg was hurt so badly the wound made him limp for the rest of his life. And God said to Jacob, "Now you are whole." Jacob became more human on a deep level because of the wound he had to bear. Suffering and loss provide us all with that same opportunity—to be more whole.

Picture this image—a giant rock arch with the ocean blasting through the center of it. Now, think of these words: "The only way out is through." If people don't go through their grief completely, it will splash out and saturate their lives forever. But the opposite is true too—when we deal with our grief, we can become free.

I remember the former happening with my first client—a twenty-three-year-old graduate student who had to come home because he was having uncontrollable anxiety attacks. In therapy what came out was unresolved grief about his mother's death when he was fifteen. When his mother passed away, his father didn't cry and made him go to school the next day. He never had the chance to grieve. And now, eight years later, his grief came splashing out.

Grief in children is different from grief in adults. It's sporadic and a lot of it can be nonverbal. This is so for kids of any age. Grief can be triggered periodically at different developmental stages of their lives. With children of all ages, grief is often acted out rather than talked out. I once had a seventeen-year-old girl whose mother brought her to me. She had been suspended from school for punching another girl Her mother said she was incorrigible.

When the girl talked to me, she revealed that her parents were divorced and her father had died a year and a half ago. Her mother was so angry that she wouldn't let her grieve. The girl started crying and opening up to her grief. That was the beginning. By dealing with her grief, the girl was soon able to soften and reconnect with her mother. She also completely turned around at school, stopped fighting, and improved her grades. Before releasing her grief, she was holding her anger in so tight it spilled out onto the world.

My advice for parents is to *listen* and follow your child's grief path. Don't try to lead. Children will express what they have to say then go off to play. As parents, we expect them to sit and talk for long periods of time. That's not how it works. With kids, things come out in small doses. If parents try to press for more, children close up.

I always encourage children and adults to move toward grief, not away from it. One way this happens is by having them write to the loved one who died, talk to them in their minds or even aloud. For most people the loved one lives on in spirit. Part of the healing process is keeping a continued connection with that person.

It's also valuable for parents to share their vulnerability with their children. Parents often think they always have to be strong, but that's not true. Find the balance of expressing how you feel without getting carried away. Also don't use your child as a confidant. If a parent has a lot of unmet needs, it's important to find adult support.

Young children understand more about grief and loss than we give them credit for. I believe that children should be given the choice to go to funerals. When my two-year-old son died of cancer, his brother David was four. He wanted to go to the funeral and I'm so glad we allowed him to. At the grave site his eyes were riveted on the casket. As he watched it being put in the ground, his grandmother cried inconsolably. David put his arms around her and said, "Grandma, didn't you know that Noam was very sick?" As young as he was, he accepted Noam's death.

When I lead grief workshops, I draw a line down the middle of a large paper and say, "When you think about loss, what feelings bubble up?" On one side I write words people suggest like sadness, loneliness, betrayal, despair, hopelessness. Then I ask what they think is on the other side of that line. I get responses like strength, sensitivity, community, spiritual growth, love, closer friendships, greater intimacy with God. As the result of confronting difficult feelings, people in grief discover these resources within themselves, their families, and their communities. Loss is not only despair, it also leads to the potential for change and deeper spiritual and emotional growth.

Kahlil Gibran once said, "We can only fill our cup of joy as fully as we've filled our cup of pain." We must accept, even embrace, our grief. Loss is an inevitable part of life. It doesn't always happen as the result of death. Loss can come through divorce, health problems, moving, losing friends. The challenge is to transform loss into a journey of growth rather than a tragedy that shuts us down to life.

RON LEWIS, M.A., is a grief counselor and pastoral psychotherapist. He has been working with children and families for twenty-one years and currently serves as Clinical Supervisor at Aldersgate Youth Service Bureau.

Ron Lewis recommends a wonderful website you can visit for very sensitive information on helping your child through the grieving process. It's called the Dougy Center (www.dougy.org/adult_grievchild.html). The information below is based on recommendations from their guidebook, *35 Ways to Help a Grieving Child,* which you can order by calling 503-775-5683.

Ways to Help Your Child Through the Grieving Process

Answer their questions; don't avoid the difficult ones.

Let your child know that it's okay to talk about whatever is on his mind. Be as honest as possible without going into an overabundance of detail, and keep the conversation appropriate for your child's age level. The Center advises you to use real language, not figurative. They say it's better to say "died" than "passed away." Kids do better with words that are concrete, not vague.

Encourage your child to speak about the person who died.

Use the person's name. Help your child recall memories of that person and talk about experiences they shared. Keep sharing your memories too. This gives your child permission to keep the person alive in spirit. The Center advises you to hold on to keepsakes from the person who died, particularly things of emotional significance. They give an example of a twelve-year old boy who saved his father's work boots. Another child saved his father's flannel shirt to wear it when he goes fishing, something he and his father had once shared together.

Allow your child to make choices.

If your child wants to attend the funeral, let her. When six-year-old Hannah lost her grandfather three weeks after losing her grandmother, she wanted to be at the funeral to say good-bye.

Some children want lots of pictures and memorabilia around; others don't. Allowing your child to make choices gives her a feeling of control in the face of loss. Each child in the family may choose to express grief in different ways. Try to honor each individually.

Every person grieves in his own way. Understand this.

Listen when your children want to speak about their feelings. Encourage them to let their feelings up and express them in any way possible: writing, drawing, crying—whatever matches their unique needs and personality. Validate whatever your child's experience is. Some may be angry, some confused. Be there, listen, comfort, and affirm. Don't try to talk them out of how they feel.

Support groups are also very important. Ron Lewis says, "Approximately 5 percent of all children lose parents before they become adults. That's literally millions of children, thousands in every community across America. Yet many of those children feel isolated because there are no other children to talk with who've been through the same thing. They need this along with outlets for their creativity and anger."

The same holds true for you. If you have lost a loved one and you have not already joined a support group, do it now. At the end of this chapter there are many wonderful resources for healing from grief. By the way, the Dougy Center provides books on grieving for teens and adults also. You can order them by calling the number listed earlier.

Is it really possible to transcend crisis and trauma in our lives? What do we need to know to do this?

PATRICE GAINES: A resounding yes, it *is* possible to transcend. I didn't know this when I was younger but my life has taught me what is actually possible. Now I believe there are very few things that are impossible. For me finding hope wasn't a straight path. Even though I was lost and thought I was nothing, when I could look around and see other people living better lives, it gave me hope for my own. Even the smallest amount of hope helps.

Sometimes getting through starts with a decision. In my books and speeches I talk about the day I made up my mind to change my life. I had gotten arrested for possession of drugs and was in jail. My mother came to visit me and she was holding my two-year-old daughter. When I looked out of my cell and saw my daughter in her arms, I said, "I have to change—I have to be there raising my child." At that moment, it was like the thought came out of a place I didn't know. If you decide you have to do something, you have to believe that somehow there's a way you can. I didn't know how I would do it, but I knew I had to. To believe and to have hope are so crucial. If a person doesn't have hope, then nothing changes.

When I look back, knowing that I had a family who loved me was a source of hope. Growing up I didn't think I was lovable, but there was still a memory of having been loved. People who don't have love find it harder. They must discover other ways to hope.

I correspond with several prisoners serving life terms. They say, "I wish I had you in my life when I was a kid." What they mean was they wish they had been loved. Because there was no memory of ever having been loved, it's been hard for them to have hope.

These men never learned to connect with feelings. They never learned to feel what they felt and to respect themselves. They never learned to love themselves. They both ended up murdering people.

When I was little, I thought I wasn't smart enough because I was black, and not strong enough because I was a girl. I absorbed this thing that a girl always had to have a guy. The guy I ended up with led me even deeper into this pit. I wasn't the stereotypical kid who gets into drugs. I had a nice middle-class upbringing, nice clothes. Yet I was having a difficult time inside. That's why people need to know that even kids who look fine on the outside can be suffering on the inside.

We don't teach our kids enough about genuinely loving themselves. Like if you're a little kid and you have buck teeth, that's fine. The core of who you are is not that. We need to teach kids that they are just magnificent. Every person needs to give children these messages, not just their parents. And the most important one is to respect yourself.

So how do we transcend? Sometimes you have to start by looking at people you admire and start acting like that. It's a form of pretending. Before I really knew I could change, I had to act out the part. I knew what worked for other people, and I tried somehow to act like they did. Changing is hard. But if you get hung up on thinking how hard it is, you'll be paralyzed. So start with one little thing. If you're depressed, break things down to the smallest steps you can take. Ask for help. That's a big accomplishment. Or smile, that's another.

Also pay attention to your life. Think in the third person. I talk to myself and say, "Okay Patrice, why did you do this or that?" It causes me to reflect on my actions, and I gain insight.

That's something you can teach a kid to do. Find out why the child did what they did, help them unravel their thinking process, and teach them how to reflect. It's very freeing to start understanding your own motivations.

For me there's a higher power piece too. But I had to figure out how I was going to define it. The process of determining what a higher power meant to me was very important. The beauty is in figuring it out for yourself. If you just go with what everyone else tells you, it's not yours. As you question and learn, you make it yours. As a child, I didn't think I believed in God because I thought God was a white man and white people didn't like me, so God didn't like me. But as an adult, I reconsidered that. I began to read and read. The thing that made me start to believe was approaching it through the psychic and intellectual. I came to realize there was something profound in the universe.

It's important to define what you believe. One of the prisoners I work with told me he didn't pray because he felt like God wasn't listening. I told him to talk to God like he was talking to a good friend. He tried it, and the next time we spoke he said that when he talked to God he started to cry like he'd never cried before. He's still praying.

The other guy I work with said he couldn't see a reason to live, and I told him there's so much there for him, worlds he can travel through even when he's in prison. I said, "You still have a purpose." He's trying to discover what it is. One day he sent me a "student of the week" certificate he'd been awarded in his G.E.D class. He was so proud, he had to show me. Can you imagine, a convicted murderer feeling so proud of being student of the week? I see these guys learning, and knowing they can learn in the circumstance they are living in defines hope for me.

Working with these men has taught me that even under the worst circumstances the human spirit can still have hope. We're pretty amazing beings. These men have really helped me help others. They are a gift. I get this because I give. I told my friend, she doesn't know what she's missing.

I believe if these men had been loved sooner, they probably wouldn't have become violent. So I really do believe that love is the answer to violence. Their growth was stunted from the lack of love. Because I love them, they are healing. Every day, they give me hope.

PATRICE GAINES is a former reporter for the *Washington Post*. She overcame abuse and drug addiction to rise to the top of her field. She is the author of three books, including *Moments of Grace*.

RAISING PEACEFUL KIDS

How do we raise moral, compassionate children in a cruel and violent world?

DR. MICHELE BORBA: We have to prioritize our children. The number one thing we need to do is commit ourselves to raising them as compassionate people. I think we sometimes spend more time planning our summer vacations than planning how our kids are going to turn out. Kids don't learn compassion in a textbook. They learn it by seeing it. This is particularly critical because our children are being desensitized by seeing so much cruelty.

When we teach kindness and compassion, we're going against the current, because all of the support systems we have are counter to this: cruel images in the media, cruelty among peers, the Internet, movies, videos, TV shows, and computer games—in all of these, often the tough guy wins and no one thinks about the victim. We're raising kids in a climate of cruelty instead of a climate of caring. But you have the ability to change that.

The best question you can ask yourself each night is: "If my kids had only my example to watch, what would they have learned today?"

Then spell out what you want them to learn so they know what it is. Show them in everyday examples. Don't assume they know. Be intentional, and point it out as it happens. Expect and demand your kids behave in kind, respectful ways. If you want your kids to be compassionate, then your overriding standard needs to be *"In our house we treat each other with kindness, and in our world we do the same."*

Be sure to reinforce when your child does it *right*. When we only point out what they do wrong, we rob them of knowing how to do it right.

As far as morality—the best news is that it's learned. There is no moral gene. Kids aren't hard-wired for it. Morality is learned through a series of skills and behaviors that we need to teach. The most important core moral value is empathy. Kids are born with a jump-start for moral growth because they are born with the *potential* for empathy, but don't assume it's going to develop naturally in a morally toxic world.

Empathy needs to be nurtured, and if it's not, it will lie dormant or extinguish. The first three years of your kids' lives are critical for making this happen. The first sound a child will respond to is another child crying. When we nurture and reinforce this type of response, we see it continue. We've all had those moments when our two-year-old curls up in our lap and pets us because we're distressed, but we don't boost that wonderful potential for sensitivity. If we don't nurture it enough, it'll be extinguished as soon as they walk out our door into this toxic culture.

We don't tune up empathy enough in our sons. By second grade they're already starting to extinguish it. The reason is that we talk about emotions more with our daughters and and we mask emotions with our sons. So our boys are already handicapped in moral growth because they lack a vocabulary for compassion. How can you feel for someone when you can't recognize and read their emotions?

If you want to build empathy, the two best questions you can ask your child are: "How would you feel if that happened to you?" and "How do you think she feels right now?" Follow up these questions with, "What does she need to feel better, and what can you do for her?" *Your whole goal in parenting is to stretch your kids beyond themselves so they can see the other person's point of view.* Once this happens, you have set the groundwork for a peaceful child. Why? Because if you can get into the shoes of another person and feel how they feel, it makes violence and cruelty unthinkable.

> DR. MICHELE BORBA is an internationally recognized authority on child development and self-esteem and moral intelligence. She is the author of numerous books. Her latest is *Building Moral Intelligence: The Seven Essential Virtues That Teach Kids to Do the Right Thing.*

How can we groom this generation of children to live in harmony with one another and to accept differences?

DR. RHEA V. ALMEDIA: The notion of peace and justice is not just a distant idea. It starts in our homes and places of work. But too often we don't take the time needed to explain the most important things to our children, or even to discipline.

The tide is against accepting norms that are more justice and equity-based. So our children grow up with mixed messages. We have to work hard to develop and maintain a different kind of community, and we have a responsibility to the next generation to teach them differently. In a country this wealthy, all of our kids should have the same access to a good education. The level of literacy would drastically improve, and so would problems of inequity.

Parents need more time and space to be with their children and communities. This is critical. Otherwise the value system of the work force starts to permeate everybody's life. It's happening now—we all have cell phones, and people are bombarded with business calls even in their spare time. It becomes the dominating influence in our families.

I grew up in Uganda and my school was an extension of Cambridge University. My education prepared me really well, yet we only went to school from 8:00 to 1:00. And we were able to get into the top colleges. So I question the amount of hours our kids are in school here. Kids are more productive if they have a shorter day, and a shorter week. They need time to think, play, reflect.

Kids are missing out on this larger sense of community and connectedness. Try doing an exchange in your neighborhood—plan to alternate meals at other people's homes. Being connected to the community helps kids relate better, learn better, and become better leaders. It removes the "self focus."

Finding ways to become part of communities of other cultures is important too. Discrimination comes from fear and the desire to convert others to one's way of thinking. It's important that we don't see *our* way as the only way. Unless we make that bridge into each other's communities, we'll go on living in separate isolated compartments.

Educate yourself about ethnic, religious, and other differences. Then do things together. Try visiting temples, churches, and places where other cultures congregate. Don't just go to a Chinese restaurant—go to a museum that has artifacts of the culture. Read multiethnic stories to your kids—there's great poetry and literature from other cultures we can bring into our homes. I really believe we have to do more diversity training, one that honors people who are not honored instead of trying to make them all fit into the same mold.

Also critical is demanding a certain moral code from all our kids. But *we* must model that code first. Be aware of your own biases If you don't want your child to play with someone because they're poor or from a different ethnic group, but you don't admit this to yourself or your kids, you veil the truth. We are supposedly raising our children to be smart and understanding—yet we don't speak honestly about a lot of things. We need to give our kids another consciousness, one that conveys more honesty, more equity.

Be aware of having a different set of rules for girls and boys. We look at little boys being really aggressive and say, "Boys will be boys." It's crucial to pull our boys aside and teach them a different way. At a national conference I attended, Gloria Steinem called some of the violent crimes we've seen in suburban schools "crimes of entitlement" where young white boys raised to believe they can have what they want become enraged when they don't get it. Kids need to be resocialized—we must give them a clear understanding of differences and the need for acceptance. They need to rethink the choices they make in the way they treat others. We need to touch their consciousness.

> DR. RHEA V. ALMEIDA, a family therapist, is regarded as one of the nation's foremost experts on family/community violence. Creator of the Cultural Context Model, Dr. Almeida is the author of *Transformations in Gender and Race: Developmental and Family Perspectives* and other books.

What can families do to raise kids who care about the larger world and are willing to get involved?

JIM VOGT: There are lots of things parents can do. When our four kids were younger, we involved our children in a variety of activities that have helped them grow up to be compassionate, socially responsible people. When they were about four or five, we started having family nights where we'd teach them about peace and social justice issues. Ultimately the children "caught' our values. It's how you live, not what you say. An important commitment we made as parents was to try to be intentional about the way we lived so that our lives reflected our values.

Another thing we did was to "adopt" a refugee family from southeast Asia. When they moved to our community, we agreed to help them get integrated into our culture. This gave our children the experience of dealing with different kinds of people. Most of us live our lives with people just like we are. If that's all our children experience, they miss a lot. They need to experience racial, ethnic, religious, and economic differences because so many people are *not* like us.

We would also take bike rides through poor neighborhoods or neighborhoods of a different ethnic mix where our kids could see that people live in different ways and struggle with things we don't. Then we'd talk about it so our children could learn about likenesses and differences. It's very healthy for children to be exposed to this. Doing it can raise some fears, but where better to address fear than in your family?

We would invite different people into our home too, an international student at the university, for example. Having the exposure to someone from another part of the world was another opportunity for our children to get a glimpse of what the rest of the world is like, how it's so much bigger than just "us." We have a large map of the world in our home and we refer to it all the time. It's one more way of reminding ourselves of how big the world is.

Sometimes we would cook ethnic dinners. The kids would grouse about it, but they'd end up tasting different foods and got to experience what people in other parts of the world eat. The combination of all the things we did gave the kids an expanded sense of what other people and cultures are like.

In our world we have too many people who are intolerant, too great a divide between the haves and have-nots, a perpetual state of war in different parts of the world. As much as possible we must encourage our kids to have a sense of global community. This needs to be an intrinsic value we live by.

We must teach our children to be tolerant, hopeful, good listeners, and to realize that *they have a responsibility to leave this world a better place.* They need to have a vision and values beyond themselves, to know that it really *is* better for them if they're sensitive and caring to others.

Getting our children involved gives them a sense of hope. Also, unconditional love. Did you know that 85 percent of prisoners in jail for violent offenses said the first place they experienced violence was in their families. People who experience peace in the family are better for it. The odds are so much higher of them succeeding and being contributing members of society.

Another challenge for parents since September 11th is to not get caught up in this black and white way of thinking we've been seeing—good versus bad, righteous versus evil. It's much more complex than that. We must help our children have critical eyes and ears so they're not just swept up in the direction everyone else is going. The task is to step out of our little piece of the world and see things through larger eyes.

JIM VOGT is Administrator of the Parenting for Peace and Justice Network, a transnational organization that helps parents teach peacemaking, equity, and social responsibility.

How do I explain the contradictions to my children—we say we want peace but we're at war?

COLEMAN MCCARTHY: Tell your children there are two ways to deal with any problem—either through violent force: fists, guns, armies, and verbal violence—or through nonviolent force: the force of dialogue instead of monologue, honesty, justice, ideas, morals, and love. In order for nonviolence to be effective, it has to be active. This means working hard to resolve conflicts. Not everyone has learned how to do this, and the more who do, the more we'll be able to solve our problems without all the violence we see in the world. Sometimes violence comes from not knowing there's another way.

We also need to work on prevention. Kids need to know that we must sit down and talk, and stop killing each other. We can also use legal solutions—the World Court where Slobodan Milosevic went on trial. The first people who tried to blow up the World Trade Center have been prosecuted in a court of law, and we didn't bomb anyone to make that happen. We need to do this more.

We must let our children know that violence doesn't solve problems. A study was done by the Senate Judiciary Committee that determined 95 percent of children's cartoons have violent themes. Kids get the message that if you've got a problem, go belt somebody or push them off a cliff. Study after study has shown that this is the first introduction to solving conflicts with violence. If you want to help, cut back on TV.

Let your children know that there are many people who do not believe the way to stop killing is by more killing. Tell them about the peacemakers—Gandhi, King, and others. Many people don't agree that war and hurting people are the way to deal with problems.

The idea that killing people solves problems clearly hasn't solved them, or they would have been solved by now. If we can start seeing that war is not the answer, there will be much less violence in our homes and in the world. This is what we need to teach our children.

COLEMAN MCCARTHY is the Director of the Center for Teaching Peace in Washington. He is a nationally recognized speaker and author of *Strength Through Peace* and other books.

CREATING PEACE

How can people of opposing views and varying perceptions live together in peace?

IMAM MAMED AHMED CHELBI: When I lived in Lebanon, I tasted war from 1974 until 1982. Since I've been a citizen of the United States I've lived in peace—until September 11th. To accomplish true peace we must talk about our differences before we talk about the common things. You can't understand the light until you walk in the darkness. We must focus on the roots of war, so we can avoid repeating the same mistakes. Only if we are smart enough to learn from the mistakes of the past can we have peace. People who have never lived through war, and haven't known the color of blood, don't really know the price we pay when we choose violence.

From the day I came to this mosque, we have been teaching peace, walking peace, and opening our doors to every human being. We continue to talk about peace because the name "Allah" means peace. The work of peace is on our tongues, in our daily prayers, and in our lives. We have to keep working until we accomplish peace in ourselves and with the rest of humanity.

How can we have peace for our children? This is the million-dollar question. In Islam we teach our children—God in heaven respects every child of Adam, male or female, and we must respect others too, regardless of religion or gender. We have only one earth, and it is open to all human beings. We share the same air, water, and land. We should not put boundaries between any human beings: blacks and whites, Christians and Sikhs, Arabs and Jews, people who practice religion and people who don't. When we are able to teach our kids there are no boundaries and divisions, our kids will live better lives than their parents have.

We have actually been practicing this in our town. One year we invited our youth to speak at different houses of worship. My son Mohammed spoke at the synagogue, and my daughter Mariam spoke at a church. We need to create more programs like this so our youth can know each other and learn to live peacefully.

Our clergy association has been working together since the day I came here. Every Thanksgiving we celebrate in each other's houses of worship: one year in the mosque, one year in the synagogue, one year in church. We rotate like this so we can give people the sense that all of us are the children of God and everyone of us has the right to join together, yet pray in different ways. When all of the clergy stand on the pulpit hand in hand, the community sees the reality of what it means to live in peace.

IMAM HAMED AHMED CHEBLI is the leader of the Islamic Society of Central New Jersey.

RABBI MARCIA PRAGER: A terrifying window onto the everpresent insecurity of life in this world opened on September 11th, bringing fear closer to home for many Americans than ever before. As we live through our horror and astonishment, our pain and rage, perhaps we can also find a call to compassion for all who live with fear and insecurity woven into the fabric of their daily lives. For myself, as a teacher and guide among the Jewish people, it is so clear how the generations of dislocations and attack has affected us. Can we not see how people who are minorities, or living under tyranny, suffer the uncertainty and the fear of assault that is now experienced by everyone? For many Americans, everything has changed. For most of the people in the world, little is changed. Let us live in such a way that we can make a difference! When power supports injustice, that system cannot stand.

I have long noted the curious relationship between the Hebrew words *lechem*, "bread," and *milchema*, "war." One day I realized that both of these words exemplify two choices: food or war. Yeasty bread and war are both, after all, a kind of "uprising." The appearance of the same root letters in these two seemingly different words seems to say: When there's no bread—where there is starvation, poverty, disease, pollution, and exploitation—will there not also be war? The prophet Amos once proclaimed, "Let justice flow like water and right-action like a mighty stream." Now would be a good time to teach ourselves and our children to not only talk this talk, but walk this walk.

I am reminded of a small incident that took place when my little boy was six. He came home from school one day and asked, "Mommy, why are some kids bad?" A bullying child had once again tormented a weaker boy in the school yard. I asked my son, "Do you know what is underneath 'bad'?" We thought together, agreeing that underneath bad, was probably "mad." Could there also be something underneath mad? We thought again, and realized it was "sad." What happens, we asked, when you are sad, but no one cares, no one listens, and there is no one to fix it? Don't you get mad? Yet if no one sees that you are mad, and still there is no redress, no repair—only then does the behavior start that we call "bad." Even though the pummeling from the bully must be stopped, the caring question to ask is, "Why is this child angry, what has happened to him to make him feel this way?" We soon discover the angry child is deeply sad, and the condition that engenders the sadness must be uncovered. In this talk my little boy discovered his own compassion.

How do we help our children strive for justice, hold compassion, and embrace the oneness of G-d in all people and things? Both the powerful and the powerless have the ability to act out their pain with horrific and destructive consequences. We have seen this. Yet the world has now become a village where even the affluent cannot live in walled communities imagining that the pain and humiliation of the destitute will not enter. Not only is it a moral imperative, it is in the self-interest of all of us to share the earth's abundance. We must remember that each human being is in the image of G-d. The abundance of the earth belongs to all.

RABBI MARCIA PRAGER is a nationally known speaker and rabbi of P'nai Or Synagogue in Philadelphia.

Creating Hope

Is there reason to be hopeful about the future?

MICHAEL LERNER: I personally feel hopeful about the future because there has been a huge spiritual opening since September 11th where more and more people are asking themselves how their lives can embody the kind of compassion we saw in the fire fighters and rescue workers.

More people are now challenging the dominant materialism and selfishness of American society. That's one reason to be more hopeful—this change in the mass psyche. Witnessing the incredible self-sacrifice on the part of ordinary people showed us that there is tremendous goodness in the American people. Unfortunately most people haven't felt comfortable showing their generosity and goodness except in the face of public disasters and national emergencies. But on 9/11 we saw the goodness has always been there.

There's reason for hope because a great deal of goodness has been demonstrated, and a great deal of goodness is out there ready to be tapped. *The key is for individuals and groups to act on their highest vision of good.* When we do this, we empower others who have previously been too scared to show their own generosity, and idealism. It creates a ripple effect.

This is how we will have more safety in our world. We're never going to get it through wars and bigger armies. If there's one lesson we should have learned from 9/11, it's that there will be no security in this world if there are so many people who are so downtrodden and oppressed that they are willing to lose their lives to get us.

But the world is changing. We're starting to change it now. Recently there was a conference held in New York where over 700 people from all over the country gathered to build a new national movement called the Tikkun movement. *Tikkun* is the Hebrew word for "healing, repair, and transformation." Our goal is to build a new society which encourages us to be more loving, caring human beings capable of responding to the world around us with awe and wonder. We are seeking to support each other to develop as individuals, as communities, and as part of an interrelated network.

Social change and inner change go hand in hand. It's time to realize that it is in our own personal self-interest to ensure a world in which everyone is invited to be part of loving, spiritually deep, emotionally satisfying, and materially thriving communities of their own choice, and to live in a world in which mutual respect and care are the commonsense truths by which we live. Herein lies the essence of hope.

MICHAEL LERNER is the author of *Spirit Matters: Global Healing and the Wisdom of the Soul* and other books, and the editor of *Tikkun* magazine.

Can regular people really make a difference in the lives of others?

ARNIE ROPIEK: If you believe in yourself and believe in this world, you can make a difference. And it's absolutely necessary that we each do this. When my granddaughter turned seventeen, she didn't know how to make a difference, but she wanted to find a way. She said, "I'm trying to throw my arms around the world." Over the years, I've met so many people who *have* thrown their arms around the world and made a difference. Regular people like you and me.

One of the most courageous people I ever met was a young African-American woman. She was only twelve years old, but she put a rapist behind bars. Her stepfather had assaulted her. They were so poor that her mother was terrified of her testifying because she thought she might not able to feed her children without this horrible man's help. To the mother it was a matter of survival. But the young woman said, "No, Mom. We'll find a way to eat, but we have to do what's right. I want to put this guy in jail."

So this twelve-year-old garnered the strength to sit in a courtroom, point directly at the man who had raped her, and tell the court what he had done. He ended up going to jail for fifty years, and she ended up graduating at the top of her class. She was offered scholarships to some of the top schools in the country, but she ended up turning down a scholarship to Princeton because she felt she didn't have decent enough clothes. She ended up at a small women's college where she did very well. But it makes me sad to think how she'd survived rape, had tremendous courage, but still didn't have enough clothes to wear. Nevertheless she triumphed in life, went on to become very successful, and supports her mother. She stands out in my mind as a person who really made a difference. If it weren't for her testimony, that guy would still be out on the streets.

There's another woman who stands out in my mind for the difference she's made in another way. This woman had two little children both with Down syndrome. The younger one almost died. She was on a feeding tube and was up every two hours throughout the night. Her mother not only takes care of her, but decided to become a spokesperson for the Association for Retarded Citizens. She brings this message all over: "Don't forget about these children—they belong to the world too." Her courage is overwhelming. Because of her, people are helping retarded citizens in many more ways than ever before. She makes me remem-

ber that we are all one beating heart and we have to keep taking
each other's pulses and caring about each other.

I've seen my own impact as a journalist many times too. One
that comes to mind was when I'd heard about how the local rescue mission had run out of many basics: toothpaste, soap, sham-
poo—the little things of life the rest of us take for granted. Their
heating bill had gone up so much they could no longer afford
these supplies. I decided to write a piece about this. Within days
supplies started pouring in by the truckload. If we can save one or
two people along the way, there would be fewer lost souls in the
world. I saw how just a few words affected other people's lives.
Knowing I can make a difference gives me the courage to go on.
We all need to know this, and we all need to *do* it.

We must teach this way of thinking to the children. Whenever
I speak to kids, I ask them to do one thing for me—take care of
my world. I tell them, "I've sandpapered the rough spots, but it'll
belong to you soon. You've got to keep taking care of it when I'm
gone." I have the kids cup their hands together and I say, "I'm
putting the world in your hands now, take care of it." I'll always
remember when a young man came to me after a speech, cupped
his hands together, and said, "I *will* take care of your world." I
started to cry.

I also tell the kids that our world is not built of steel and
spaceships, it's made of words. Words are forever. If we work toward using the words of peace instead of the guns of war, we will
have a ten times better world than it is right now. If we find the
right words for peace, we will cut deeply into prejudice, hatred,
greed, selfishness, and lack of understanding. We will cut into illiteracy, and that alone will save millions of lives.

I tell the children, "You find the right words for your generation, and they'll find the words for the next. The right words can
encourage the right action. By talking about peace instead of war,
your very words will pull the world up. There is no limit. Weapons are temporary; words are forever. Words inspire action.
They inspire understanding, and understanding will help people
contribute to the world instead of just extracting from it.

We have to reach for each other and find ways to touch hands.

That's how we'll make the biggest difference of all. Peace will start in a home or classroom where we'll teach a generation about peace, and they'll teach the next, and they'll teach the next. That's the greatest difference we can each make.

> ARNIE ROPIEK is senior editor of *Times of Trenton* and former managing editor. During fifty-three years in journalism he has met thousands of people who have touched his life.

How can we reach peace in a world at war? What do we need to know?

REVEREND ROBERT MOORE: Prevention is the solution. If we had proactive programs that addressed the roots of violence over the past twenty years, the acts of September 11th might not have ever taken place. The climate in countries in poverty is one that gives rise to violence. People can be only frustrated and oppressed for so long before it explodes. We would have a much more secure world and society if we gave more humanitarian aid. These investments are relatively cheap in contrast to our military budget. Also we need more diplomacy. We must stay with negotiations that we start, and follow through. Doing each of these will help create a more secure global environment.

There are paradigms we have forgotten about. We apprehended everyone from the first World Trade Center bombing. We used the law and brought them to justice. We can start apprehending people earlier and earlier by working together worldwide. We must not accept as a given that military is the only option in dealing with international conflicts. We tend to think we either must capitulate or send in this massive dose of violence. This simply isn't true.

Our international criminal courts are another avenue, and we must create broader world coalitions that include people from all countries to apprehend perpetrators, not just do it unilaterally. Also, we must limit the use of force, not eliminate it, but limit it. Have it be the last option we turn to, not the first. But this takes patience. In our culture we want instant results on everything. You've got to be patient when you use nonviolent alternatives.

Our United Nations must be used preventatively not just in re-action to crisis. Right now nation-building is more important than ever. Did you know that all of the UN agencies combined are getting about 10 billion dollars from all of us. If we were to give about 40 billion dollars more, we could essentially eradicate the worst poverty in the world and provide basic nutrition, clean water, and access to education to every person living in poverty. By now we've probably spent more than that on the current war. If only we had spent it ahead of time, we may have prevented what happened.

Humanitarian and foreign aid also would have helped address some of the issues that lead to war—poverty and hunger. Yet we've been cutting our humanitarian aid. In recent years it has sunk to .1 percent of our Gross Domestic Product. Yet a full 1 percent is given by Scandinavian countries in humanitarian aid.

Aside from these issues, peace needs to begin at home. We must practice peace toward each other, use peacemaking skills, and listen to each other's needs. That can make a huge difference. It will make an eventual difference in our foreign and domestic policy because the children we are raising now will grow up to be our leaders someday.

Discuss these issues with your children. Bring things out in the open. Talk about negotiations and diplomacy as a means of deal-ing with problems. Ask your schools to teach peace. It starts with you.

Reverend Robert Moore is the founder and director of the Coalition for Peace Action. He is internationally recognized for his work.

Is it possible for regular people to help bring peace to this violent world? What specific things can they do?

William Ury: Yes, it is possible for regular people to help create peace in our world. In fact, peace is *only* going to come through ordinary people taking the future into their hands. Peace is much too important to leave to anyone else. Creating peace takes more courage, persistence, and patience than war. Imagine taking all the resources that go into war, and putting them into peace. It will take everybody pitching in to make this happen. It's like the old Irish saying—"Is this a private fight, or can anybody get in?" There are no private fights in this world anymore. Each of us has to get involved, and it has to be at all levels—in our homes, schools, communities, nation, and world.

Our world is going through wrenching changes. Yet these changes hold the potential for making peace—*if we seize the opportunity*. We have the capacity for peace, and if you look at the big picture, there have been long periods of time where there have been no wars between nation-states, only *within* nation-states. In fact, for half a century, we haven't had a war on the scale of World War II. In the Middle East, we're seeing hundreds of people die, not millions. Even terrorism hasn't taken the amount of lives lost in past wars. Not to diminish its horror, but more people die from bee stings each year than from acts of terrorism.

In the 200 years that we've known real democracy, there's been no instance of one democracy making war with another, and for the first time in human history, more states than ever are democratic, and the number is increasing. Take a look at Western Europe. For 1,000 years, it was the most wartorn part of the planet. Yet for the past fifty years, all the European countries got together and realized it makes more sense to work together and cooperate. *If it can happen there, why can't it happen elsewhere?*

The unprecedented danger now is nuclear weapons. We are on a razor's edge. The human genius for devising new and wonderful tools for cooperating has also had us develop new and terrible ways to destroy all life on earth. Unless we change our ways of handling conflict, our future and the future of our children are in question. That's the urgency. But we can take hope that there are many people out there working to create a coculture of peace.

We can all be part of this, and we need *your* involvement. One role you can play is right in your own home and neighborhood— notice signs of escalating conflict and do something about it, instead of remaining silent. Or be a provider—help meet the basic human needs of others. Where basic human needs are met, there's a lot less violence. Get involved in organizations that do this.

Another specific thing you can do is change the "fatalistic" story. We tell ourselves that human beings are brutal violent creatures, and that war is inevitable. *This is scientifically erroneous.* We need to rear our children with the correct story—that for the first 99 percent of human history our ancestors learned how to survive through cooperation and peacemaking. Wars were more intermittent. The preponderance and consistency of organized violence is a feature of the last one hundred years of human history. People must know that there are reasons to hope.

In order to create peace we must all contribute those things we do best. Ask yourself what that is for you. And whatever role you play, infuse your life with the dimension of conflict resolution and peacemaking.

For the first time in human evolution, humanity is in communication with one another and can express its collective will. What needs to emerge is the expression of all of us—*one voice saying a loud no to violence and a loud yes to negotiation and coexistence.* We are indeed in a Race to Peace, which we can win with *your* help. I urge you all to join in.

WILLIAM URY is an internationally renowned expert on peace and diplomacy. He is the author of several books, including *The Third Side,* and is the director of Harvard's Project on Preventing War.

About the Author

NAOMI DREW is recognized around the world as a pioneering educator and one of the first to introduce peacemaking and conflict resolution into public education. She has specialized in this area for twenty years, has lectured nationally to parents, educators, elementary school administrators, and has worked extensively with children. She is the author of *Peaceful Parents, Peaceful Kids* (Kensington), which *Publisher's Weekly* called "inspiring and useful," as well as two other books: *Learning the Skills of Peacemaking* and *The Peaceful Classroom in Action,* which Jonathan Kozol praised as "gentle, ingenious, and immensely practical." She currently serves as an advisor to the New Jersey Association of Professional Mediators. The mother of two sons, she lives in Lawrenceville, New Jersey. Visit her website at www.learningpeace.com.

If you would like to schedule a workshop or keynote in your area, you can reach Naomi Drew at win47win@aol.com. You can subscribe to Naomi's e-newsletter *Peaceful Parenting* by going to www.learningpeace.com.

REVEREND DR. ARTHUR CALIANDRO succeeded Dr. Norman Vincent Peale as senior minister of Marble Collegiate

Church in New York City. For ten years he has also served as chair of the Partnership of Faith in New York City, an interfaith group including Jewish, Catholic, Protestant and Muslim clergy. He is the author of four books, including *Simple Steps: Ten Things You Can Do to Create an Exceptional Life* and *Lost and Found: Personal Freedom in a Time of Uncertainty.*

Index